"Mare",

May you find Jesus
in these pages & your life.

Love,
Fr. John

MYTH MAN

≈

JOHN R. AURELIO

≈

MYTH MAN

A Storyteller's Jesus

CROSSROAD • NEW YORK

1992

The Crossroad Publishing Company
370 Lexington Avenue, New York, NY 10017

Printed in the United States of America
Typesetting output: TEXSource, Houston

Library of Congress Cataloging-in-Publication Data
Aurelio, John.
    Myth man : a storyteller's Jesus / by John R. Aurelio.
      p. cm.
    ISBN 0-8245-1106-9
    1. Jesus Christ—Biography. I. Title.
BT301.2.A974 1991
232.9′01—dc20
   [B]   91-21856
                                         CIP

The Gospels tell us something of what Jesus said and did.
But not all. How did he feel? What did he think?
What about the Apostles?
This is the domain of the mythmakers.
Using the findings of biblical scholarship
and remaining faithful to the times and conditions
in which Jesus lived
and the Gospels themselves,
we attempt to fill in the blanks.
This book is affectionately dedicated to all who wonder.

CONTENTS

≈

1

THE BIRTH OF JESUS

A CHRISTMAS CAROL

First Stanza   *Tempo: Piano*

In the beginning, before the world began...
before the sun came to be,
when there were no planets, no comets, no galaxies stretching
    beyond imagination,
before the first star was ever made;
in the beginning there was God
just God — only God
Spirit-God without form or shape

> – Father without white robe and flowing beard since there
>   was no one to imagine them,
> – Son without gentle eyes and tender hands since there was
>   no one to need them,
> – Holy Spirit without wind or fire or feather since there was
>   no one to see them,

endless Spirit-God without beginning and without end;
Spirit-deep and wide to infinity,
immense God, powerful God, awesome God,
Love-God.

Second Stanza   *Tempo: Andante with feeling*

>In the beginning God loved Himself.
>There was only God to love...
>Spirit-Father loving Spirit-Son,
>Spirit-Son loving Spirit-Father.
>Holy Spirit joining love into One Love sigh!
>Emptying and filling,
>Breathing,
>Moving in rapture... together!
>Pulsing,
>Flowing,
>>and overflowing into stars,
>>galaxies,
>>earth.

Third Stanza   *Tempo: Crescendo*

>In the beginning Love abounded.
>In the beginning Love created the heavens and the earth.
>In the beginning Love created life as all love must.
>Boundless Love giving birth...
>>flowers everywhere,
>>birds filling the sky,
>>fish swimming the deep,
>>creepy, crawly things,
>>invisible things,
>>small things and mighty things,
>>Man,
>>Jesus!

Fourth Stanza   *Tempo: Fortissimo*

>In the beginning there was Life.

EPILOGUE

Books don't begin with epilogues. Not usually. The only other one I'm aware of that does is the New Testament. Historical evidence indicates that the first and central message of the Good News was the death and resurrection of Jesus. In modern parlance this is called "the hook." It is what captures the people's attention and makes them want to hear more. This was followed by the Gospel accounts as we know them — teachings, parables, healings, miracle stories, and so on. The earliest account of the Gospel, designated as Q (Source) by biblical scholars, from which Matthew and Luke drew much of their material, contained no narrative of the birth and infancy of Jesus at all. In fact, it probably didn't contain "the hook" either.

Some have used the latter as an argument against the historicity of the resurrection account, claiming that if the original source material didn't claim so important an event, there is every reason to believe that it never took place at all. They theorize that it was an embellishment of later writers who had already begun to manipulate the material. To deny that as a possibility would be blind-sided. To accept it as the only possibility would be short-sighted.

The Gospel was originally and essentially an oral tradition. Stories, teachings, genealogies, and entire histories were memorized and transmitted by word of mouth. The Jewish culture of those times was more than just infatuated with learning and wisdom. These were almost an obsession. Hellenization (Greek influence) merely fanned the flames ignited during the reign of Solomon. Jesus must be examined in the context of his times.

Jesus was a Jew first, last, and always. He never denied or repudiated his Hebrew roots. What he decried was "the sin" of the people. That "sin" was and continues to be the violation of the First Commandment — straying from God and panting after false loves. Sin was misdirected love and Jesus passionately wanted to direct it back to the Father (see, e.g., the story of the prodigal son). He would no more abandon his people than a good shepherd would abandon his sheep.

He answered, "I was sent only to the lost sheep of the house of Israel."

(Mt 15:24)

The way Jesus chose to accomplish this was through teaching. The miracles were used only to authenticate his teaching. He was not simply a wonder worker. He was a rabbi, a teacher.

You call me Teacher and Lord; and you are right, for so I am.
(Jn 13:13)

His teachings, and not necessarily the miracles, were what made him stand out. The Jews had a tradition where other wise and learned rabbis backed up their teachings with miracles. As wonderful as those miracles may have been it was the teachings that differentiated one teacher from the other, that made one rabbi more special than another. And there was no lack of audience to remember and collect these "sayings."

Thus it was that such wise and memorable teachings were collected and passed on by ancient Bartletts whose quotations would eventually become familiar. The birth and death of the teacher, as uneventful or remarkable as they may have been, were not at issue, any more than were the origins or circumstances of the authors of all the wise sayings contained in the Wisdom literature. "The hook" or lack thereof was the proselytizer's concern. His wisdom was the collator's.

So it is not unexplainable how the infancy or the death/resurrection of Jesus were not mentioned in the earliest Gospel source. It was the Evangelists who felt the need to expand on the sayings, to put them in context and give them life, and to make the lessons more dynamic and easier to learn, remember, and pass on.

In the human context, "the hook" always comes first. Then follow the important events and facts that surround it. When it came to Jesus, the good news was that death had been overcome. This far outweighed any other consideration, from clever aphorisms (love life and you shall lose it) to multiplying loaves and fish for a hungry crowd. The oral tradition would place his death and resurrection first. Once the people's attention had been assured it would then proceed to the salient features that related to it (miracles, teachings). The writing came later.

I can easily visualize three streams flowing from the great death/ resurrection event: first, an oral telling of the story beginning with the death and resurrection, followed by the miracles, teachings, and other significant happenings in the life of Jesus; second, the collection of the sayings and such related events, especially miracles, that gave them significance (prescinding from any controversy about his death and resurrection), in other words, a scholarly collection as was sometimes assembled for other rabbis of the time; third, the Gospel accounts as we know them, which present a "theography" and not a biography of Jesus.

Although the Evangelists were not out to write biographies as such, they did write their accounts in a somewhat biographical mode. The literary genre (style) for this type of work was not much different from today. Mark and John chose to get right to the heart of the matter, the baptism of Jesus, which inaugurated his public career. Almost as an afterthought Matthew and Luke include a birth and infancy narrative. I call it an afterthought because their material varies considerably and there is no progression from that to the public life. It is as if it were just dropped in at the last minute. This would follow logically from an orally transmitted tradition. First, the big event, "the hook." The death/resurrection story would most likely be followed by "he did some other wonderful things." After the miracle accounts, which would bolster the faith of the listeners, one can surmise the people asking, "Can I resurrect from the dead the way he did? What do I have to do?" Logically, the teachings would follow. These would be arranged in some kind of order that would make them easy to remember. Perhaps, then, in the idleness of an evening's relaxation after the essentials had been taken care of, someone might inquire about Jesus' birth. Only in the few spare moments of waiting for the imminent return of the savior does one speculate on something that has nothing to do with salvation. Thus, the Nativity was an epilogue even if it comes first in the Gospel accounts.

THE NATIVITY
A PLAY

The stage is set up like an anteroom to an office. The office door is closed. There is a couch with a coffee table and a standing lamp on one side of the room. Next to the couch there is a magazine rack. The other side of the stage has a large picture window that looks out at clouds.

There are two men in the room. One is seated on the couch paging through a magazine he took from the rack. The other is looking out the window. They are both older men sporting white hair and beards.

The door opens and a younger man enters, closing the door behind him. Both men turn and give him their attention.

GABRIEL: Everything is to go ahead on schedule.

MOSES: What are the rules?

ELIJAH: How like you, Moses, to worry about the rules before anything else.

MOSES: You have to have rules. How can people function without rules? You would have chaos. No one knows that better than you prophets. It's when people break the rules that you make your appearance.

ELIJAH: (*Laughing*) So what you're saying is you'd like to eliminate us.

MOSES: You know perfectly well Elijah that given the state of humanity there will always be the need for prophets. I simply want to help them before they get into trouble. You'll be there to help them after they get into trouble.

ELIJAH: I guess we're two sides of the same coin.

MOSES: Which brings me back to my question. Are there any rules?

GABRIEL: The same as always. The same as was done with Job. You may set the stage. You can create the scene. You may provide whatever characters you wish. But, as you know, you cannot write the dialogue. There's no giving in on that point. *He's* always very definite about that. Each person must respond the way he or she chooses. You have *carte blanche* with the situations you put them in but they must be free to respond as they wish. That is not negotiable.

MOSES: We understand.

GABRIEL: (*Looking at Elijah*) Do you agree?

ELIJAH: Do we have any choice?

GABRIEL: (*Throwing his hands up*) Prophets! (*He goes back into the office*)

MOSES: I think it's a wonderful idea.

ELIJAH: I do too. Only I would have preferred a little more latitude.

MOSES: Latitude! They have too much already. That's what causes them problems.

ELIJAH: Rules are what causes them problems. If they had fewer they wouldn't break so many of them.

MOSES: That only proves what I've always thought. That you prophets are the most unruly of all.

ELIJAH: And you lawyers have to have rules because you are the most insecure of all.

MOSES: We've had this go round before. Let's just get started and do some planning. (*He takes a tablet and pencil off the table*)

ELIJAH: (*Under his breath*) Spare me. The man has a thing for tablets.

MOSES: (*Joins Elijah at the window. Stage right fades into darkness.*) Think of it, Elijah. What we hoped and prayed for. A Messiah. Now he's ours to plan.

ELIJAH: Plan but not program. Remember what Gabriel said.

MOSES: As much as I'd love to, I'll let him handle things his own way.

ELIJAH: Big of you.

MOSES: But I can plan the circumstances.

ELIJAH: *We* can.

MOSES: I can see him now. He's entering Jerusalem and a huge crowd is cheering him. (*Outside the window Jesus passes by with people cheering and waving palm branches*)

ELIJAH: (*Almost cynically*) Are you going to plop him into Jerusalem full grown or is he going to grow his way there? I know you can't wait for him to get right down to business and that will come in due time. In the meantime there's a whole life for us to talk about. (*He laughs*) There are some rules even I can't get around.

MOSES:	(*Seriously*) I know. I know. But I'm going to want that Jerusalem scene.
ELIJAH:	Let's get him born first.
MOSES:	Let's approach this logically, one step at a time. First of all, he should be announced. Granted you can't just plop him down into the middle of things. People will have to get ready for someone this special. Besides, every great person should make some kind of auspicious entrance. Agreed?
ELIJAH:	Agreed. But what?
MOSES:	How about an angel? (*Gabriel comes out of the office*)
ELIJAH:	Good. I'm partial to angels. Then what?
MOSES:	I know! Zechariah.

Assistant angel #1 and Zechariah emerge stage right. The angel places a sign reading ZECHARIAH on an easel that stands outside the curtain and exits. Zechariah is carrying a burning censor. Gabriel crosses over to him.

GABRIEL:	Do not be afraid, Zechariah. Your prayer has been heard. Your wife, Elizabeth, is to bear you a son and you are to give him the name John. He will prepare the way for the Messiah whom the Lord will send.
ZECHARIAH:	Impossible! I am an old man.
GABRIEL:	Do you dare doubt the Lord? For doubting you shall not speak again until you utter the name God has chosen for your son . . . and praise Him for it. (*Stage right fades into darkness*)
ELIJAH:	You certainly have a flair for the dramatic, Moses. You should have been a prophet. (*Laughs*) Well, you have the tablet. What next?
MOSES:	Where? Where should he be born? Obviously, it should be Jerusalem.
ELIJAH:	I say Bethlehem.
MOSES:	Bethlehem? And why Bethlehem, of all places? It's nowheresville.

ELIJAH: I owe it to Micah. (*Moses looks at him bewildered*) He's a friend of mine.

A prophet type enters stage right. He walks out a short way and pauses. Assistant angel #1 walks over to the easel and places a sign on it that reads MICAH.

MICAH: And you, Bethlehem, in the land of Judah, you are by no means least among the leaders of Judah, for out of you will come a leader, who will shepherd my people Israel.

Stage right fades into darkness again.

MOSES: That's the *last* place I would consider. What's it got going for it?

ELIJAH: David. He was the *last* of Jesse's litter and he was from there. The least of the litter became the best later.

MOSES: Cute! Nice alliteration. Only here's the one the whole world's been waiting for since the time of Adam and you want him born in some obscure village in Judea. Be serious. Messiahs and kings should come from kingly cities. Like Jerusalem.

ELIJAH: He (*pointing to the office door*) likes his kings and prophets to be humble, or have you forgotten that already? When this one makes a name for himself he should have nothing going for him, not even his hometown.

MOSES: No problem if he comes from Bethlehem.

ELIJAH: Give me this one and I'll give you one.

MOSES: I can't believe you want to hide this shining light, this bright star, in obscurity.

ELIJAH: I'll give you a star.

MOSES: And a king! At least give me a king to acknowledge his presence.

ELIJAH: And a king. I'll even throw in some magi. But that's two concessions for one.

MOSES: Bethlehem demands it.

ELIJAH: Conceded.

Two assistant angels come out. Assistant angel #2 climbs a ladder and places a star on a sky hook. Angel #1 places a sign that reads BETHLEHEM *on the easel. They exit.*

MOSES: Now for the mother.

The door opens and Gabriel enters.

GABRIEL: That is not for discussion, gentlemen. *He* has already picked her. It's Mary of Nazareth.

Gabriel leaves.

MOSES: I told you Bethlehem wouldn't work. She's from Nazareth. It's not much better, if you ask me. But at any rate, Bethlehem's out.

Assistant angel #1 comes out and places a sign that reads NAZARETH *over the* BETHLEHEM *sign.*

ELIJAH: If Bethlehem's out, then so is the star.

They watch as the other angel comes out with his ladder and removes the star.

MOSES: On the one hand *He* tells us we can set things up the way we want.

ELIJAH: Then on the other hand...

MOSES: The Lord giveth...

ELIJAH: And the Lord taketh away.

Just then Gabriel comes into the room. They both look at him and say:

MOSES AND ELIJAH:
Blessed be the name of the Lord.

Gabriel does an about-face and returns to the office.

ELIJAH: Too bad. I really liked the idea of Bethlehem.

MOSES: I rather liked the star, too. It had a certain dramatic flair.

ELIJAH: Maybe I can still work Bethlehem in. After all I think we owe it to David and to Micah.

MOSES: How are you going to get her from Nazareth to Bethlehem?

ELIJAH: That should be no problem. How about going down to visit a relative?

MOSES: While she's pregnant? Be real. Pregnant women don't go traveling unless they have to.

ELIJAH: Then let's make her have to.

MOSES: It would take a decree from Caesar himself to make a woman in those days go traveling while she's pregnant.

ELIJAH: Fine. Then we'll make it a decree from Caesar Augustus himself. The Messiah really should be born in Bethlehem.

MOSES: As I said, I'll concede Bethlehem.

Assistant angel #1 looks for the BETHLEHEM *sign and places it over* NAZARETH.

Now, about the girl.

ELIJAH: A virgin.

MOSES: A virgin?

ELIJAH: Of course, a virgin.

MOSES: Why is it you prophets always have to go to extremes. Why not just a good woman like Ruth?

ELIJAH: Face it. Everybody who's anybody had some kind of miraculous birth. Abraham's wife Sarah was barren, but she gave birth to Isaac. Isaac's wife Rebecca was barren, but she gave birth to Jacob. Jacob's wife Rachel was barren, but she gave birth to Joseph. Does that say anything to you?

MOSES: How about, like father like son?

ELIJAH: Clever! Try, God likes impossible odds.

MOSES: Yes, but being born of a virgin? Who'd believe it? Why not just have her be barren? That'll put the Messiah in good company.

ELIJAH: That's precisely the point. He's got to be different. Better. Look what these people do to their leaders and prophets. This Messiah's going to have to stand head and shoulders above the rest to get anywhere with them. She has to be a virgin. Nothing else will really do.

MOSES: It won't work. I prefer the barren woman idea.

ELIJAH: How about a compromise?

MOSES: Like what?

ELIJAH: How about this?

Stage right lightens. Mary is sleeping on the couch. Gabriel enters and approaches her.

GABRIEL: Hail Mary!

Mary wakes up startled.

MARY: Who are you? What are you doing here? What is it you want?

GABRIEL: Do not be afraid, Mary. I have good news for you. You have found favor in the eyes of God. You are to conceive and bear a son and give him the name Jesus. He will be great and will be called the son of the Most High. The Lord God will give him the throne of his ancestor David, and he shall rule forever.

MARY: How can this be since I am a virgin?

MOSES: What did I tell you.

ELIJAH: Be quiet and listen.

GABRIEL: The Holy Spirit will come to you and the power of the Most High will overshadow you. Thus the child will be called the Son of God.

MOSES: I hate to admit it, but that's not such a bad idea after all. But you said a compromise, and so far I've made all the concessions.

Elijah points back to Mary and Gabriel.

GABRIEL:	Know this too. Your cousin Elizabeth has, in her old age, herself conceived a son, and she whom people called barren is now in her sixth month.
MOSES:	Wait a minute. Zechariah was my idea.
ELIJAH:	And Elizabeth's sterility is mine. So there's your barren woman.
MOSES:	All right. I'll concede that. Still, the idea of a virgin? What are you trying to prove?
GABRIEL:	Nothing is impossible with God.
MARY:	Then let it be done to me as you say.

Elijah looks at Moses.

MOSES:	Conceded.

Right side of stage fades into darkness again.

What about my star?

Assistant angel #2 returns with the ladder and hangs the star. When he's finished assistant angel #1 places a MAGI sign on the easel. Three magi enter from stage left. They stop not quite beneath the star.

MAGI 1:	It seems to have stopped. Let us rest while the star rests.

They sit.

MAGI 2:	The holy books say that it will come to rest over the place where the Special One will be.
MAGI 3:	How are we to know where? All stars rest over every place. The traveling star may have alerted us to seek him, but there is no telling over which place it stops.
MAGI 2:	True. But we must assume that a divine hand guided our journey. Now that the star has stopped we must have arrived.
MAGI 1:	But where are we? And where is he?
MAGI 3:	Just ahead is Jerusalem. I have been here before.
MAGI 2:	We will proceed there and make inquiry. The wise men of the king's court will know how to advise us.

They move off stage right. A woman carrying a child enters from stage left.

MOSES: Who is this woman?

ELIJAH: It is Hannah.

Assistant angel #1 places a HANNAH sign on the easel.

MOSES: Was she not the wife of Elkanah in the time of Eli the priest?

ELIJAH: She was. And I might add that she was barren.

MOSES: You might also add that she became the mother of the prophet Samuel who anointed David king. Surely, you don't want to bring Samuel back to anoint this Messiah.

ELIJAH: I'm not bringing her into this for his sake but for hers. (*He points to Mary who enters stage right*)

MARY: (*Calling out*) Elizabeth! Elizabeth!

MOSES: I ask you again, why have you brought this woman Hannah into this? I conceded the point on virginity. This woman was barren. What place has she here?

ELIJAH: I repeat that I have brought her here for Mary's sake. This woman bore the shame of sterility and was the reproach of her neighbors. God saw her plight and removed her reproach by allowing her to conceive.

MOSES: Yes. Everyone knows that. But what has that to do with this virgin Mary?

ELIJAH: The joy, Moses! She will help her to express that inexpressible joy.

Elizabeth enters and embraces Mary.

ELIZABETH: Mary, when I heard you call, the child within my womb leapt for joy.

MARY: Oh, Elizabeth, it's true! God has taken away your reproach . . . (*pauses and looks into her eyes*) . . . and mine.

ELIZABETH: (*She touches Mary's womb and then hers and smiles*) Of all women you are the most blessed. And blessed is the fruit of *your* womb. (*The two women laugh*)

HANNAH:	(*Facing the audience and holding her baby up to God*) My soul magnifies the Lord.
MARY:	(*Facing audience with arms outstretched*) My soul magnifies the Lord.
HANNAH:	My spirit rejoices because God is my savior.
MARY:	My spirit rejoices because God is my savior.
HANNAH:	He raises the poor from the dust. He lifts the needy from the dunghill and gives them a place with princes.
MARY:	He raises the poor from the dust. He lifts the needy from the dunghill and gives them a place with princes.
HANNAH:	He has come to the help of Israel his servant, mindful of his mercy.
MARY:	He has come to the help of Israel his servant, mindful of his mercy.
MOSES:	According to the promise He made to our ancestors — to Abraham and his descendants forever.

Hannah lowers the child at the word "promise," as if remembering, and walks off stage left.

ELIJAH:	(*As she's walking off*) And Hannah left the child with Eli the priest because she had promised Yahweh to give the child back to Him.

Stage darkens. Assistant angel #1 places a HEROD sign on the easel. When lights are raised Herod is seated on the couch. The magi enter with some others.

HEROD:	What have you discovered, my learned friends? Is the Messiah truly come?
MAGI 1:	Of that, great Herod, there is no doubt. The question was where.
HEROD:	Then where is he?
ADVISOR:	Bethlehem. According to Micah the prophet he is to be born in the town of David.
HEROD:	Can this be true? This fantasy of a star is true?

ADVISOR: It was foretold. By Balaam the seer in the Book of Numbers. "I see him — but in the future. I behold him — but still at a distance. A star from Jacob." It is there, my lord, in holy writ.

HEROD: Then I must know where in Bethlehem. Go seek him out and offer your presents, but I exhort you to return hence straightaway so that I too may go and offer my respects.

Stage darkens.

MOSES: Gabriel!

Gabriel enters from the office.

I do not trust this Herod. The magi should be warned of his deviousness.

GABRIEL: I will see to it. (*He returns to the office*)

ELIJAH: I can't take this waiting much longer.

MOSES: Everything must be just so.

ELIJAH: How much more can we set the stage.

MOSES: Well, let's see. There was Zechariah.

ELIJAH: He was yours.

MOSES: Elizabeth, his wife, was yours. So too was Bethlehem.

ELIJAH: The star, the king, and the magi were yours.

MOSES: Yes, but Herod turned out to be a rotten apple. Then there's the virgin, Mary. By the way, Hannah was a nice touch.

ELIJAH: Moses! We forgot something. Her husband — Joseph! How's he going to take all this? What if he doesn't believe? About the pregnancy, I mean.

MOSES: That's what I tried to tell you in the beginning!

ELIJAH: But it's too late now. It's done.

Gabriel enters.

GABRIEL: I've taken care of Joseph. (*Moses and Elijah look at each other startled*) I explained everything to him in a dream.

MOSES: Like Joseph of old who interpreted dreams.

GABRIEL: I thought it a rather nice touch myself. After all, we angels are not exactly at a loss over what to do without you humans.

ELIJAH: How did he take it?

GABRIEL: Splendidly.

ELIJAH: Good old humans! We're really not much less than angels when you get down to it.

MOSES: Then that should take care of everything.

GABRIEL: Good. Now let's get on with it, shall we?

ELIJAH: Just one more thing.

MOSES AND GABRIEL:
           Now what?

ELIJAH: I'd like some shepherds.

MOSES: Shepherds are out. The people consider it an unclean profession.

ELIJAH: How can they be unclean when God Himself told Ezekiel that He would come and shepherd the people?

MOSES: Well, to be honest with you, I never said they were unclean. Some lawyers interpreted that.

ELIJAH: See. What did I tell you about lawyers?

GABRIEL: Never mind. The shepherds are in. I'll take care of them myself. Now can we finally get on with it.

Moses and Elijah look at each other and nod.

Good. (*He exits*)

Moses and Elijah direct the entire setting up of the stage. Appropriate Christmas music is heard in the background. Assistant angel #1 enters and places a NATIVITY sign on the easel while assistant angel #2 comes out with a ladder and polishes the star. The two of them then move the couch to center stage. Moses directs the magi holding their gifts to the right of the couch. Elijah shepherds in the shepherds and places them to the left of the couch. Mary and Joseph are directed to the couch where they sit. Moses and Elijah stand at center stage at the apron appraising the setup. Moses goes over to Joseph and has him stand behind the couch over Mary's shoulder. Elijah nods his approval. He looks questioningly at the scene and then goes over and knocks on the office door. Gabriel emerges and is directed to climb the ladder. Hesitatingly, he does so.

Moses and Elijah return to center stage.

MOSES: I don't know. Something's wrong. Something's missing.

ELIJAH: The baby's missing! That's what's missing.

He goes over to Mary and whispers in her ear. Mary rises and goes to the office door. She knocks and enters. When she comes out, she is carrying a child. She leaves the door opened. The sound of angels singing joyously emerges from the office and fills the house.

Mary sits on the couch. Joseph looks over her shoulder at the child. The others stare in wonderment. A dazzling light floods out of the office door and spotlights Mary, Joseph, and the child.

ELIJAH: Perfect! Pretty as a picture, if I do say so myself.

MOSES: Definitely a masterpiece! And if the Almighty would indulge me in a little pride, I would like to do what all artists do after they have completed a great work. I would like to sign it.

ELIJAH: Why not? He's so pleased right now I'm sure he would grant us anything.

MOSES: Seeing the child here reminds me of my humble beginnings. Remember, Elijah? The pharaoh wanted to destroy me, just like Herod now wants to destroy this child. I was placed in a little reed boat and set adrift on the river.

ELIJAH: There is no river here. And no boat.

MOSES: True. But there is a manger.

He brings the magazine rack over to the couch and places it in front of Mary. She lays the child in it.

ELIJAH: You surprise me, Moses. As I said before, you do have a flair for the dramatic. Well, you've left your mark on the nativity of the Messiah.

MOSES: What about you, Elijah?

Just then the light emanating from the office goes out. Gabriel descends the ladder and the others begin to break up. During the commotion Elijah goes to the child and places his hand in blessing over him.

Pity, the scene broke up before you could sign it.

ELIJAH: Yes, a pity. But then we prophets are not so proud as you lawyers.

MOSES: Just remember, Elijah, prophets don't get the last word. We lawyers do.

ELIJAH: Yes. A pity.

Joseph and Mary carrying the child come to center stage and pass in front of Moses and Elijah. They both look at the baby.

MOSES: We will see him again. We'll see to it.

ELIJAH: Yes. Later, when he's grown. There's nothing more we can do for now.

Mary and Joseph nod and exit stage right. Moses and Elijah watch them until they are gone and then slowly follow them.

MOSES: Elijah, you did leave your mark after all, didn't you?

ELIJAH: What are you saying?

MOSES: The baby. I looked at the baby as they were leaving.

ELIJAH: Yes?

MOSES: You made him look like you.

ELIJAH: I tell you what. You give me this one, and I'll give you one.

MOSES: Like what?

ELIJAH: How about me setting it up so that he can give com-
            mandments the way you did?

MOSES: On a mountain.

ELIJAH: A hill.

MOSES: Ten of them.

ELIJAH: Eight. And instead of calling them commandments,
            we'll call them beatitudes.

            *They walk off arguing stage right. Assistant angel #1
            enters carrying a sign that he places on the easel. It reads
            TO BE CONTINUED.*

REFLECTIONS

Christmas

Christmas is a wondrous time. In spite of the current trend toward de-
mythologizing the scriptures and the strident quest for historicity there
is a sense of the faithful that no rational scholarship can reason away.
Nowhere is this more evident than in the birth and infancy accounts
of Jesus.

   Scholars have time and again explained the rationale of these narratives, the language, style, and literary forms that comprise them, but
never the *need* for them, the human, emotional need for the Incarnation to be expressed first in terms of a helpless child. In a scientific and
critically oriented scholarship there is no room for the emotional. It is
undemonstrable in terms of biblical criticism. But it is there; otherwise
how else can we account for these narratives? Mark eliminates the Nativity entirely and John philosophizes beyond it. The discrepancies in
the Matthew and Luke accounts can be explained only by myth. Some
fear that the biblically illiterate may misinterpret this to mean that the
accounts are pure fabrication or total fiction.

I maintain, however, that there are two levels of biblical interpretation — the scholarly level with its critical, interpretive analysis, and
the *sense of the faithful*. Both are needed and both are valid. Because the
former is more exacting and definitive it can be a valid guide to keep
us carefully on the path of truth. But the latter can also express truth in
another sense, even though there may appear to be a greater danger of
straying off the path.

The sacred authors weren't always expressing facts in the strictest
sense (witness the numerous discrepancies in the four Gospel accounts).
If indeed, as we are told, there is no real, provable historicity in the infancy accounts, how else can we explain the reason for those narratives?
The sense of the faithful had need of them. They express a truth on a
different level.

So one Evangelist pieces together an account centered on the prophetic proclamations and expectations concerning the Messiah, and the
other does it in terms of the themes and expectations of the living Christian community. Historical validity is not the point. Whether Mary and
Joseph lived in Bethlehem at the time of Jesus' birth or moved there from
Nazareth is immaterial. The need for the Incarnation to express God becoming a human being also needed to be expressed as God becoming a
child. That is very much to the point. Such is the power of the sense of the
faithful. The Spirit is as much alive here as it is in the more defined sense.

There is no question that the central point of all Christian faith is the
resurrection of Jesus. Theologically speaking it is the foundation stone
of our faith and the pinnacle of the liturgical year. The celebration of
the resurrection is preceded by forty days of preparation and expectation (even more so in the older rites with Septuagesima, Sexagesima,
and Quinquagesima Sundays) and elaborate rites of celebration. Passion
narratives are read, palms are distributed, feet are washed, crosses are
carried, paschal candles are lit, exultets are sung, waters are blessed, and
bells are rung. By contrast there are only four weeks of Advent and no
special rites for the Christmas liturgy. Yet, in spite of all this, the faithful
are more excited and delighted over Christmas. One biblical scholar explained this by saying that Easter is the feast of the (institutional) church
and Christmas is the feast of the people.

We may justifiably decry the rampant commercialism that has tainted
the celebration and even some of the maudlin sentimentality surrounding it, but never was the cliché more appropriate: "we must not throw
out the baby with the bath water." Christmas was created by the people

and will endure with them. There is a truth here that endures beyond the rational and the critical. Jesus had to be born, had to be a baby, and birthing is a wondrous time.

The Birth of Jesus

Children have a puzzle game they play called Connect the Dots. There is a series of numbered dots you connect with a pencil, which when completed reveals a mystery picture. You aren't sure what you're going to come up with until the end.

In explaining the scant knowledge and conflicting accounts of the infancy of Jesus, scripture scholars have averred that such sketchy information is not unusual when dealing with historical figures. Birth and infancy have little import when compared to that part of the person's life that had an impact on the world. What more than passing knowledge is known about the beginnings of such great personages as Alexander the Great, Napoleon Bonaparte, George Washington, or Abraham Lincoln? The same may be assumed of Jesus. Remember too that his public ministry was short, less than three years. By the time he gained popularity he was already on his way to Calvary. Thus, personal knowledge of him would be limited. One may also assume that referring to his roots was a touchy subject with Jesus, since it occasioned harsh criticism of his hometown for belittling and rejecting him.

Only in the end did his birth receive any attention. As already mentioned, Mark's Gospel, the oldest of the four accounts, skips it altogether while John's speaks of it only in philosophical, cosmic terms. It was left for Matthew and Luke to fill in the blanks.

Matthew seems to have done precisely that. Knowing what he did about Jesus and the scriptures relevant to the Messiah, he apparently connected the dots of scriptural passages about the Messiah and drew them into a picture of Jesus' birth. Historicity was not the question. Authenticating Jesus was.

Luke has Mary and Joseph traveling to Bethlehem from their hometown of Nazareth, while Matthew has them living in Bethlehem at the time of the birth of Jesus. Before this discrepancy can be resolved, you must understand first the forces that are at play here. The common perception of the nativity is actually a composite of the two Gospel accounts. People have joined them together into one flowing narrative. Thus, the popular understanding is that Mary and Joseph traveled to Bethlehem as did the magi who followed the star. This is a longstanding, deep-rooted tradition dear to the hearts of the people. You cannot do violence to it without shaking the people's faith even though the evidence of the discrepancy is present in the scriptures. Second, our generation was nurtured on the scientific method with its obsession for objectivity. Scientific and historical truth demands that it be either one or the other: Either Mary and Joseph were living in Bethlehem when Jesus was born or they were not. It cannot be both. The literalists hold that both Matthew and Luke are right since the word of God cannot contradict itself, and they leave it to others to come up with a plausible explanation. Modern scholarship admits the discrepancy but speaks of a kind of truth different from the historical or scientific.

What is the truth that is at stake here? That Jesus is the Messiah — foretold in the scriptures, approved by God in his teachings and miracles, and vindicated by his death and resurrection. To the scientist we assert that this is a religious truth unprovable by empiric evidence. It is a faith statement. Matthew's Gospel believes this and wants its hearers to believe it too. So Matthew begins with this belief and fits the scriptures into a picture of Jesus.

First, the Messiah must be of the line of David. Therefore, his account begins with a genealogy to attest to that fact:

> The book of the genealogy of Jesus Christ, the son of David, the son of Abraham. Abraham was the father of Isaac, and Isaac the father of Jacob, and Jacob the father of Judah and his brothers, and Judah the father of... Obed the father of Jesse, and Jesse the father of David the king. And David was the father of Solomon by the wife of Uriah, and Solomon the father of... Jacob, and Jacob the father of Joseph the husband of Mary, of whom Jesus was born, who is called Christ.
>
> (Mt 1:1–16)

Matthew had another problem with his genealogy. Heredity followed the male line. However, he does not list Jesus as being born of Joseph but of Mary. The genealogy should have been of her ancestors, but there were no listings for women. So Matthew accommodates, which is what this account is all about.

Now that he has shown Jesus to be of the line of David (the first dot of the puzzle), he then had to be of the city of David:

And you, Oh, Bethlehem, in the land of Judah, are by no means
least among the rulers of Judah; for from you shall come a ruler
who will govern my people Israel.

(Mt 2:6; cf. Mic 5:2)

The city of David was Bethlehem. There was an added nuance here
that could be lost to non-Jews. David was the last child of Jesse, the one
least expected to be anointed by the prophet. Samuel is reminded that
it is God who does the choosing and not human beings (1 Sam 16:7).
Was this also meant as a sign to the Jews who were resisting Jesus as
the chosen one?

The birthplace of David would become the birthplace of the Messiah, so connect the next dot to Bethlehem. Matthew had Mary and
Joseph living there so Jesus could be born there, while Luke, knowing
that Nazareth was Jesus' hometown and families lived in the same town
for generations, got him to Bethlehem by means of a census the likes of
which we can find no evidence for in those times. Trying to find historical evidence for that peculiar census is like trying to find what celestial
phenomenon occurred around December 25 two thousand years ago.
No one knows the date or season of Jesus' birth. December 25 is an arbi-
trary date picked for its symbolic significance. It is the time of the winter
solstice. From that time on the days get longer. Jesus is called, "the light
of the world." From the day of his birth his light increased the way day-
light begins to increase at that time of year. Moreover, that particular
day was picked to supplant a popular pagan feast that was celebrated
at that time. People are reluctant to give up popular holidays, so the
early church simply superimposed its own to give the pagan holiday a
Christian significance.

Furthermore, if Halley's Comet or some other "star" occurred back
then, how could you possibly tell if it stopped over Bethlehem? In the
Book of Numbers there is an obscure reference to a star like the equally
obscure reference to Bethlehem from the Book of Micah quoted above:

I see him, but not now; I behold him, but not nigh: *a star* shall come
forth out of Jacob, and a scepter shall rise out of Israel; it shall crush
the forehead of Moab, and break down all the sons of Sheth.

(Nm 24:17)

This prophecy emanated from a pagan prophet, Balaam. In context,
it is meant to signify that even the Gentiles will come to recognize the

light that shines from Israel. Thus, we have gentiles (astrologers) and a star in Matthew's account. Connect two more dots.

Next, add something from the prophet par excellence, Isaiah:

Therefore the Lord himself will give you a sign. Behold, a virgin shall conceive and bear a son, and shall call his name Emmanuel.

(Is 7:14)

The final dot has been connected.

Dare I add that to the Jewish mind steeped in ancient lore one might add color to the picture by invoking the image of an angel announcing an extraordinary birth, much as the angel did with Sarah (Gn 18:1–15), inaugurating a *new race* of people?

To the analytical and critical mind this appears to be no more than story weaving. In fact, it is. But it is not pure fiction as in fairy tales. It is myth in the biblical sense. Aesop told a fable about a boy who cried wolf. Would the hearers be offended if they were to discover that Aesop never saw that wolf or heard a boy who did the crying? There is a truth there that's at the heart of the story, not that the boy's name was Harry or the animal was actually a fox.

I once told a story in a homiletics class in the seminary. Afterward, a classmate asked me if it really happened. I said no. He said to me, "Then you lied." I'm afraid that my friend will never understand the scriptures, that he and others like him will be scandalized by current scholarship, that their preaching and teaching will be forever crippled: "What if there were a boy and what if there were a wolf and what if the boy were to cry, 'Wolf,'" and so on and so on.

The quest for the historical Jesus fails to look at him and his mission in a faith context. One must understand that Matthew had a prior bias, namely, that Jesus was the Messiah. Everything in his Gospel is colored by that belief. Matthew sees links that others might question or refute. Admittedly, fitting the facts or connecting the dots after the fact is easier than trying to anticipate the facts, but to Matthew Jesus was unquestionably the Messiah and, therefore, all Old Testament texts had to refer to him. Being born in Bethlehem did not make him the Messiah. Nor being born of a virgin. Nor the presence of a star and magi. Not even all of them put together make Jesus the Messiah. He was the Messiah because God made him so. Matthew knew that. The where and how of his birth was just wonderful window dressing.

Where Matthew was an arranger who connected dots between material that came before Jesus, Luke was a composer who worked with themes that became important after Jesus. These themes were the return of Elijah to herald the Messiah and the importance of the poor and lowly in the ministry of Jesus. Elijah makes his reappearance in the miraculous birth of John the Baptist and Jesus is born in a stable with shepherds in attendance.

If Gospel literalists take umbrage at such interpretations, choosing to accept the nativity accounts as true and historical as recorded, that, of course, is their right and prerogative. They would then have to come up with some other plausible explanation to account for the differences and discrepancies in the narratives. Those I have offered do no violence to truth in the *literary* sense. To have Jesus born by dropping miraculously out of the sky would do violence to the Gospel theme of Jesus as the Son of Man, as would having him be born amid the riches and splendor of a kingly court without some kind of later conversion experience. Such literary fantasies were not unknown in the early church, but they were rejected out of hand.

Today, we have continued the tradition begun by Matthew and Luke by weaving their two separate accounts into one. Every retelling, every reenactment blends them into a satisfying literary whole. Every Christmas creche has the Matthean magi and the Lucan shepherds in the same setting. If we allow such latitude now, why not then?

A Virgin

> Therefore the Lord himself will give you this sign: the virgin shall be with child, and bear a son, and shall name him Immanuel.
>
> (Is 7:14)

There are times when all of us could use a miracle. King Ahaz of Judah needed one badly. Syria and Israel (Northern Kingdom) were trying to persuade Judah (Southern Kingdom) to join them in a coalition against Assyria. Ahaz was in terror.

> When the house of David was told, "Syria is in league with Ephraim [Israel]," his heart and the heart of his people shook as the trees of the forest shake before the wind.
>
> (Is 7:2)

Isaiah was trying to prevent him from forming a counteralliance with Assyria, so he invited the king to ask for a sign from God, even if it be in the deepest depths or the highest heights (Is 7:10). Ahaz refuses:

> But Ahaz said, "I will not ask, and I will not put the LORD to the test."
>
> (Is 7:12)

What may seem like humility was not humility at all. Ahaz was saying that he didn't want to hear God's response. How many of us want to hear what God has to say when it runs contrary to what we want?

God was not pleased:

> And he said, "Hear then, Oh, house of David! Is it too little for you to weary men, that you weary my God also?"
>
> (Is 7:13)

The situation was desperate so only desperate measures would suffice. A sign. A miracle. Isaiah foretells a special birth that is to occur to a virgin (Is 7:14).

This prophecy has been the subject of no small amount of interpretation and controversy. The dispute centers on the word "virgin." Did he mean simply a young maiden, the other meaning of the term in Hebrew? I find the argument specious. In numerous European and Eastern cultures a girl is called a young maiden or virgin before she is married. The terms are synonymous. If anything else were intended the prophet would have used "madam" or "married woman." He certainly knew the words and the distinction. Then consider the context. Isaiah is trying to convince this recalcitrant king to follow his advice. To prove his point he tells Ahaz to ask anything, no matter how outrageous it may seem and God will grant it (Is 7:10). When Ahaz refuses would Isaiah counter with such an insipid, lackluster proposal as the declaration that a girl is going to have a baby and name him Emmanuel? What's so remarkable about a girl giving birth? Would such a prophecy knock Ahaz off his feet? Would such a pronouncement bring him to his knees? The context itself cries for some extraordinary sign that would convince this stubborn prince. Would telling him that a young girl somewhere, at some time was going to have a baby do it? Hardly.

Here is a God who demands impossible odds. Like when God promised barren, postmenopausal women that they would conceive and bear sons; like when God led the Israelites across the Red Sea; like when God defeated more than thirty thousand Midianites with just Gideon and three hundred men. To a king steeped in the lore of his people, breast-fed on the accounts of the wonders God had done, would the prophecy, "Somebody's going to have a baby!" stir him to the depths of his being? It had to be a virgin!

Again, consider the context. Isaiah is trying to convince Ahaz that God is with him, with Judah. In exasperation he is saying, "What will it take to convince you? If it takes a virgin giving birth to do it, then God will do it. We'll even call the baby Emmanuel." Emmanuel means, "God is with us." I dare say that what Isaiah said in the heat of the moment went beyond even his expectations. Moreover, if Isaiah was less in control because of his apparent exasperation, then the prophecy was all the more of God.

Even so, how potent a prophecy would it be since it was not to take place for hundreds of years? But we know that only in retrospect. Ahaz did not know when this great sign was to take place. Second, kings as well as commoners gave greater attention to posterity than we do today. A man lived on through his lineage. While he didn't want to hurry his departure, he certainly didn't want to go without leaving someone behind. Here was the definite promise of a dynasty. Third, it would not be just some ordinary scion, but one born of a virgin. If the prophet spoke the truth, and Ahaz had no doubt about Isaiah's credentials, then there could be no doubt about who the Father of the virgin would have to be. If God could allow sterile women to get pregnant, God could make a virgin conceive. And this remarkable offspring would be of Ahaz's lineage. Finally, would the world have had to wait seven hundred years for the coming of Jesus if Ahaz had not eventually been found so wanting?

The Genealogies

Matthew deals with the humanity of Jesus for a people and a tradition that could understand messiahship only in human, Judaic terms. Therefore, there could be none greater than Abraham the Father of Nations, from whose loins dynasties were to endure until the end of time. The physical presence of countless Jews was testimony enough of his greatness. Egypt, Babylon, Assyria, and Greece had come and gone. The Israelites had undergone slavery, persecution, and the sword. Yet they endured. The promise was verified by their continued presence in the world. Here alone there was more than sufficient reason for their faith. God was with this people as with no other. What else could account for their indomitable spirit, their defiance, their arrogance? They had only to look around to see Emmanuel (God is with us).

For all his greatness Moses, the Lawgiver, is not in the genealogy. To the non-Semitic mind this might appear a glaring weakness. Certainly, as a Hebrew he was a descendant of Abraham. To include him would assuredly add prestige to the lineage, which includes an usurper (Isaac), a conniver (Jacob), a harlot (Rahab), an alien (Ruth), and a whole host of unsavories and unknowns. When in so many other places historicity is stretched, why isn't artistic license utilized here?

Part of the reason is that prophets, the greatest and the least, can be called by God according to God's own discretion. God can raise up children to Abraham from the very stones irrespective of human considerations. Family trees may be important to human beings but God chooses whom God wills. No caste or lineage restricts God. This leaves room for hope even among the lowliest. Therein lies the strength of their faith.

Another reason that helps explain this genealogy, undoubtedly the more important, has to do with David. David is the Messiah par excellence in the minds of the Jewish people. That God can call and sanction this enigmatic man as ruler of his people is ample witness of divine condescension. David's accomplishments were indeed monumental, although his methods were far from praiseworthy. For his sins he would pay the price, but the legend that surrounded him would live on. The dreams of a divided and beleaguered people to be united, to conquer and stand unbowed among the nations became so rooted in the Davidic kingship that David's reign would stand forever as the bright star in the annals of their long and turbulent history. The prophetic promise was that another Messiah would spring from his loins. Any future messiahs would be measured against David. It would be difficult if not impossible to conceive of a Messiah in any other way. David would be the litmus test of authenticity. Messianic validity extended backward from David to Abraham and forward to any reputed Messiah.

The lineage of Joseph is traced back to David so that Jesus may lay claim to messiahship. True messiahship, however, may extend beyond any one line, for all genealogies can be traced back to Adam and hence to God. So Luke allows for the sensitivity of the Jewish tradition but traces Jesus back to his Father, the ultimate source of all authenticity.

The inclusion of the genealogies in the two infancy accounts satisfies both the critical needs of the tradition and the inner needs of all people. Divine election is not determined by human requirements but by the free choice of God. No lineage is too exalted or lowly or spotted for God. God chooses whom God wills and where God wills. Tradition tells us that many women dreamed of being the mother of the Messiah. Would such a dream have been possible if God were as restrictive as human beings?

A Star

The two accounts of the birth and infancy of Jesus differ because both Evangelists approached the topic from different perspectives. Matthew wrote his infancy account around the prophecies of the Old Testament. Luke wove his around the theme of poverty. Matthew wanted to demonstrate that Jesus was the promised Messiah. Luke accommodated his version to the Christian theme of poverty.

The star appears only in Matthew. "Where is he who has been born king of the Jews? For we have seen his star in the East, and have come to worship him" (Mt 2:2). The allusion is to an obscure passage in the Book of Numbers. Balaam, a pagan oracle, was hired by king Balak to utter a curse against the approaching Israelites. In the desert the Hebrews had grown to be a mighty nation, defeating in battle the fierce Amorites. Fearing a similar fate for Moab, Balak wants to enlist God in his cause. This would give him assurance and his troops confidence since Balaam was regarded as an upright prophet. Balaam refuses because he foresees the destruction of Moab. Instead of cursing the Jews, he blesses them three times, as directed by the Lord. When he sees the sprawling encampment of the Israelites, he utters:

> How fair are your tents, Oh, Jacob, your encampments, Oh, Israel! Like valleys that stretch afar, like gardens beside a river, like aloes that the LORD has planted, like cedar trees beside the waters. Water shall flow from his buckets, and his seed shall be in many waters, his king shall be higher than Agag, and his kingdom shall be exalted.... Blessed be every one who blesses you, and cursed be every one who curses you.
>
> (Nm 24:5–9)

These are hardly encouraging words to a rival king who is looking for confidence. Finally, in his fourth oracle Balaam utters:

> I see him, but not now;
> I behold him, but not near.
> A star will come out of Jacob;
> A scepter will rise out of Israel.
>
> (Nm 24:17)

Three blessings and a prophecy. Any time someone proclaims something three times in the scriptures it is a sign of definitiveness. Once you repeat a statement three times there is no recanting. It is so.

True oracles and prophets were persons of vision able to read astutely the signs of the times. No doubt Balaam had heard of the exploits of this people emigrating from Egypt; otherwise how could he have described them so accurately?

> God brought them out of Egypt;
> they have the strength of a wild ox.
> They devour hostile nations
> and break their bones in pieces;
> with their arrows they pierce them.
> Like a lion they crouch and lie down,
> like a lioness — who dares to rouse them?
>
> (Nm 24:8-9)

Did it take much discernment to see how God had blessed this people? If God had not been with them, how else could they have come so far? Balaam was not just prophetic, he was courageous. It was not uncommon for the bearer of bad news to be executed. At the risk of his life Balaam told the truth.

What of the star? Oftentimes oracles had two levels of meaning — the apparent surface meaning and the deeper symbolic one. The obvious significance of the star was much the same as it is today. Someone special will arise from among this people. The deeper symbolism is that no matter how dark the world becomes for a people or a person, a light will eventually penetrate the darkness for those who remain faithful.

You must bear in mind that this account is taken from a Jewish book and told from a Jewish point of view, so it would be understandable that it might be somewhat embellished. But there is also some internal evidence that gives the story its own credibility. One might excuse a man whose life is at stake if he hedges a little bit:

> I see him, *but not now;*
> I behold him, *but not near.*

Was this that little bit of hope that Balak needed, that the impending doom of his kingdom was not quite imminent? Did it spare the life of the messenger?

Matthew uses the star in both senses, real and symbolic:

> We saw his star in the east and have come to worship him.
>
> (Mt 2:2)

A star to mark the birth of a star. Goodness and light are always the signs of the presence of God. These themes abound in the scriptures and were prevalent at the time of Christ. Israel would be a light to the nations and Jesus to the world. Only the wise would come to it. The foolish are an abomination.

The symbolic meaning is also present:

> When they had heard the king they went their way; and lo, the star which they had seen in the East went before them, till it came to rest over the place where the child was.
>
> (Mt 2:9)

Have you ever stood outside on a starlit night? Which star is directly over you? They all are. How could you tell if one of them, even if it were as bright and as close as the moon, were over a particular village? The light of God shines over every city, house, village, and person where there is deep and abiding faith. The darkness will not prevail. The star of Bethlehem is a message to all of us who now and again live in darkness.

Santa Claus and Angels

> In the sixth month the angel Gabriel was sent from God to a city of Galilee named Nazareth.
>
> (Lk 1:26)

I don't remember exactly when I learned there really wasn't a Santa Claus. I know that the discovery did not traumatize me since the discovery left no emotional scars behind. I must have just taken it in stride.

Now that I'm older and wiser, I have come to believe in Santa Claus once again. Not as I did when I was a child. Differently but no less really. I believe that there is such a special spirit that flourishes among people at Christmas time, a spirit that is so pervasive that it is almost palpable, that we just had to give that spirit a form, a body. That's what we call Santa Claus.

Are angels any different? Angel means "messenger," and in the Bible they were bearers of good news. (It wasn't good news, however, if you were bad. Sound familiar?) Angels told Sarah that she would bear a child in her old age. An angel told the barren wife of Manoah that she would bear a son, who later became the great Samson. Gabriel brought good news to Elizabeth and outstanding news to Mary. When the spirit of good, the spirit of God is so tangibly present we just have to give that spirit a form. It is the only medium we understand, something we can see or hear or touch. So we give angels bodies, wings, and haloes. Does that make angels any less real? Does it make Santa Claus any less real?

Scripture scholars tell us that more than likely angels had the appearance of men. They looked like just ordinary people. But they brought a message from God, a gift from God to the people. Intrinsic to the message was that it brought hope.

Does not our modern-day Santa Claus bring a message of peace, hope, and joy wherever he goes? Are not the gifts he brings merely a substitute, another word for grace? Does it make any difference if he wears a red suit and whiskers rather than a halo and wings? Is Santa Claus any less an angel?

The invitation to be angels, messengers of God, is open to all human-kind. Still most of us would hesitate to take on the role. Samuel Taylor Coleridge writes that in Ratzeburg, Germany, in 1799, children at about seven or eight years of age were let in on the secret about Santa Claus. He found it curious to observe how faithfully they kept the secret. We have evidence here that from 1799 on and perhaps before, millions of children and adults have dressed up and taken on the role of Santa Claus themselves to keep the "myth" alive. What a remarkable thing that God uses a red-suited, white-whiskered, jolly old man to do what the great angels of scripture were unable to do, even if it is only once a year!

Not believe in Santa Claus? You might as well not believe in angels.

The Incarnation

> And the word became flesh and dwelt among us.
>
> (Jn 1:14)

The treatment of the birth of Jesus would be incomplete without taking into account the remarkable perspective of John the Evangelist. John looks through and beyond the temporal to the eternal. For him the birth of Jesus has cosmic implications. The Incarnation begins with the dawn of creation.

To say that the Incarnation began with Mary's *fiat,* "Be it done unto me according to your word," that it began when Jesus took flesh within her womb, would be far too short-sighted. Even if we were to speak in biological terms, we would have to go beyond that moment, precious as it is. Biologically one may say that when the substance of the man (sperm) enters into the substance of the woman (egg), incarnation begins. In the same way, then, we would have to say that when the substance of God *initiated* creation the Incarnation actually began. "*In the beginning* was the word" (Jn 1:1). At the very moment creation began God — Father, Son, and Holy Spirit — penetrated all of it. The faith picture presented by John the Evangelist was precisely that all creation from the first moment of its existence was affected by Jesus. "Through him all things came into being, and apart from him nothing came to be" (Jn 1:3).

Bethlehem began at the dawn of creation.

Christian faith believes in one God consisting of three divine Persons — Father, Son, and Holy Spirit. Although they are one, they are separate and distinct from one another, each having its own personality. Like in a cup of sweet coffee, water, coffee, and sugar permeate the whole of it, yet they each have their own distinctness. The three Persons are totally present in all that God is, yet each has its own uniqueness, its own individuality. This trinity according to revelation is Love (1 Jn 5:16).

This is the foundation stone of Christianity. It is upon this that everything is built.

The Father loves the Son with the totality of all that God is. It is like saying, "Every bit of me loves you." The Son loves the Father in exactly the same way: "All that I am and all that is in me loves you." The Holy Spirit is the personification of the love of the two of them. The Spirit is the love that moves between them. They are all one in a perpetual state of giving and receiving.

Therefore, love is a trinity. All love is trinity.

I am a trinity. My father is in me. My height, my weight, my receding hairline, the fire of my emotions are the presence of my father within me. My mother is in me. The color of my eyes, the shape of my face, the gentleness of my affection are the presence of my mother within me. The way I blend all these and the way I use them are the unique me. I am three in one. Even in this small way we are made in the image of God.

God is love and love is like breathing.

We inhale and fill ourselves with the exhilaration of life-giving air. But it doesn't stop there. It cannot. We must exhale. In the same way, love must first be taken in. We cannot know love unless we have breathed it in.

And we have. All of us have. Love was breathed into us at the very moment of our conception.

Then the Lord God formed man of dust from the ground, and breathed into his nostrils the breath of life; and man became a living being.

(Gn 2:7)

We, for our part, love, because he [God] first loved us.
(1 Jn 4:19)

We have inhaled the life-giving breath of God, and, as when we breathe, we must also exhale. To capture love and try to hold onto it would be like inhaling without exhaling. We would die and love would die. Love and breathing are sustained by giving and receiving.

What does love give? Gifts. I express my love for you by giving you a gift. I try to express the depth of my love by the value of the gift. The more I love you, the more valuable the gift. The Father expresses the infinite love He has for His Son by giving Him an infinite gift — the universe. A billion galaxies, each with a billion stars, stretching countless trillions of miles. All for His Son. All things were made through the Son and because of Him.

Creation was the egg God fertilized and Mary was the womb for the Incarnation of the Son. Bethlehem began at the dawn of creation. And Jesus was the firstborn of all creation.

He is the image of the invisible God, the firstborn of all creation.
(Col 1:15)

What is the significance of this added insight? The commonly held idea of the Incarnation as between God, Mary, and Jesus is much too limiting for what the Bible tells us is the full scope of the meaning of Jesus. God is the medium in which we exist. Like a fish that lives and moves in water, we live, move, and have our being in God. Every rock, every tree, every blade of grass, every animal, every man, woman, and child, every living and existing thing is permeated by God and sustained by God. All of this is because of Jesus. This is why Saint Paul can say:

We know that the whole of creation has been groaning...until now.

(Rom 8:22)

From the very beginning pregnant creation groaned like a woman in labor for the coming of Jesus. Creation takes on a greater stature because of Jesus. It exists because it is the gift of the Father to the Son. It is a good gift. Indeed, a very good one (Gn 1:31). Because God chose the time, the place, and the woman for the entrance of His Son into the world, we may rightly assume that the selection was made with special care. The time was the right time for it to happen. Bethlehem was the right place. And Mary was just the right woman.

Rejoice, Oh, highly favored daughter! The Lord is with you. Blessed are you among women.

(Lk 1:28)

She was the right woman because God had prepared her to be so. Is it not reasonable to assume that the womb that would bear the immaculate Son of God would itself be made immaculate?

All creation breathed in God's love when it came into existence and all creation must breathe it back. But only human beings can speak. Only human beings can express love like God. So human beings speak for all creation.

Then God said, "Let us make man in our image, after our likeness; and let them have dominion over the fish of the sea, and over the birds of the air, and over the cattle, and over all the earth, and over every creeping thing that creeps upon the earth."

(Gn 1:26)

When humankind speaks, it speaks for all creation. Adam cannot say to God, "I love You." He must say, "We love You!" All creation rises and falls with the love of humankind.

Love says, "I do!"

My father stood before the altar of God and said to my mother, "I do!" My mother looked at my father and said, "I do!" In that breath they pledged their all to one another. That breath is creative. I am its creation.

God stood before creation and said, "I do!" Humankind responding for creation said, "I do!" In that breath they pledged their all to one another. That breath is creative. Jesus is born!

> For God so loved the world that he gave his only Son.
>
> (Jn 3:16)

Jesus is the reason for creation. Jesus is the pinnacle of creation.

> He is the image of the invisible God, the firstborn of all creation; for in him all things were created, in heaven and on earth, visible and invisible, whether thrones or dominions or principalities or authorities — all things were created through him and for him. He is before all things, and in him all things hold together. He is the head of the body, the church; he is the beginning, the firstborn from the dead, that in everything he might be pre-eminent. For in him all the fulness of God was pleased to dwell, and through him to reconcile to himself all things, whether on earth or in heaven, making peace by the blood of his cross.
>
> (Col 1:15–20)

2

PRELUDE TO MINISTRY

Before dealing with Jesus in the New Testament let me preface my comments by saying that it was much easier dealing with the Old Testament. I assert this primarily because dealing with the Old Testament is pretty straightforward. One does not have to deal with the thorny problems associated with the divinity of Jesus.

Asserting the divinity of Jesus is not without its ramifications for objectivity and historicity. There is a tendency to read the material of scripture with bias or to read into it what was not originally there. Modern research is aptly skeptical of *a prioris* (pre-sentiments, preconditions). They have a way of forcing you to fit the evidence into your own conclusions. The *a priori* approach is tantamount to saying that you may investigate all you want so long as you come up with my solution, which is the only possible and correct answer. That may be true, but this approach certainly does distort one's objectivity. Besides, what does such narrowness say about faith? If we are honestly seeking truth any conclusion could never disagree with objective truth. So why then need we begin with *a prioris?*

Certain contemporary factors should be taken into account that may have a definite bearing on our present-day understanding of Jesus, his person, and his mission. *First, we do not live in a theocracy as they did then.* This means that in Jesus' time God was perceived as directly involved in the personal and (especially) the social affairs of His people. No aspect of life was without the people's consciousness of divine involvement. Today religion is not so pervasive. For us religion simply stands side by

46

side with other factors of life — like Sunday is worship day as Monday is wash day, and Tuesday market day, and so on, rather than Sunday permeating all of them. *Second, the ordinary person's concern today is coping with life.* God is not immediate to us unless there is some want or need. The constant consciousness of God is gone. God is no longer in the language of our greetings and partings. God does not begin and end our days, our meals, our business transactions, our special events. *Third, there is a tendency in our times to relate to religion as magic or superstition.* This is especially true when it comes to the unexplainable or uncontrollable — sickness, tragedy, death, fate. *Finally, religion today is looked upon for its practical value.* It is seen as useful for living an orderly and peaceful life. Where it ceases to be practical it is disregarded.

All of this is not without its effect on both the researcher and the person in the pew. The Christian researcher tries to uphold the divinity of Jesus, yet understandably struggles with Jesus' ignorance of the last day. The person in the pew wants the reassurance of the resurrection and salvation but not especially Jesus' advice about turning the other cheek or giving everything away to the poor.

The territory is fraught with dangers. I have not come to proclaim the stereotype as I seriously doubt much of its "truth." Nor do I come as an iconoclast, for I truly believe in the person, mission, and divinity of Jesus. If virtue then lies somewhere in the middle, I am reminded of the wisdom of Margaret Thatcher, who said, "You then get hit from both sides of the road." In the end if this book pleases and displeases both the liberals and the conservatives it may vindicate me in my attempt at objectivity.

ESCHATOLOGY AND JESUS

Jesus and his message cannot be understood apart from the Jewish understanding of eschatology, the Jewish conception of the end of the world. The notion was so prevalent in his day that it shaded everything he said and did.

After the return of the Jews from exile and the eventual deterioration of their condition following the Maccabean revolt, their hope for the coming of the Messiah became intensified during the period of subjugation to the Greeks and then the Romans. The time was right and ripe for a savior. All the signs pointed to it. There was talk of it everywhere. Only those who were comfortably well off, those who fared better than the poor and destitute, had no interest in the matter. For them there was no need of a savior since there was nothing they wanted to be saved from. The establishment was content to maintain the status quo. All too often, such established bureaucracies and institutions live by the mottos, "Don't rock the boat," "Don't make waves."

However, a boat that makes no waves is going nowhere. It lies stagnant in the water. Stagnation is never progress, especially in the spiritual life. It is regression. This is what the prophets and Jesus came to fight against.

Jesus was very much a man of his times. We may take it that apart from considerations of his being divine, he grew in age and wisdom as did everyone else (Lk 2:52). He was no doubt a precocious child and a voracious learner. The religious atmosphere of the times was saturated with ideas about the imminence of the eschaton everywhere he went. One could escape this atmosphere no more easily than escape the very air one breathed. This, of course, is understandable. Every captive dreams of freedom, every prisoner of release. Jesus quotes Isaiah in speaking of his mission:

> And he came to Nazareth, where he had been brought up; and he went to the synagogue, as his custom was, on the Sabbath day. And he stood up to read; and there was given to him the book of the prophet Isaiah. He opened the book and found the place where it was written, "The Spirit of the Lord is upon me, because he has anointed me to preach good news to the poor. He has sent me to proclaim release to the captives and recovering of sight to the blind, to set at liberty those who are oppressed." ... And he said to them, "Today this scripture has been fulfilled in your hearing."
>
> (Lk 4:16–18, 21)

This "Day of the Lord" was in the air Jesus breathed while he was growing up. It was the food of his adolescence and the wine of his maturity. It colored his life and his mission.

Consider if an alarm clock goes off while you were in bed and you decided to ignore it. How long can you endure its persistent ringing in your ears? How long can you lie there and do nothing about it? It is almost impossible to take absolutely no action whatsoever, even if it's just to cover your ears with a pillow. If the ringing continues unabated, you must respond to it. The very notion of an alarm is to "alarm" you, to force you into action. Solace comes only when you turn it off, when you satisfy its demand.

Jesus heard the alarm of the eschaton ringing in his ears all the time. It was persistent and insistent. He could no more ignore it than we can the ringing of our alarm clocks. He was the ultimate man of action. The only way he could silence the alarm was to hasten the time of the eschaton's fulfillment and save as many of the remnant (the faithful who remained) as would listen. His teachings were replete with "Stay awake!" "You do not know the day or the hour." "Be ready." "It will come like a thief in the night."

Jesus was an alarmist. The Day of the Lord was coming and he was driven to do all that he could to prepare the people for it. From the very beginning of his mission this was what he was about. Matthew's Gospel states that Jesus began his public ministry at the arrest of John and describes its inauguration in the following words:

> From that moment Jesus began his preaching with the message, "Repent, for the kingdom of heaven is close at hand."
>
> (Mt 4:17)

The question is, How does the imminence of the end of the world affect people? How would it affect you if you knew that at any moment the world would end? Would you squander what precious little time remained for you? Would you want to spend your remaining hours starting trouble, holding grudges, fighting, lost in drunken oblivion? Undoubtedly there are some who would not care. In the scriptures these are the ones who are already lost, "who have ears but hear not." Or would you live it as fully, joyfully, and peacefully as you possibly could? Would you spend it gathering with those you love and sharing a final agape (love banquet) with them? This is the message inherent in the true prophetic call. This is not doomsday negativism that gloats over the destruction of sinners. This call does everything in its power to seek out the straying sheep and weeps over the loss of even one as a parent would mourn the loss of a child. It is not pessimistic when it says, "Tomorrow you die," because it looks to make one live today fully.

It is also the only truly honest approach to life, for the fact is not that someday, sooner or later, we will die, but that death is now! Each moment is a lived moment that dies the instant it passes. It is gone. Lost. Irretrievable. Nothing can bring it back to life again. Nothing can make it present again. The message of the true prophet is that if our lives would be different and changed because of the prospect of our impending death, then change it now, because death comes at every moment.

Every moment is a precious gift of life from the Father. It is meant to be lived to its fullest, that is, in harmony with God. That is what being "perfect as your heavenly Father is perfect" is all about. God's will is "living in peace with everything," and our will should be the same every moment of our lives.

Just as there is death at every moment, there is also life. New life. The old passes in a way that cannot be retrieved and the new comes in a way that cannot be denied. This is resurrection. This too is at the very heart of the message behind the Day of the Lord.

Jesus heard the alarm ringing. It was not some distant sound that he heard. He heard it around him, every moment. As that moment died it became a poignant reminder of his own impending death. And ours. So out of love for us, he had to speak out. He had to do something. He wanted his followers to hear the alarm too and to understand.

NAZARETH: JESUS AS A BOY

They were laughing at him. It wasn't funny. Well, maybe to him it wasn't since the joke was on him. The others were overdoing it and more than just a little. Some of the boys were bent over guffawing and slapping their thighs, while others pointed at him and brayed like jackasses. That's what they are, he thought. Jackasses!

Now he could see it. He had been led like a lamb to slaughter by none other than the rabbi himself. How could he, when Jesus was his best student and the rabbi knew it? Jesus was embarrassed and hurt. He had been dipping into the honey, answering the questions, even elaborating on how much more he knew than was required, savoring the sweetness of the moment, when the bee stung. They were all reveling in his humiliation.

Not all. Rabbi Ezra ben Johanen wasn't. He just looked Jesus straight in the face, showing neither triumph nor displeasure. He was frustratingly noncommittal. Of course, this gave Jesus pause. The others would have sulked longer and always did, but Jesus, having felt the flush of anger, now had to move on. "A dog that stays behind to lick his wounds misses the meal," the rabbi once said. Jesus had never been one to lick his wounds and forfeit the meal. Or to waste his time gloating. That's what made him so precocious as an adolescent. Rab Ezra knew this, so while the other boys laughed he simply stared at Jesus.

The anger was gone. It had left its footprint. His face was still slightly flushed and warm, but that was fading fast. Jesus had moved on in search of the meal. He knew that when he found it he would be the one rejoicing. Like a woman who forgets her pain once the child is born. The rabbi had taught them that, too.

He mentally retraced his steps. The lesson had been on Gideon and the Midianites. Jesus had been answering and interrupting the rabbi from the very beginning, hoping to please him with how well he knew the story. At one point the rabbi looked at him for the briefest of moments and then continued. That was the juncture, the warning Jesus had missed. He was sure of it.

"Gideon told his soldiers as the Lord commanded him that if they were frightened they may go home. Twenty-two thousand went home and ten thousand remained. How many soldiers ... "

"Thirty-two thousand," Jesus answered before the rabbi had finished the question. Some of the boys looked at him and smirked. There were times that they would have given anything to have Jesus get his comeuppance. The rabbi continued the lesson, telling about those who went to the water and lapped it up like dogs.

"Nine thousand seven hundred did." He didn't pause the way he usually would have to give the boys time to figure it out. Had Jesus not been so eager he would have caught it. "So tell me ... how old was Gideon's mother?"

"Three hundred!" Jesus blurted out.

There was a momentary pause as what had happened sunk in. Then came the uproar. Jesus saw clearly now what had happened and how, but not why. Once the hysteria subsided and the lesson continued Jesus pondered the question, keeping only surface attention to what the rabbi was saying since he knew the story well. Was the teacher out to humiliate him for being such a know-it-all? That's what the others called him when they wanted to jibe him. No. That would have been out of character for the rabbi. Was he trying to teach him to temper his enthusiasm for the sake of the others? Jesus decided that was it, although there was just the niggling hint of a doubt in his mind. He didn't like doubts. More than anything else he had experienced thus far in his young life, he hated doubts. He had this irresistible need to always be sure. He couldn't wait for the lesson to end and the others to go so that he could question the teacher and be sure.

"Why?" That's all he needed to say. He knew it. So did Rab Ezra.

"Why do you think?" The Greek influence, answering a question with a question. With the others he would have simply given the answer. But not with Jesus. There was more here, and they both knew it.

"To remind me to give the others a chance." He said it, but there was still that gnawing little doubt.

"Not entirely."

Jesus was right.

"During the lesson, did you see me look at you?"

Jesus knew exactly what he meant. "Yes," he said.

"And you let it pass."

"I suppose I did. What should I have done?"

"At that moment I decided to test you — to be Satan, your adversary. You should have been prepared for me." He would not have tested any of the others in this way, and Jesus realized it. He had always demanded more of Jesus because Jesus had so much more to give. "To whom much is given, much is expected," he told Jesus when Jesus once complained about being treated unfairly.

"What is it, then, that I should learn from this?"

Leave it to the boy to cut right to the heart of the matter, the rabbi thought. He was precocious and there was no doubt about it. Any one of his other bright students down through the years would have wallowed in anger, or righteousness, or self-pity. This one was special and the rabbi was both proud and wary. Such a pupil never comes in the lifetime of most teachers. When he came to Nazareth after his own special training in Jerusalem, the rabbi had lost all hope of ever finding one. Now he worried about being equal to the task. He was doing his best. This pupil would one day certainly be greater than his master. But the Lord had put this Yeshua in his hands and he would teach him as well as he could. Was it possible that this one would become the Savior that his name implied? He shrugged. Not likely. Not from Nazareth? What good could come from Nazareth?

Jesus waited patiently for an answer.

"Proverbs," the rabbi said. " 'War is won by sound thinking.' You must always be ready to meet an adversary. Even when you least expect to have to."

"That is what Gideon learned," Jesus replied, "when with a paltry force of three hundred he was able to defeat an enemy of more than thirty thousand. 'Better the wise man than the strong, the man with knowledge than the brawny one,' " he continued, quoting from the preceding verse of Proverbs.

Rab Ezra could not help but marvel at this boy. He was a wonder indeed. "But what should Gideon have done if the fleece he had put before the Lord had not come through the test and he had to face a superior force and the Almighty was not with him?"

Jesus smiled. Rab Ezra made reference to the test again. What a wonderful teacher, he thought. He knew exactly what the rabbi was up to and what Gideon should do.

"Sue for peace," he said and they both laughed.

QUMRAN: JESUS AS A MAN

Restless. That's what he was. Restless. There was something inside him that seemed to be always, constantly, relentlessly pushing him on.

When he was a boy everyone took it for what it was — excitement. Excitement over every new discovery, every new experience, every new fact that he learned. It was more than just youthful curiosity. He had an insatiable appetite for whatever life put in his way. He examined, tasted, and devoured, all in one motion. And he never seemed to forget anything. It would almost have been better if he could; that way he would know the joy of rediscovery. But that was simply not possible for him. Nor did he need it. His mind was so agile that he could fit whatever he discovered into dozens of new applications and find excitement in that. It was when he ran out of challenges that he got bored — and restless.

So he went out looking, for God only knew what. He had something to do or somewhere to go but he didn't know what it was. All he knew was that he couldn't sit still and wait for whatever it was to happen. He had to go out and look for it and make it happen.

It was like that time at the Temple on the occasion of his *bar mitzvah*. He had been jumpy for weeks beforehand. He could barely eat and he couldn't sleep for wanting to rush the days. He went through his chores in half the usual time. He ran everywhere he went and when he sat down he moved his legs ceaselessly like a pent-up stallion. He ran ahead of the caravan all the way to Jerusalem.

When he got there it was all that he hoped it would be and more. It wasn't just the endless array of sights, sounds, and smells that assaulted the senses and fed his voracious curiosity, although they were all wonderful enough in themselves. It was the time he spent in the Temple with the elders. He had learned all that Rab Ezra could teach him. He was starved for more. Sitting in the midst of these wise and learned scholars was joy unsurpassed. He sat there entranced by the way they quoted the Law or the Prophets to solve the most complex of issues. He had only had a small taste of this in Nazareth. But the questions there were far simpler and the solutions relatively easy. It was only when some thorny issue arose and the discussions among the men of the synagogue got heated, and Rab Ezra didn't know the answer but promised to raise the point with the elders of Jerusalem when he next went there, that Jesus got restless to go to Jerusalem and see them for himself. Now that he was there he could not tear himself away, not even to eat. This was food for him.

The next day he again sat there all day and listened. He discovered that there were differing opinions on points of the Law, and he was completely surprised by it. Back in Nazareth there was only one opinion about the Law. Rab Ezra was the last word. Jesus was intrigued to learn that there were great and learned men on two sides of the same issue. Before long he learned that there was the beloved Hillel, whose disciples interpreted the Law leniently. Then there were the disciples of Shammai, who were always serious and strict whenever they spoke. Jesus listened to how they quoted a vast array of scriptures and the opinions of other learned scholars to bolster their arguments. Along with the crowd he would applaud when a convincing argument was put forward on one side. Then when the other side countered with an equally interesting and convincing argument, he applauded them too. He derived no end of delight in these debates, which took place all day long. When his parents told him that they would be leaving for home the next day, he reminded them that he was a man now and that they shouldn't concern themselves about him any longer. Early the next day he hurried back to the Temple precincts for more of the same. His excitement was becoming even more intense because he was beginning to catch on to the method and was interested in testing his own wings.

It was not common for those in the crowd to comment on a debate other than to cheer or jeer the arguments presented. No one would dare offer an opinion when with a mere look or deftly turned phrase the sages would put all would-be interlopers embarrassingly in their place. Jesus had seen a young rabbi try it and get decimated. The crowd laughed so hard that the poor man walked off shamefacedly — which is why Jesus had his heart in his mouth when he ventured to speak.

The discussion was about a case of a merchant who had loaned money to a certain centurion. The centurion was called off to duty in another land so he came to repay his loan with interest. However, he came on the Sabbath, when it is forbidden to conduct business. The merchant had no alternative but to accept the money or lose everything when the centurion left. The question was whether the merchant was allowed to keep the interest on the money since that was considered the fruit of labor and it was the Sabbath. The debate raged back and forth through a strict interpretation with rigid rules that said that he could not keep the money, to a loose interpretation that claimed that the interest could be considered as a treasure found. Jesus was bursting to jump into the discussion. But for a boy his age to do so would have been the height of impropriety, if not audacity. He knew this so he had to enter into the discussion in a way that would not give offense. He did so by asking a question.

"Excuse me, venerable fathers," he said. All eyes looked at him. It was so unheard of for a youth to break into a debate that he took them all by surprise. Jesus seized the momentary silence to venture on. "Did not King David eat the Showbread at the time of the high priest Ahimelech?" When the crowd told him to be quiet and mind his manners, one of the sages came to his defense.

"This is now a son of the Law," he said, recognizing that Jesus had just come of age and acknowledging his new stature to the gathering.

"He did," the old man answered, curious as to why the boy should pose such a strange question.

"Was it permitted for him to do so?" Jesus pressed on, grateful to the old man.

"It was not permitted him since it was consecrated to holy use."

"How then was he able to eat it without incurring guilt?"

"David and his men had assured Ahimelech that they had abstained from women as they were going into battle and so were undefiled. And they had consecrated themselves for their journey."

"Since they ate what was forbidden, should they then have been forbidden to reap the fruits of that meal, the strength for battle?"

"Clearly, that is absurd," the disciples of Shammai interjected. "Let us get back to our discussion."

"There is no need to," the old man said and smiled. "This new son of the Law has just answered it." Turning to Jesus he said, "Well done, young man." The crowd gaped in amazement.

He could have stayed there forever, listening to the debates, learning the arguments, quoting the scriptures, foiling the foolish, amazing the scholars. He could have stayed there for good, but his parents were not pleased.

"This is what I should be about, now that I am a son of the Law," he told them.

Joseph patiently answered him, "The Law says that you should honor your father and your mother."

He had been hoisted by his own petard and he deserved it. He went home with them, his tail between his legs.

But the stallion had only temporarily been subdued. He studied all the more after he returned to Nazareth. He took on work in surrounding villages just so that he could learn from other rabbis. He traveled to Jerusalem as often as he could, staying with his relatives in Bethany when he did so. He loved going there not solely for the excitement he found going to the Temple, but because his cousin John was so much a kindred spirit. Like Jesus he was a restless soul. But over the years Jesus had watched John's flame turn to fire. He loved being with him and talking about Jerusalem because it was so unlike Nazareth. Jerusalem was where everything that was anything was happening and John not only knew about it but was getting increasingly more involved in it. He had joined a group called Essenes, who were convinced that all the signs indicated that the end was coming. He had spent days and weeks listening to John and joining in their discussions. So much of what they said moved him, but he just wasn't sure. Or ready. Or something. Still, whenever John spoke his fire was contagious and Jesus could all but sit still. Something more was needed for him, but he didn't know what yet. After his last time with John in Jerusalem, he had gone back and read the prophets over and over again, especially Amos, Zephaniah, Joel, and Micah. The cauldron within him had begun to boil. He had never been political. His interest heretofore had been solely religious. John had berated him for quibbling and nit-picking with others like hens pecking at one another over a tiny morsel of food while the executioner was hastening into their midst with an axe to cut off their heads. Jesus got angry at the remark, but being angry at John was as unavoidable as making up with him.

He had begun to look critically at life around him. The quiet of village life in Nazareth had shielded him from the reality of the bigger world of Israel. The more he traveled, the more he saw. The rich got fat on the sweat of the poor. The powerful lorded it over the conquered, and there were many who emulated them. Those learned in the Law, the Scribes and the Pharisees, used the Law to bludgeon and burden the lowly, while at the same time they found ways to get around it or use it for their own benefit. Cheating, lying, stealing, and immorality were rampant and he had not taken notice. He had been so enthralled with learning that, like so many other scholars — for that's what he had become — he had removed himself from what the learning was for and about. It was for the people. It was about people. It came like a thunderbolt revelation. John had tried to tell him only he was too caught up in the heady heights of learning even to hear him. Now it was all crashing down on him. Ezekiel warned that God would shepherd the sheep Himself because the shepherds were busy taking care of themselves.

He needed to talk to John again. When he got to Bethany he was shocked to learn that John had joined the community of Essenes living in the desert at Qumran. The Scribes considered the group excommunicates. The Pharisees counted them as ultra-fanatics. The people themselves had mixed feelings. Many admired them for their ascetic way of life and considered them all holy men, as in the days of the schools of the prophets. Others found them too extreme to follow. The Essenes thought of themselves as the Chosen Remnant of Israel. The most dedicated of them left the towns and villages where they lived to practice their strict beliefs within the desert community to await the coming of the Messiah and the Day of the Lord.

They and others like them were having no little impact on the people, especially the poor. The rich have no need of a Messiah. Like a desert brushfire the conviction was spreading that the conditions were ripe for his coming. Jesus knew, because he knew the prophets thoroughly and intimately, as did John and the Essenes, that the Day of the Lord would be a terrible event. The prophets had warned the Israelites that it wouldn't be what they were expecting, that God's Messiah would overthrow the foreigners and establish them, the Jews, as rulers of the world. On the contrary. They would be as accountable for their lives as much as the pagans who oppressed them. God's winnowing fan would separate all those who were evil and not just the so-called foreign vermin. The Day was coming and Jesus could feel it breathing down his neck. In Jerusalem the feeling was so strong it frightened him.

All the more now he had to see John, so he journeyed into the desert. The Essenes' code of purity was so strict that they would not allow Jesus entry. Instead, John came out to him. It turned out to be one of the most memorable days of both their lives.

John had become incredibly gaunt. His white robe glistened in the bright sun. John told him all about the purifications they went through many times a day. These constant baptisms were meant to keep them ritually clean. Since the scriptures declare that even the just man falls seven times a day, they wanted to be sure that they would be clean and ready when the Messiah came. There was no doubt about the imminence of his coming as these washings indicated.

"But why have you come here?" Jesus asked.

"To be ready for him when he comes," John replied. "I want to be in the forefront of his army when the battle begins. I am not afraid. This is what I have been waiting for all my life."

"But why have you come out here? What do you hope to accomplish out here?"

"We are an army in training. We must prepare ourselves for the great battle that is to come. That is what we are doing here."

Jesus so admired John. John never did anything halfway. This was so typical of him to join such a group. But it also wasn't typical of him. He had chided Jesus for being a country bumpkin and remaining uninvolved in the affairs of the world. Now here he was running away from the world. It made no sense and Jesus told him so.

"You would be right, Jesus, if I were to remain out here indefinitely. But the Messiah is coming soon and I shall return."

"When?" Jesus asked.

"I don't know. Except soon. Perhaps any day now."

"In the meantime what will you do?"

"Be ready."

Jesus turned and looked into the horizon. The sun shimmered over the sand, casting a strange, eerie glow over everything. He felt all the stirring that John did, except he still wasn't certain.

"If only I could be sure," he told him.

"Why? How would that make a difference?"

"It would make a big difference. I suppose I will marry soon. It would be difficult. . . . "

Before he could say another word, John exploded. "And you would be swept away with all the others! The fox is at the henhouse even now. Can you not see the signs? Tell me that I have not been wrong about you all these years, cousin. Do you not feel the call of the Lord deep within you? Have I not seen your own restlessness like mine since we were boys?"

"Yes," Jesus responded, surprised at the sudden vehemence of his outburst.

"Have you not felt like me that the Spirit is urging us on?"

"Yes. But what are you getting at, John?"

"How, then, can you think of marriage?"

"What do you mean? What does that have to do with it?"

"Everything! Right now, it has everything to do with it. Jesus, believe me, the Day of the Lord is coming. It is already upon us. We Essenes are soldiers for that battle. You know the Law. No man going into battle may have intercourse with a woman or he shall be considered unclean. How can we join the Messiah and the cause of righteousness if we are not ready to go out with him the very moment he comes. I tell you he will pass us by and we shall be left behind. If we run after him and catch up with him, he will surely say that he does not know us. Then we shall together weep and gnash our teeth with all the defiled." He looked hard at Jesus and threw out his challenge. "Cousin, you must search your heart. If you believe, there is no time for marriage."

It was so like John the extremist! He never did anything in half measures and expected others to act likewise — especially Jesus! It was all or nothing. But marriage? Jesus had always seen himself as married and with children. Now this desert voice, this prophet, was challenging him. And his very commitment to God! John and these Essenes were denying themselves for the sake of the kingdom of God, the way David and his men denied themselves for the sake of the kingdom of Israel. Could he do any less?

Jesus felt cornered. Trapped. He shuffled restlessly, thinking of the implications. It was overwhelming. If John was right, it could change everything. Why, if the Day of the Lord was really imminent, think of what that would do to marriage laws. Marriage laws! He almost laughed out loud. Who would be getting married? My God, everything would change! Until now Jesus had been getting fairly settled and confident about things. Suddenly he was uncertain again. He was feeling the old excitement he knew as a boy in Jerusalem when the prospect of learning the Torah was ahead of him. Now the Day of the Lord was ahead of him, and he had to mull over what that would mean. He shuffled and paced, unable to keep still. He had to get away from there and think things out.

But there was one thing he had to do before he left. Something he had to get out of his system. John had bested him. But in rabbinic debate every good argument required a worthy rejoinder. He turned to John and said, "And you, John, will you stay out here and keep yourself nice, clean, and undefiled, while the people out there will be swept away for not knowing?"

He had hurled the challenge back at John and he felt better. Now he was restless to get started and think through these new things. As he walked back into the desert, he wondered. What if John were wrong?

It was a temptation and he knew it. John wasn't wrong, and he knew that too! He cast the temptation aside. He must not pick it up again. Marriage would have to go. But if that was the case, then the Day of the Lord had better come soon.

REFLECTIONS

Precocious: Jesus at Thirteen Years Old

Precocious. What else would you call a thirteen-year-old who knows considerably more than he is expected to? You wouldn't say miraculous. Nor would you say incredible. "Precocious" is the word for Jesus at thirteen years old.

When Jesus was questioned by the elders at the Temple in Jerusalem, they must have thought the boy precocious. It was not altogether unusual to find a bright and ambitious young man well versed in his catechism. After all, did not the Talmudic tractate *Pirke Aboth* declare that "at five he must begin his sacred studies; at ten he must set himself to learn the sacred tradition; at thirteen he must know the whole of the Law of Yahweh and practice its requirements; and at fifteen he begins the perfecting of his knowledge."

Although the Law prescribed the Jerusalem pilgrimage for three major feasts — Passover, Pentecost, and Tabernacles — it was disputed whether this injunction applied to women and children. That Mary and Jesus came to Jerusalem at that time was more an indication of their piety than the need for some prodigious, youthful manifestation of divinity. In fact, spurious accounts of the fantastic and miraculous in the boy Jesus' life were discounted by Luke, who simply asserts that like other boys "he grew in age and wisdom." In his infancy narrative Luke had given ample evidence of the divine nature of Jesus' birth and was careful not to overstate his case when it came to the boy's youth. Jesus was a boy, a real boy and not some mythological creature or demi-god like those of Greek and Roman legends.

To deal with the real humanity of Jesus in no way diminishes his divinity. After all, we are dealing with a mystery. That a human can be divine is in itself incomprehensible. How could the infinite be made finite? The limitless, limited to a human body? To make Jesus more than a real human, however, would be to destroy the total meaning of the Incarnation and the redemptive value of his life. Jesus would not then be truly "bone of our bone and flesh of our flesh" (Gn 2:23). Nor would he have "emptied himself, not considering divinity something to be grasped onto" (Phil 2:6). Nor would his suffering have had any real meaning. A divine Jesus would have been as repugnant to the Jews as a divine Caesar, even if the idea might have been a possibility to Luke's Greek mind. A divine intervention at birth was far more understandable and acceptable than a child-god. Besides, miraculous feats may have been required in mythology, but Jesus was no myth to Luke and his listeners.

Where scripture was careful not to make Jesus more than he was or to have him do more than he did, pious custom or imaginative thinking should be extremely wary of embellishing. Jesus' youth was the same as any boy's. He ate, played, went to school, and did his chores. He played pranks on his friends and got reprimanded when he came home late for supper or neglected his chores. He was a bright and inquisitive boy who more than learned his lessons, for "he amazed the teachers in the Temple with his understanding and his answers." He must also have tried his teachers with his questioning. No doubt some of his peers and neighbors thought of him as arrogant. Didn't they later say of him, "Isn't this the carpenter's son?" (Mt 13:55) as much as to say, "Who does he think he is?"

His own mother didn't always know quite what to make of him. If your thirteen-year-old took it upon himself to be gone for a day or two or three, would you not be upset and frantic? Was there not a little touch of adolescent rebellion in Jesus' rejoinder to his mother's reproof when he said, "Why were you looking for me?" What would he expect her to say, "Drop me a line and let me know when you want to come home"?

Jesus was a real boy. And yet there was something more there. In a culture where Yahweh was the unutterable name of God, at a time when God was considered totally other, awesome, and unapproachable, where would this thirteen-year-old ever come up with the idea of calling God "Father"?

3

PUBLIC LIFE

MYTH MAN

There is a story about a convict who is new to prison sitting in the dining hall getting adjusted to his new life. Someone yells out a number, there is a sudden outburst of laughter, and then everyone settles back to normal conversation. After a while another number is shouted out and again it is followed by raucous laughter. This occurs several more times before he asks about what is going on.

"In prison we hear the same jokes over and over again," he is told. "So what we've done is number them. Then instead of going through the whole joke when you want to tell it, all you have do is call out its number. We remember the joke and laugh."

Wanting to be considered one of the boys, he studies all the jokes and their numbers and waits for the moment to spring them on the group. One day he finally decides to try his hand. During a lull in the conversation he yells out, "Twenty-three." He waits anxiously, but no one laughs. The normal table conversations continue. He tries again. "Fifteen!" he shouts. Once again no one responds. After a few embarrassing minutes he decides to give it one last try. "Six!" he screams. There is a quiet in the hall. Everyone turns to look at him. Then without so much as a smirk, they resume where they left off.

"I don't understand it," he told his friend. "How come no one laughs when I do it."

"Don't blame me, kid," he answered. "You know how it is. Some guys just can't tell a joke."

Some people can't tell a joke and some can't tell a story. That's just the way it is. We've all experienced the agony of listening to people who couldn't rouse our interest if their lives (or ours) depended on it. If they were to tell one or ten stories they would all be equally forgettable. Yet others could talk about the most mundane things and keep you absolutely enthralled.

What could we expect if these two types were to experience the same event? The meat and potatoes man would simply relate what happened and that's that. The gourmand would add a nuance here, a dash there, and perhaps top it off with a tangy sauce. In both instances you would be getting the meal, but with a difference.

Even the meat and potatoes man adds a little seasoning to his meal, even if it's just salt and pepper. So it is with every story. No matter how outstanding the story may be in itself, it is inevitable that we spice it up, especially after we repeat it a few times. Our embellishment serves to make a good story even better.

I was told that the French developed great sauces to cover up the poor grade of meat that they had to serve. As good as the sauce might be, they would never consider serving the sauce alone since there would be no substance to the meal. Nonetheless, there is always a temptation to forgo the meat for the sauce. It is as true with stories and people as it is with food.

For many years I have said that it would be wonderful to arrive at a point where we don't need God any more. The emphasis is on the word "need." Perhaps, then, we could love God for God's own sake and not ours. Is that not some sort of spiritual ideal — to be able to love and have that love completely devoid of self-interest? Would that not be the highest form of love — to love the other completely for the sake of the other — to love the other because the other is so completely lovable in himself or herself. Of course, this is a chase after wind. Only God is capable of such love. This is pure trinitarian love. It is impossible for creation not to need God for God sustains it in existence. Still, we may at least mentally consider the possibility and struggle toward the ideal. The less self-interest there is in my love, the purer it becomes. Are we not called to be perfect as our heavenly Father is?

Would not the same hold true in our love of Jesus? How much of this love is permeated with self-interest, like bread is permeated with yeast?

I need Jesus to be healer, consoler, teacher, admonisher, miracle worker, savior, messiah. Does it not follow then that if I want my love for him to be purer I should refine away self-interest the way fire refines gold? Then I would be loving him for his sake and not for mine. It is probably no more realistic to hope that I can arrive at a point where I will no longer need Jesus than it is to hope I will someday not need God. Our need is inescapable because of Jesus' divinity.

But we are also dealing with his humanity. I can say to another human being, I don't need you. There is nothing you can do for me. I love you for your sake and your sake alone because you are lovable in yourself. My love doesn't depend on any supports. How great is that love! It is divine love and we are capable of it. But is it possible to love Jesus that way? Without supports?

Jesus was an event. He was a unique and remarkable event. It was inevitable that his story would be told. Down through the centuries two types have contended repeatedly about the telling of his story. The literalists (meat and potatoes people) are interested only in the facts. Others add spice and become myth makers. Because of historical reasons too complicated and numerous to go into here, it is exceedingly difficult to determine what is meat and what is sauce or, to put it in Jesus' words, to separate the wheat from the chaff.

It is important to understand that Jesus was a real person who did some amazing and remarkable things in his day. First, we must come to love him for himself. If we can get to know the person presented in the Gospel accounts and can love that person, then we can put all the embellishments and sauces into some perspective. If, however, we are primarily and essentially drawn by the signs and wonders or the remarkable teachings, we are unquestionably building our house on sand. Jesus must stand on his own. Simply put, the Jesus of the Gospels comes across as a wise and perceptive teacher, a fiery yet compassionate man, someone to whom people are more precious than laws or customs. He taught some profound but not altogether new moral principles and performed some remarkable but not entirely unprecedented acts. This is the one whom I must love, all other considerations notwithstanding, not even his resurrection. If I can love this Jesus, then I can move on with faith to delve more deeply into the man and the myth.

If, however, my faith in Jesus is based on his miracles, I precondition myself against any real objectivity in examining his works. The miracles of Jesus cannot be proven. Neither can his resurrection. Given all our current biblical knowledge we might justifiably wonder if his miracles were all that we have made them out to be over the years or were they the embellishments of gifted storytellers? Our recent translations of the scriptures have reflected this new awareness. Those possessed of evil spirits have become epileptics. Not all lepers had leprosy, as traditionally understood. Did these accounts mean at the time of their writing what we have later understood them to mean? Were there meanings beyond the merely obvious and apparent? Without sincere and complete objectivity we can never truly love Jesus, we love the façade or the need that he fulfills for us. I might even make so bold as to correct Saint Paul, who claims that if it were not for the resurrection of Jesus our faith would be in vain (1 Cor 15:14). In my opinion, he is putting the cart before the horse. It is only because of faith — his and mine — that we believe in the resurrection.

However, people cannot live without myths. Myths are not the same as fictions. They are the embellishments, the sauces of life. But they are sauces for substance and are not pure fluff. There is meat there. Pure substantial meat. Meat that is necessary for life. Once Jesus spoke, it was inevitable that those who transmitted his words would theologize. We have been doing it since the time of Adam and Eve in the garden. God told them not to eat of the fruit of the forbidden tree. A few verses later Eve tells the serpent that they mustn't even touch it (Gn 3:3). We are forever interpreting, elaborating, adding nuances. The search for the bona fide, unadulterated words of Jesus is as frustrating as the quest for the historical Jesus. The Gospels are not history but theology. They are statements of faith. This cannot be emphasized too much at the outset. The essence of faith is belief in the face of uncertainty. When it comes to Jesus certainty is not merely elusive but well nigh impossible. And not without reason. Should we be any more sure of Jesus than we are of God Himself? When it comes down to it, it is not just Thomas who doubts, but all the Apostles — and us.

Just as a tapestry requires many threads blended and interwoven to produce a final product, there were many special events in the life of Jesus that the Evangelists wove into the Gospel accounts. What follows is not a retelling of some of those events but a reusing of the same threads to create a mythmaker's weave.

"What if," said the skeptic to the romantic, "I were to show you that the woman you love is not all that she makes herself out to be?"

"I would still love her," he sighed.

"What if," he continued, "I were to prove to you that she is not at all that you think she is?"

"I would still love her," he repeated.

"What if," he pursued undaunted, "I were to strip away all the masks, all the façades from both you and her and there is nothing left? What then?"

"Then," he replied, "I would still have known love." In the end, only one thing shall remain — love.

JESUS AND JOHN THE BAPTIST:
THE TEMPTATION IN THE DESERT

"What is it, my brooding cousin?" asked John.

Jesus sat with his back against rocks staring pensively at the setting sun. John stood above him ragged, dirty, looking not so wild as he did when he harangued the crowds. He followed the gaze of Jesus to the setting sun.

"Is it setting for me?" John continued.

"It is inevitable. You know that as well as I do. It has always been so."

Since their youth they both had an insatiable love of the scriptures. It went beyond simple childlike curiosity or the desire to show off before adults. They had both been marked from their births as special to God, although even this was soon overlooked among a people much too busy with their own lives to remember the miraculous in the lives of others. After all, old women had given birth before Elizabeth and who but Mary and Joseph knew of their special visitation.

As children they had studied separately under different teachers, and when they came together they argued the Torah the way the old men did. This was hardly an engaging pastime for the other boys their age who merely fulfilled what was required. John and Jesus found their delight in the Law and the Prophets.

John was drawn to the prophets as surely as a lion is drawn to prey; he had the heart of a lion who found in the prophets fearless champions. Their fire, their outspokenness, their disregard for themselves and social conventions, their heroic deaths served as kindling for the fire that was growing within him. Jesus had the fire too, but his passion was knowledge. He devoured the Law and the words of the prophets and the teachings of the great rabbis. John the hero. Jesus the teacher. These were the childhood dreams that so consumed their lives.

Of course, the Essenes had attracted them. Both of them. Their Spartan lifestyle attracted John, and their devotion to the scriptures drew Jesus. John had sojourned with them, but that was over. Isolation was not the answer. Not for God's people. It was too selective, too exclusive to fulfill the total will of God. Yet there was much to learn from them, and they had learned. But they moved on.

It was inevitable that John would break out into ministry first. His target was no less than that of the prophets before him — the king. Herod had taken as wife Herodias, the wife of his brother Philip, and the die was cast. The affront to God was too great for such a champion to ignore. The appointed time had arrived.

When the news reached Jesus anguish seized his heart. Should he stand idly by while his cousin fought for the Lord? How much longer could he remain a carpenter in Galilee while the sheep were being dangerously led astray? As with Amos the shepherd, zeal for the sheep began to gnaw at him. But like all Galileans he had an aversion to Judea with its peacock airs and its disdain for other Jews. It was John's time, not his.

Still the anguish would not leave him. His nights had become restless and his days troubled as more and more reports reached the village of John's exploits, until he had an irrepressible need to get away. He would go to the desert away from the distractions. He would go to the desert to pray and to think.

The desert brought him to John. Somehow he knew it would, although he had not purposely set out to find John. He had found a cave where in the solitude of the desert he could pray and settle his heart. But the next day a crowd gathered below him. He was about to move on when John and his disciples arrived. Curious, Jesus made his way into the crowd and listened.

John began calmly enough, calling the people back to the Law and repentance. The crowd itself was an odd assortment of people. Besides the usual rabble, there were Scribes in their distinctive robes, no doubt ready to write down any incriminating remarks that prophets often injudiciously make; there were soldiers on their guard, watching for any signs of sedition brewing; there were Pharisees ready to make a show of their vaunted knowledge. John quickly saw through their hypocrisy and began to castigate them.

"You brood of vipers! Who told you to flee from the wrath to come?" The fire of God burned within him as he charged through them, rebutting their futile arguments and casting aside their spurious objections. They were no match for this conflagration, so they made their exits disdainfully. Those that remained were baptized.

Through it all Jesus remained a silent observer. When John was about to return to the desert he caught sight of Jesus standing there. He hastened over to him and embraced him. Then he invited Jesus to follow him to his camp.

The next few weeks were spent in prolonged but intermittent conversations. John was a driven man. After a few days of solitude in the desert he became restless. He and his disciples would then return for another foray among the people, leaving Jesus behind to brood.

Jesus wandered through the dry, barren wilderness, remembering that, according to current lore, this was the domain of Beelzebub. His fasting had made him hungry. The temptation to return to his peaceful village, abandon this austerity, and fill himself once again was very strong. He saw people there feasting in reckless abandon. The men were well dressed and prosperous. They lived in splendid houses with ivory walls. The women reclined at table, plump and heavily adorned. It was not all together an unpleasant mirage.

"Cows of Bashan!"

The prophet Amos intruded on the scene looking strangely like his cousin John. He knew well that men all too often make idols of their stomachs. First the stomach. Then the body. Then the house until sin abounds. To deny the flesh is the first step toward purity.

Yet while the flesh may be deprived, it cannot be denied. The gnawing in his belly pushed aside thoughts of the prophets and the writings. His lips were parched and cracked from thirst. He walked faster and faster to distract himself, but it was increasingly difficult to be sure-footed because of all the stones that littered his path.

When he stumbled, he lay face down on the ground. The more he sought to distract himself, the more of an obsession the temptation became. He stared at the stones that lay strewn about him everywhere.

"Would that they were loaves of bread!" he screamed. Then the voice came. "If you are the Son of God, as you sometimes imagine, command these stones to turn into bread."

Suddenly every stone became a loaf. Everywhere he looked people were reclining on the desert floor feasting. Men, women, and children with full faces and laughing eyes were eating their fill of the sweet-smelling bread. He wanted to run into their midst and laugh and feast with them. He wanted to pass among them and share their bread, but no one made a gesture to offer him any. Nor anyone else.

"Cows of Bashan!"

"It is not by bread alone that man lives but on every word that comes from the mouth of God!" he shouted.

He turned his back on the desert and returned to John's camp.

≈

"Cows of Bashan," John said referring to Herodias and her notorious daughter Salome.

"Such talk is certain to get you in serious trouble," Jesus said.

"I do not fear trouble, my serious cousin. I welcome it." Passion and fire blazed in his eyes. "There is an evil in the House of Israel and it must be rooted out and cast into the fire. The people are sheep without sense and this shepherd will lead them to destruction. Does Herod think that because he plays the harlot with Rome, he is safe? Can the sheep make friends with the executioner? The fool! If he has no backbone, then it must be given him. He is a scandal to the people. The word of God is made a mockery in the palace and in the sight of the nations. God will not be mocked!"

Jesus couldn't sleep. When he did, his sleep was fitful and filled with nightmares. He dreamt of John standing before Herod. John with his gnarled long hair and rough clothes and Herod dressed in a robe the color of blood. John pointed a long, bony finger at the king and shouted repeated condemnations. Herod, seated on his throne holding the orb of power in his hand, raised his arm and cast the orb at the prophet, striking him on the head. John fell to the ground. Jesus hurried to his side. He was mortally wounded. Before he gasped his last he stared with those burning eyes into Jesus' eyes and whispered, "It's up to you now."

Jesus woke in a sweat. He assured himself that it was just a dream by looking over to the place where John lay sleeping. He dreamt again.

John was preaching in the Temple precincts when the crowds took up stones to kill him. He turned and fled with the screaming mob in close pursuit. He found refuge behind a door where stairs led up a tower. He could hear the angry shouts of people as they banged on the door. He fled up the stairs. Suddenly it was no longer John but Jesus himself who emerged on the high parapet. The mob had battered in the door and was making its way up the stairs. Jesus was trapped. He looked down from the tower. The people below were raising their fists and shouting at him. Those in pursuit were now battering at the door of the tower. In a moment it would give way and they would be upon him.

Then the voice came again. "If you are the Son of God, throw yourself down. Scripture has it: He will bid His angels take care of you."

Angry, Jesus shouted back, "You shall not put the Lord your God to the test."

His shout had awakened the others. After he assured them that everything was all right, he went back to sleep. But not before he saw John staring intently at him.

≈

"Tomorrow I will leave again," John said. "The sun is setting for me, but it is rising for you. I wish you God's blessing, cousin." They stood and embraced.

When Jesus awoke from another fitful night's sleep, the camp was broken and he was alone. He climbed to the top of the hill to see the rising sun. As its rays broke over the land, Jesus could see for miles. There was Jericho. Off in the distance was Jerusalem. Farther out was imperial Rome. The world and all its kingdoms lay spread out before him.

Once again the voice came to him. "All these will I give to you if you will side with me."

Down below and not far distant was a trail of dust. He could see John and his disciples making their way toward the Jordan.

"Away with you, Satan," Jesus shouted. "The Lord is God and Him alone. I will serve no other."

It was time to leave. Forty days in Beelzebub's wilderness was enough. He had passed the test. It was time to begin his own work.

JESUS: *BATH KOL** —
THE BAPTISM OF JESUS

"The time is now!" he screamed. Of late, John seemed to be more frenetic. It was as if he was deliberately goading Herod. Herod's spies were in the crowd and Jesus knew it. So did John.

John pointed at them, singling them out, even though they tried to lose themselves among the bystanders. "What makes you think you will be able to flee the destruction to come? You will be the feast of the worm as surely as will Herod and his slut for defying God!"

The rage he stirred in them was written on their crimson faces. He could not continue to defy Herod in this way with impunity much longer. But John knew this. It was as if he realized that he had run his course and there was nothing more for him to do than he had already done. It was the journey's end for him.

He continued speaking to the crowd, but he regularly stared directly and for prolonged periods at Jesus. Jesus knew what he was getting at. Like David, John had gathered his five smooth stones and gone after Goliath. There was something in his manner that said he was now slinging his last stone. But at whom? Herod or Jesus?

"Sir, our master has told us to ask you if you are the one or should we look to another?"

John was pushing him to decide, to end his overlong procrastination. If the judgment of God was at hand then there must be no more delaying. The battle was about to be joined and he must take a stand for one side or the other. In this war there would be no middle ground. There never is in the battle of good against evil.

Jesus had tested the waters in the synagogues and found ready listeners and eager hearts. He was even beginning to have a following, although they were more curious than committed. The more he spoke the less hesitant he became to challenge his listeners. At times he seemed to get carried away, as if the spirit of God took complete control over him so that words and wisdom flowed from him as if with a will of their own.

It was on one such occasion that a remarkable thing happened. A man deeply troubled in spirit came forward and stood before him.

---

*Hebrew for a voice from heaven.

"Teacher," he said, "I know that you must be a man of God for no one can speak the way you do unless God were with you. Please help me."

"What is it you want of me?" Jesus asked.

"Master, I have an evil spirit that plagues me. I fall into violent rages without my willing it. I beat my wife and children until they ran away from me. My friends have abandoned me. Even now it seeks to overwhelm me. Please rid me.... " Before he could finish his plea he began to shake and froth at the mouth. His eyes, which not a few moments before were humble and beseeching, were suddenly fiery and venomous. Jesus was momentarily stunned and frightened by the sudden transformation. But he immediately got hold of himself in a way he had never had to do before. The Spirit in him was strong, and he quickly regained his composure. God was with him and no evil, no matter how powerful, could withstand the power of God. The fear left him never to return again. He was not the least bit intimidated even when the man raged at him, raising both arms to attack him. Jesus stared him into immobility.

"What have you to do with us? Have you come to destroy us? I know who you are," he said.

"Silence!" Jesus commanded, preventing the evil spirit from naming him. "Be gone, Satan!"

The unclean spirit, convulsing the man and crying out with a loud voice, came out of him, doing him no further harm. The people in the synagogue were amazed. Jesus himself was shaking from the impact of the experience. From then on he kept building momentum and courage. The people who came began to bring their sick and troubled with them.

However, it was at Cana that God had lain in wait for Jesus and he wasn't expecting it. Since his discussion with John at Qumran he had come to prize the value of marriage as never before. (Do we ever realize the full import of something until confronted with the possibility of losing it?) Still, he had not yet made up his own mind. He knew well the teaching of the prophets and the speculation about the eschatological banquet as the nuptial feast of Israel and the Lord. He had spoken of it often enough himself. He also knew well the implications of what John had said and tradition held about men going into battle. Every man must face his *shibboleth** and this was Jesus': to desire the intimate union of marriage and to deny oneself of that pleasure because of the impending Armageddon. It was as if somehow Jesus had subconsciously decided

---

* The word was used by the Hebrews to test foreigners and spies who found the word difficult to pronounce. It means a test.

that deciding either way would be catastrophic. To marry would be to deny the imminence of the kingdom of God. To deny marriage would be like inviting the final war to begin. So he put off making a decision. Until Cana. The beauty of the nuptial and the joy of the occasion were so overwhelming to him that he was about to decide once and for all ... to get married. That would be his sign of the kingdom. Until they ran out of wine. And Peter in his blundering, inimitable way wondered if that was what they might expect of the messianic banquet. Jesus knew then that it was all or nothing. He had to decide and get on with it. He was as much challenging God as he was the wedding guests with the water. It was a wonderful miracle. A remarkable event not just for what it signified but for inaugurating the public ministry of Jesus, the kingdom of God, and the final times. Now that he had put his hand to the plow there would be no turning back.

So Jesus was ready when John pointed to him and said, "He must now increase and I decrease." He knew the full implications of what that meant. The battle command was being passed on. Jesus was ready. He entered the river to be baptized. Never was a more momentous step taken. Heaven and earth gasped at the moment. "This is our beloved son!"

JOHN: THE CALL TO DISCIPLESHIP

The synagogue was hot and especially uncomfortable for him because he hated the smell of human bodies. Too many people were packed into the small room making it all the hotter, making everyone sweat all the more and stink all the more. The odor where he stood was overpowering. He looked at the man elbowing him on the right. It was Hayim the fishmonger. He was short and grizzled looking. His tunic bore the stains of at least six months' sweat. He also wreaked of fish. Dead fish.

He was a fisherman and not a fishmonger. There was a difference. He worked out at sea where the breeze purified the air and made everything smell sea sweet. Even when the days were hot, the men just shed their clothes so they were never laden with the burden of sweat. When they finished with the hauling, they dove into the sea naked, cleaning their bodies and refreshing their spirits. If their clothes did smell a little, they dove into the water with their clothes on. Fishermen didn't smell. Fishmongers did. It didn't take long for fish out of water to get sticky and smelly. Their odor clung to clothes, hair, and bodies. The joke was that the great fish couldn't stomach the cantankerous Jonah and vomited him out, so whoever dallies with fish smells of its vomit. He didn't think it was funny, but there was no denying the truth of the stench. He moved back to get away from Hayim.

This put him almost in the back where he couldn't see the action very well. Simeon the Scribe was in Capernaum attending the synagogue service. Whenever he was in town visiting his relatives, he packed the synagogue on the Sabbath. He was a wise and learned old man who knew the Law like none other in the area. So everyone flocked to hear him. To small town people not given to Roman and Greek forms of entertainment, this was about as exciting as things could get. The service began with a passage from scripture but it rarely remained there. Before long there were questions about everything from inheritance rights to swatting flies on the Sabbath. Rabbi Nathan always took a back seat on these occasions. After all, Simeon was a Jerusalem Scribe who sat on the Sanhedrin and such deference was not only expected, but with him, demanded. He carried his great weight around like his prestige. Everyone was made to feel it. The townspeople were too subservient to even imagine that he was pompous and overbearing.

He didn't particularly like Simeon, although most of the others did. He didn't like the Scribe's blatant snobbery or his overbearing manner. Nor did he like his perfume any more than Hayim's stench. It was just a cover-up and he knew it. He'd wager a week's catch that the old man hadn't bathed in several months.

But he was worth coming to listen to, even on a hot day. After all, what else was there to do on the Sabbath? The service started off normal enough with Simeon expounding on the scripture passage he chose to read. This was the boring part, but it was the price you had to pay. It would get better the minute he finished and someone would ask him questions. Then anything was game, and he had to admit that the old man was never at a loss for answers. Not that he always liked what he said. It was just that there was something about the way these lawyers could quote laws and scripture and other learned rabbis until you were overwhelmed with their prodigious learning.

He got past the sermon rather quickly, he thought. It must be the heat. Then the questions began. Simeon lived up to his expectations. He waxed eloquent from subject to subject. He even seemed to get bigger as he went along so pleased was he with himself. It was almost over when someone asked a question about *korban*. There was no hiding anything in a small town, so even though no names were used, everyone knew that it had to do with Isaac the miller. When his father died, he took over the mill and was prospering. However, his mother was an old woman in dire need. Because she was a shrew throughout her life, Isaac refused to provide for her. Rabbi Nathan had offered him a way out of his duty. He could declare what he owed her as *korban* and give it to support the Temple. It was revenge pure and simple. Even though there was some heated dissension about the advice, most of the townspeople were in sympathy with Isaac. Because his mother was the miller's wife everyone in town sooner or later came into contact with the abrasive woman, so it was the consensus that she was getting what she deserved. Simeon, of course, knew of the situation and quoted pertinent passages from the Law. It would have passed and been forgotten except that someone spoke up in objection. On the street, this might have been tolerated. But in the synagogue with Simeon the Scribe expounding on the Law, it was unthinkable. The assembly gasped in amazement. All eyes searched for the offender.

It was the gaunt carpenter from Nazareth standing not very far from Simeon. He had heard the man expound in the synagogue several times and was intrigued by him. The carpenter knew the scriptures well and at times dumbfounded even Rab Nathan. But taking on Simeon was getting in over your head. He was going to leave but quickly changed his mind. He was sure that Simeon would skewer this hapless commoner with a few well chosen verses. That was unfortunate because he rather liked the carpenter and disliked the Scribe.

Simeon glared at the interloper. He immediately expounded on pertinent passages from scripture from which the practice of *korban* had emerged, backing up his arguments with a whole array of decisions from outstanding rabbis down through the centuries.

"Does the young man require further corroboration?" He smiled facetiously as he looked around the congregation. The implication was obvious. Calling him a young man, though he obviously was not, was meant to put him in his place. Young men are considered fools.

"I do," the carpenter said.

Simeon glared at him. He would not lose his composure over this trifling. "If you wish, I could add the names of the High Priest, the entire Sanhedrin, and anyone else you wish."

"There is one you have missed."

The crowd was getting angry at his brazenness. "This Nazarean should have more respect." "He will give our town a bad name in Jerusalem." "Who does he think he is challenging a respected member of the Sanhedrin."

"Oh!" Simeon made a grand gesture. "Is it your name I have failed to include. You must forgive my ignorance. The world has yet to know who you are?" The congregation guffawed. They thought it was wonderful of Simeon to take this effrontery with such kind deprecation.

"Not my name," he answered.

He has flare for the dramatic. I'll give him that, he thought.

Simeon was beginning to lose his composure. "Whose?" he snarled.

"God's!" The eruption was spontaneous and violent. Simeon had to shout to be heard over the anger of the crowd. "How dare you!" His face was blood red, the veins on his neck bulged.

The carpenter shouted above the din. "You have used the opinions of men to circumvent the command of God." He raised his arm and pointed a long, bony finger at the Scribe and thundered, "You shall honor your father and your mother!"

The crowd quieted down in deference to the word of the Almighty being spoken. Simeon was panting heavily. He shook a fat finger at the carpenter. "It is God who is served in *korban*. The things of God take precedence over the things of men."

"How is God being served?"

"The proceeds go to the Temple."

"And this serves God?"

There was an implication here that bordered on heresy, if not blasphemy. Simeon decided to trap this upstart. No one would dare speak ill of the Temple. "The Temple serves the one true God. In the midst of our enemies we build. We flaunt our God in the face of their foolish idols and like the dumb mules they are, they don't even see it. Yes, we give *korban* to build our Temple, to build it higher and higher so that it stands far above their pagan monuments, to hold our God above the false gods of this world. Nothing is more important. No one is more important."

The congregation applauded. It was time for the carpenter to shut up and make a gracious exit while he could. Instead, he spoke. "Every tower built by human hands will be destroyed."

This was unbelievable. No one had ever dared attack the Temple. Simeon frothed. Spittle bubbled at the sides of his mouth. He was in an apoplectic rage.

"How dare you!"

"Every tower built by human hands is doomed by God to be surrounded by dissension and contention."

"It is the glory of Israel!" Simeon shouted.

"It is the pride of Israel. And pride goeth before the fall!" The carpenter was relentless.

"Mind your tongue. It is the Temple we speak of."

"It is Babel!"

Simeon tore at his vesture. He looked as if he were about to suffer a seizure. Rabbi Nathan hurried over to him.

"You have offered the good of the Temple as an excuse for a man not to support his aged mother," the carpenter continued. "Yet if your son were to do the same to you, you would find a law that brings condemnation down upon his head. You hypocrites! You bind up loads for others to carry when you yourselves will not suffer the weight of them. When will you hear what the prophets shouted at your fathers? It is mercy and not sacrifice that the Lord wants from you. I tell you when the Day of the Lord comes, you will feel the full weight of the justice of the Almighty on your backs and who will plead your case then, the miller's mother?"

Simeon collapsed. The carpenter left the synagogue in shambles.

Everything was suddenly oppressive. He had to get outside into the fresh air. He walked over to the lake. The breeze was cool and refreshing. That was some synagogue service, he thought. He almost walked into the carpenter. He looked directly into his eyes. Then the strangest thing happened. He began to laugh. He couldn't help himself. Whether it was to relieve the tension or because he had never seen the pompous Simeon put down or whatever, he laughed uncontrollably. At first the carpenter was taken aback. Then he too started laughing. The two of them could not contain themselves. Even when they stopped and tried to talk they would start laughing all over again. If you had seen them, you would have thought they were crazy.

Finally they settled down.

"I have seen you here several times before," he said. "I know you're a carpenter from Nazareth, but I don't know your name."

The carpenter hesitated for a moment. To give someone your name was to put yourself in that person's hands. He wanted to be sure before he did that. "Jesus," he said.

"Well, Jesus. Let me tell you that your name should be David, the way you slew that Goliath." They both laughed.

"What is your name?" Jesus asked.

"John," he said immediately. "Well, if I am David," Jesus said, "then you are my Jonathan."

"That I would gladly be," the young man said enthusiastically. "Let's go out after giants."

The two of them walked off down the beach together. It was time to gather stones, time to call others.

PARALYTIC: BETHSAIDA*

The pain in his lower back was worse today, so he cursed. It seemed now that there was hardly ever any respite from the pain. With one arm slung over the shoulder of the man carrying him and his legs dragging uselessly beneath him, they carved a tortured path through the sick bodies strewn everywhere beneath the porches.

"Find me a place out of the sun, you jackass!" he screamed as he was being lowered to the ground. His carrier pulled him by the armpits just barely out of the sunlight and dumped him there. "Be back before the sun is fully down or I'll see to it that my father gives you pig's dung instead of a shekel." The man made an obscene gesture that the prostrate man could not see. He threw the sick man's mat down to him. Then walking away, he scratched his behind. That he can see, he thought angrily.

The sick man pulled himself together as best he could. This was another day in an endless succession of days of pain, hopelessness, and boredom. He had grown accustomed to the stench of the unclean bodies around him, but the day had been unusually hot and his absence during the midday heat had cleared his nostrils. It assailed him and taunted him now as if it were an extension of his infirmity, ever there, always waiting for him. Again he cursed under his breath, not because he didn't want

---

*Reprinted from John R. Aurelio, *Mosquitoes in Paradise* (New York: Crossroad, 1985), p. 13.

the others to hear him as his would be just another invective in a vast chorus of grumblings. It was more because of the utter futility of it all. It simply wasn't worth the effort.

He could no longer recall when it had begun — the crippling. It seemed as if it had been with him all his life. At any rate it had started some time in his youth. The physicians had applied their remedies but to no avail. Then when these charlatans could do nothing more, could extort no more money from his merchant father, they exonerated themselves by referring them to the rabbis. He had fared no better there. "It is the punishment of God for sin!" What sin could a young man be guilty of to warrant so terrible a penalty? "If not the sin of the child, then it is the sin of the father!" True, his father was not the most honest of merchants, but then which merchant was honest? So the guilt was laid upon his father's shoulders and his father paid the toll over these many years.

The heat from the sun seemed remorseless today. Even the pool some twenty feet away appeared warm and stagnant. The others kept their distance from him. He was disliked for his wealth that could provide him with litter bearers and for his temperament that voiced loudly his displeasure and disdain of the sickly lot. Why, then, did he come here? As wretched and as smelly as the place was, the pool of Bethsaida offered hope. When the waters of the pool were stirred, the first one to enter them would be miraculously healed. He had come close once, only once, to being first. One never knew when it would happen. He had kept a helper with him in those early days of waiting. They had arrived early in the day hoping to get a place as close as possible to the water. The sick who had no other place to go and stayed the night were still asleep. They had just passed the pool when they heard the rush of water behind them. They turned quickly and bumped into an arthritic old man who was on his way to relieve himself. The encounter toppled him directly into the water. He struggled for a while, but then straightened himself out and emerged healed. The old man screamed with delight. He thanked the two of them profusely for the happy accident and hurried away never to be seen again. His own response was to cuff his helper on the back of his head and send him packing. He had never come close again.

He shifted restlessly trying to get more comfortable. A crowd was entering the area, causing a little commotion. It was a rabbi and his peripatetic school. It was not common for visitors to approach the place, let alone learned scholars. The sick were considered unclean and were therefore to be avoided. Yet here was one of some stature, judging from his following. They treaded their way through the prone and seated bodies, deeply engaged in some learning. Perhaps, he thought, this is Gamaliel, the scholarly and much venerated rabbi. Here was a man of distinction and rank whom even he held in esteem.

They made their way slowly through the crowd. When they reached the paralytic, they stopped. The teacher looked down at him. There was a strange, perceptive look on his tired face. Now that he was close, he saw that he was too young to be the great man. Before he could adjust his feelings, the rabbi addressed him.

"Do you want to be well again?"

"Sir," replied the sick man, "I have no one to put me into the pool when the water is disturbed; and while I am still on the way, someone else gets there before me."

Jesus said, "Get up, pick up your mat, and walk."

He was cured at once, and he picked up his mat and walked away. He could not believe his good fortune. He hurried off without so much as a glance back. It was over and good riddance to it. He was free — free at last!

≈

Now that he was free of his crippling sickness, he wasn't sure what exactly he wanted to do. He pushed his way through the startled spectators, struggling to get as far away from the pool and its painful memories as he could. Others were waiting outside. They had seen the miracle and wanted him to talk about it. But he would have none of it. He must get away. There would be time enough later to discuss it. He decided to go home and show his father that the price for the merchant's misdeed had finally been paid. And there was the aide who had dumped him so unceremoniously not an hour before. Would he ever be surprised! He'll be even more surprised when I see to it that he's fired, he thought.

He didn't notice that two priests had broken away from the crowd and were following him. When he was some distance away from Bethsaida, they overtook him.

"It is the Sabbath; you are not allowed to carry your sleeping mat," one of them said.

The paralytic was startled by the accusation. Rolled up under his arm was the mat. He had not given it a thought, let alone that it was the Sabbath. Here was trouble again without his having had time to enjoy his new freedom. Why should he have to pay the price again for someone else's misdeed? He was simply doing what the rabbi said.

"The man who cured me told me, 'Pick up your mat and walk.'"

They asked him, "Who is the man who said to you, 'Pick up your mat and walk?'"

He cursed and told them that he had no idea who it was. Some teacher, he supposed.

"A false teacher," they quickly corrected. "Only a false teacher would command you to do manual labor which is forbidden on the Sabbath. You had better come with us to report this."

The paralytic protested his innocence all the way to the Temple. Curse the luck that would get me into trouble so soon after my good fortune, he thought. And curse my father whose sin got me into this predicament in the first place.

He had been questioned carefully with a scribe present recording exactly what he said. There was more afoot here than was apparent. Otherwise why would they spend so much time questioning him about the Messiah? What did they expect him to know of their political wranglings when he had spent most of his life as an invalid? Instinct told him to be wary of these powerful men and fear told him that he had better cooperate or his restored life would be as pitiful as his invalid one.

"If you should remember more or learn more about this false teacher, you had better report it to us or you will be in even greater trouble. Remember, we have spies everywhere, and if we learn that you have been seen with him or have joined his band, we will extract the full penalty for your breaking the Sabbath law."

He thanked them a bit too profusely for their leniency and hurried out into the courtyard. He was having more excitement in this one afternoon than he could ever remember. He didn't know what to make of it all. He walked pensively past Solomon's porticoes, still deeply shaken by his brusque encounter with the Temple officials. He stumbled right into Jesus.

"Now that you are well again," Jesus said, "be sure not to sin any more, or something worse may happen to you." That's all he said. Nothing more. Then he and his disciples continued on their way.

The paralytic was now shaking from his head to his feet. Who was this strange man? Why was he doing this to him? He looked around at the crowd gathering beneath one of the porches to listen to him. Surely, one of the Temple spies had seen the encounter. Now they would think beyond a doubt that he was one of them. Why must he suffer this way? And what did this rabbi mean when he said, "Sin no more?" What sin had he committed? He was innocent of any sin that had caused his crippling condition. Had not the rabbis told him that it was his father's sin? If this man had been a true prophet, he would have known that. Yet he healed him.

He approached the crowd. "Who is he?" he asked.

"Jesus. A teacher from Nazareth."

He had once heard of him. Among the sick one always hears of healers. He had decided at that time to stick with what was certain, the healing power of the Pool of Bethsaida, rather than go off chasing after spurious healers. He might have thought differently now after what happened to him, but at just that moment he caught sight of one of the priests who had questioned him. He had better stick with what was certain. He went back and reported that it was Jesus who had cured him.

JESUS: RICH MAN, POOR MAN

He was having another restless night. Why was it that he always felt like there was so much to do and so little time to do it? Is that what it was like to be a prophet? That's what many of the people were calling him lately. If that's what it meant, then he was surely a prophet. But was it true for everyone or only for prophets? Was the world coming to an end or just his own, like it did for John the Baptist, Jeremiah, and the others? If the Day of the Lord was coming, what must the people do to prepare for it? If only his life was coming to an end, what must he do? Was there any difference, considering that all life must come to an end?

Questions. Questions. Questions. Always questions. Was it any wonder that he couldn't sleep? That his dreams were so troubled? He simply continued working even in his sleep, trying to answer the endless questions before time ran out and he had no more left to pass on his wisdom.

Death was a surety. When was not. But he knew it would be soon. Imminent. "A man dies every minute," he said out loud. John, who slept next to him, stirred. The night air was chilly and the fire was reduced to a few smoldering embers, so he wrapped his cloak more tightly around himself. Each moment dies and passes irretrievably into eternity never to return again. If it is forgotten, it is forever lost like the souls of the unjust. If the moment is fruitful it will be in everlasting remembrance like the souls of the just. So as many moments as possible should be made memorable. That is why only very little time should be spent sleeping. Only what was absolutely necessary.

But he wasn't always able to convey that sense of urgency to others, not even to his Apostles. He tried talking to them late into the night, but they invariably dozed off long before he did. When he finally fell asleep it was from sheer exhaustion. Then he continued the work in his dreams. There were numberless, faceless people surrounding him as he tried to explain the kingdom of God to them. At first, they listened patiently like children. Soon they became bored and restless. They began pressing forward, shoving the Apostles aside in an effort to get to him. Their faces changed into distorted and diseased images. Leprous, blind, scarred, disfigured, and hideous because of their sins. He tried to tell them so and they became angry. He tried to tell them that if they loved one another, they would get well again. But they wouldn't listen.

"Give us what we want!" they shouted. "Give us what we need!" they demanded.

"The only thing you need is the Father," he pleaded.

"What we need is health. Give us eyes to see with. Give us ears to hear with."

"You have eyes, but still you do not see. You have ears, but you will not hear."

They pressed in closer like a wave building menacingly. You could tell after a while which waves would rock the boat and which ones would come crashing over it.

"Give us wealth! We want food and clothes and fine things!"

"Look at the birds of the air. They do not sow or reap because the Father takes care of them. God must come first. Then all these things will follow. If you seek them first, emptiness will follow. Sow riches and you will reap the wind because thief will steal, or rust will diminish, or moth will eat away. You must love God with all your heart and soul and mind and strength. Anything that gets in the way of this is a disease that will bring you death. Whatever stands in the way, give it away. Throw it away. If instead you clasp it to your heart, it becomes a venomous viper that will bite you and kill you."

"Give us what we want and not words! We cannot eat words. We cannot wear words."

"Where your treasure is, there your heart will be."

"Where the head of the Baptist is, yours will be!"

The crowd broke in upon him. The wave crashed upon the boat and scuttled it. He woke up shivering.

The next day he led the crowd out into the wilderness. Just as Moses had to get the people away from their meatpots in Egypt, there would be no distractions here. The bride needed to be alone with the bridegroom so that love could flourish without temptation. In the desert the Israelites exchanged vows with Yahweh but the arrangement was based on laws and failed. A new nuptial must be arranged. Only this one would be based on love because love goes the extra mile and gives the extra measure. Because true love never fails. Because love is relentless as death.

He must give them a new commandment — the Law must give way to love: to love Yahweh and nothing else before this. The world loves riches. To empty oneself of riches and the desire for them is to be filled with the Spirit. The first sign of the kingdom must be poverty.

"Blessed are the poor. The kingdom of God is theirs."

The crowd listened, trying to understand. So he explained. Their hearts were with him. He could sense it as never before. The Spirit that had moved him to the very depth of his being at his baptism was present now in power once again. He could tell that their hearts were being moved. Their old men would begin to dream dreams and their young men would be having visions.

But not all of them. A wealthy looking young man approached. The love in the crowd was so strong it was palpable. Jesus had to restrain himself from reaching out, embracing him, and never letting him go.

"Good master, what must I do?"

"Beloved. Let nothing stand in the way of your love. Give away your earthly treasure and you will have heavenly treasure."

The rich young man walked away. The blow was like a sword to Jesus' heart. Damn your wealth! Damn your riches! A camel will go through the eye of a needle before you will enter the kingdom. Your wealth will be your consolation. It will pass as surely as the grass on the rooftops. Then what will you have? Our consolation is the Lord. He is our inheritance and that will last forever, for Yahweh is for days unending.

Even though he said it, his heart was breaking. No shepherd wants to lose any of the sheep. He would give his life for this lamb but the lamb would not have it. He was getting moody. One of the disciples came up to him.

"They have no food. You had better send them home."

"Have I not told you that if you abandon all for the kingdom, He will provide?"

"Out here in the desert?"

"Manna."

"There is no manna here. Only a boy with some fish and bread."

Jesus approached the young man. "Son, will you give what you have to the others for the sake of the kingdom?"

He looked Jesus in the eyes. A grin broke across his face. In that look at that moment Jesus was more important to him than all the bread and fish in Jerusalem.

"Yes," he said without hesitation. So like a child. So like the kingdom of God — love without hesitation, without question. He held up the bread and fish for the crowd to see.

"A child shall lead them," he said. Jesus sat down on the grass and ate with the boy.

"I'm not a child and I'm not a boy," he said. "I'm a man. I'm almost seventeen years old." He was not the least bit shy. If anything he was brazenly familiar, which totally delighted Jesus. The boy had more than made up for Jesus' disappointment in the rich young man. He had made this moment in the desert memorable.

The boy's looks, like those of all young people, were deceptive. No mere boy could have followed him into the desert for three days without being accompanied by an adult. Suddenly, Jesus realized his naiveté. He frowned momentarily. Then affection softened his mouth and eyes. In human affairs is anything ever totally right?

"Where did you get the bread and the fish?" he asked.

The boy's face turned scarlet. His bravado left him. Shyly and penitently he owned up to the truth.

"I stole them from a rich looking young merchant in the crowd."

Irony. Divine irony. God continually surrounded him with marvelous insights into His plan. What else did God have in store for him? Or this boy for that matter? Jesus looked into the young man's mischievous eyes but saw his heart instead.

"Remember this, Didymus," he said. "Continue to show love and one day you just may steal heaven too."

MARY: MIRIAM

They're back, she thought.

Once again she had to deal with her mixed feelings. She wanted her son at home with her. What mother didn't? Admittedly, Nazareth wasn't the most wonderful village in Galilee. But it was pleasant enough. She had seen worse. Much worse. Anyway, with all its faults, it was home. It had been for God only knew how many generations. And she knew, probably better than most, about small towns and small minds. She had had her own difficulty in that regard. But she had weathered the storm. "People are the same everywhere," Joseph had said, "and this is where I earn my living. It is too late for me to make a change. In time, people forget." And they did. Except for a few. There are always those too, even in bigger villages.

But Jesus had left in a storm. Men and their politics! The Sabbath was meant for rest and they use it to squabble like hot-blooded roosters. Joseph was right in teaching Jesus that idle hands make for restless minds. All week long they conduct their affairs in a friendly enough way and on the day of shalom they fight like hungry dogs over a morsel of the Law. Is that what the Almighty wants of His children? Old Rab Ezra was right. The Torah is a field of briars and nettles, and only the wise and experienced can make their way through it. Then they have the effrontery to tell us that these things are better left to men, the way God intended. Men rip the clothes, but it is the women who mend them!

It was another one of those Sabbath squabbles that had sent Jesus away from Nazareth, this time for good. He wouldn't tell her why, but she knew. It wasn't that the men in the village were too proud and stubborn to see reason, although that was true enough. It was because of her. It was because if you get people angry enough they will look for any stone to throw. Even an old one. He could not abide that. So for her sake, he left.

Now he was back for another of his short stays. As usual, he brought others along with him. The faces changed over the years, but some had become regulars. She was no longer surprised to see women among them. As a matter of fact, she was pleased. Perhaps he would take one of them for his wife and settle down. That would be a blessing — for him to settle down and give her a daughter-in-law to gossip with and grandchildren to seek her favors. Was that asking too much? Did not the

Almighty Himself say that it is not good for a man to be alone? What Jesus needed was a good woman to help him settle down. A good, bossy woman. So she always kept her eyes open when they came along with the group.

There didn't seem to be any likely candidates this time. She looked again. One of them might be a possibility. A little older, perhaps, than she was accustomed to thinking about, but not as old as most of those who usually came. She also had that matrimonial look in her eye. Well, she had seen it before, but her son never did. Maybe, just maybe, an older woman might do the trick. She resolved to get this woman aside and find out more about her when the men took their afternoon rest.

≈

"Miriam!" He called again, only louder. "Miriam!"

She turned and saw him running to the well she had just left. Her heart beat faster. Just the sight of him did that to her. He was young and handsome and they were so much in love. She unshouldered her water jar and "accidently" tipped it over spilling it on the ground. David came running over to help her. "You ought to be more careful. Water is precious," he said winking at her.

"My reputation is even more precious," she said, smiling back. While it was true that young men and women could meet and socialize at the well, if it happened too often, idle tongues would wag and a girl's father might be forced to protect his daughter's reputation.

"You look beautiful again today, my Michal." It was his term of endearment for her. But it also spoke of the frustration, if not hopelessness of their situation. Marriages were arranged. Fathers negotiated and terms had to be met. Romance had nothing to do with it. Miriam's father was a well-to-do merchant, while David was a simple, apprenticed stonemason. There was little hope for him as her suitor. He could never pay the price. But hope springs eternal in the hearts of the young, and he was young and in love. Which is why he called her his "Michal." It was the commonly told story of romantic love and marriage. Michal was Saul's daughter who fell passionately in love with David. In a culture where romance and passion had little to do with marriage, their story had taken on mythic proportions. Where girls especially had nothing to say about their marriage partner, it was like dreaming the impossible dream. But dreams are the stuff love is made of, so Miriam dreamed.

Only it turned out to be a nightmare. And like a nightmare, it all happened so quickly. A passing caravan had stopped at the village, and Miriam's father negotiated the purchase of some goods. After a deal had been made, the men took to celebrating, as was the custom. The trader, however, drank too much at the dinner Miriam helped serve, and he kept eyeing her lasciviously. That night he caught her unawares, attacked her, and raped her. The next morning, instead of beating the man senseless as she expected, her father did the legal and expedient thing. He negotiated her marriage with the man, demanding the accustomed *mohar*, the payment required by law. The man signed the contract and promised to fulfill his obligation when he returned with the money he would get from the sale of his goods in Jerusalem. However, he never returned. Not that Miriam cared, for she could never live with such a despicable man, whatever the arrangement. Word arrived shortly thereafter that the trader had been beset by robbers on his way back and was killed. Miriam felt vindicated and relieved.

But that was not to be the end of her troubles. Her village was not a large one and word of her rape had spread quickly. Idle tongues are the fruit of idle minds. Women jealous of her good looks whispered that where there's smoke there's fire, while the men who were jealous of her father's wealth claimed that God puts down the mighty. All of this, as unbearable as it was, might have passed and been forgotten except that she had gotten pregnant.

Her only hope had been David. He claimed his ardor was undiminished. He would go to her father and negotiate to work in their household until he could settle the payment for the marriage contract. But the gossip had gotten to him. He came less often to the well. When word of her pregnancy got around, he stopped coming all together.

≈

"Oh, my dear. What a terrible tragedy."

Jesus' mother broke into her story. Miriam had almost forgotten that she was telling it to someone else, she had relived it so many times in her mind. Somehow though, for the first time, it didn't seem to hurt anymore. At least, not as much as it used to. She looked at Jesus' mother. There were tears in her eyes. Her story had touched her. Now the older woman looked like she was lost in memories of her own.

≈

"Miriam!"

She turned restlessly in her bed. She had been having a fitful sleep filled with strange dreams. She had been feverish that entire day and now she woke in a semi-stupor. The night was exceptionally warm, and with the fever she was perspiring heavily.

"Miriam!" the voice called again.

It was not a familiar voice. She strained to open her eyes. Even though the room was flooded with moonlight the languor of sickness made it difficult for her to see. Was she still dreaming?

When the voice called a third time, she became frightened. She did not recognize this voice. Who was it that had entered her bedroom? She wanted to cry out in alarm, but she felt exhausted and utterly helpless.

"Do not be afraid," he said as if sensing her feelings. She sat up and drew her night cloak tightly around her.

"Who are you? What are you doing here?" Even as she said it, the unreality of this stranger in her room only convinced her the more that she was delirious.

"I have come with good news for you."

"Who sends me this news?" She wanted to ask more — "who would send a message to me and at this hour of the night?" — but it was as if something were holding her back. She still could not focus her eyes. She could not see this stranger's face clearly.

"It is the Lord who sends you this good news. You are to conceive and bear a son and give him the name Emmanuel. He will be a savior to his people."

"Surely, I am dreaming," she said more to herself than the stranger. She was sterile and she knew it. It was in her family. It was the curse that so many of their women had to bear. So many of them had hoped fruitlessly. In her case there never was a doubt. There was no flow. There never was and there never would be. "Resign yourself," she was told by those who knew. "It is the will of God." Now here was this stranger telling her she would get pregnant. It had to be a dream because if it weren't she would be laughing.

Her father received the news stoically. Could he blame his daughter for what must have been his sin or the sin of some long forgotten ancestor? His only concern was whether he would ever be able to arrange a marriage for her. Not that he would mind having her with him for good, but she was a spunky girl and deserved a life of her own. In a town as small as Nazareth, however, there was no way to keep her sterility a secret. He had resigned himself to having her remain at home.

Until Joseph. Joseph was a kind and well thought of man. Like so many others in the village, he had worked long into his years as a poor carpenter before he could afford to take on a wife. When he did, she bore his children, but unfortunately died in bearing the last one. He was left to raise them by himself, a difficult prospect for a poor, hard-working man. He could have portioned his children out to his relatives as was sometimes done, but he could not bring himself to do so. He was the perfect prospect for Miriam.

"I can afford no more children than my good wife already gave me," he said to Joachim when he told him about his daughter's condition. "I would be grateful enough just for someone to take care of them." So the arrangement was made. Miriam herself was happy that, at least, she would be married. Besides, she loved children and taking care of Joseph's might distract idle gossipers from her plight.

Now here was this stranger telling her that she would have a son of her own. Either she was dreaming or he was crazy. Again, he answered her as if she had spoken aloud, convincing her all the more that this was a dream.

"Your cousin Elizabeth is sterile too, but she is already in her sixth month. Miriam, nothing is impossible with God." He then placed a hand on her head and prayed a blessing over her and was gone. So too was her fever the next morning.

To prove to herself that she had been dreaming, she went to visit Elizabeth. To say she was astounded to find her pregnant would be to put it mildly. To discover her own pregnancy while she was there was absolutely incredible.

All during her journey back to Nazareth she worried about how to tell Joseph. What would he do? They had not yet been formally married. How could he believe what she herself had not believed? The more she thought of that night, the more confused it became. The fever and delirium made it all so unreal. But her pregnancy was real enough. She went over it again and again in her mind, always stopping at the same point, always afraid to go beyond it — afraid to even consider that the stranger had done more than pray over her. "Oh, my God!" she said as she arrived in Nazareth.

It had not gone well with Joseph. He was going to do the noble thing and divorce her quietly. The women of the village already suspected. She had waited too long to tell him, and it was beginning to show, especially in someone so young and thin. Now she would carry a different shame than the one she had worried about. An even worse one.

Her only consolation came when Joseph told her about his dream. He too had found it very unreal and wondered if it wasn't something occasioned by the shocking news she had just revealed to him. He would have thought it just that and only that, except that the angel (his word, not hers) read his thoughts at every turn and had identified himself by name. She had not named the stranger in telling her story for fear that Joseph just might go and seek the man out. When he asked her for his name, she hesitated before saying, "Gabriel."

"Just so," he said and smiled. She breathed a deep sigh of relief. But somewhere, deep inside her, there remained a tiny remnant of doubt, so she resolved never to bring it up again.

She never did. But after Joseph died and she lost her protector, gossipers occasionally would. They had driven her son away to return only for short visits.

≈

For a moment she thought that she might be speaking out loud. Then she realized that she had only been thinking. This other woman's plight had triggered the memory of her own. She came back to reality. "You said you had a child," she commented, trying to pick up the thread of conversation.

When the other heard Jesus' mother speak, she realized that she too continued to be lost in her own world of memories. "No," she said. "I did not have a child. After a few months, I miscarried." She sat silent for a moment and then continued her story.

"I admit I was glad I lost the child. I didn't want anything to remind me of that awful man and that terrible night. I had lost everything and the child was the least of it. Shortly afterward I began to bleed. I went to the doctors and they said it would pass. It didn't. Again and again I went to them, but they could do nothing. The women said it was punishment for my sin. What sin? I was an innocent child! I did nothing!" She raised her voice so that both women looked toward the room where the men were napping. No one stirred. Then she continued.

"For years it continued. I am not without means," she said, and Jesus' mother nodded. It was apparent from the way she dressed and from the smell of her perfume. "But it was hopeless. I had to move out of the house because it was affecting my father's business. Well, you know what men think of a woman living alone. It didn't take them long to slander me. Even the village boys would make cat calls whenever I walked by. I hated men."

Jesus's mother caught the past tense. "Did you go to the rabbi for help."

"Hah!" she laughed. "He told me that I was unclean so I hated God, too."

Again the past tense. "Then what changed you?" she asked, presuming the obvious.

"Your son. Your son changed me," she said softly. Her demeanor changed. Suddenly, the harshness was gone. She became soft and tender. You could hear it in her voice. "I heard him speak one day and was deeply touched by what he had to say. The anger I had borne in my heart for so many years, like a knife wound making me bleed, seemed to melt away as he spoke. I listened with my heart as well as my head, for the first time in years. I listened and I cried. Maybe all men aren't so cruel, I thought. For the first time since I could remember, someone made me feel good. Then suddenly he finished teaching and started to leave. People flocked around him to talk to him, but he hurried away as if he had to go somewhere. I don't understand what came over me, but I had this overpowering urge to touch him. Imagine me, an unclean woman, wanting to touch a rabbi? He would probably scream at me or rebuke me, but I didn't care. He would go and I would never see him again so I didn't care. I had to touch him. I broke through the crowd and reached out as he passed by.

"Then it came. 'Who touched me?' he asked. I was terrified. He was going to holler at me in front of all these people. He was going to belittle me like so many men before him had. I couldn't bear it. I turned to run away. He called out again. 'Who touched me?' I don't know where I got the courage but I stopped and said, 'I did.' He looked at me and said, 'Your faith has healed you.'"

When she said this, she started crying. The men began to stir in the other room. They would have to prepare something for the men to eat, but Jesus' mother had to know what happened. She had to hear the end of this story. "Did my son heal you? Did the bleeding stop?"

"The bleeding?" She quickly dried her tears. "Oh, yes, the bleeding. Yes, that stopped. But as it turned out that was the least of it."

"There's more?" his mother said. "Save it for later," she whispered. "For now we had best prepare for the men."

The two women worked quietly side by side, again lost in their own thoughts. Jesus' mother broke the silence. The thought that they both lived in a small village, that they both had been hurt by the gossip of small-minded people, and so many other strange related things caused her to remark quite unexpectedly, "We have more in common than you realize."

Jesus called for them. They gathered up the baskets of fruit and started for the courtyard. Jesus' mother was attracted to this special woman. Somehow she knew that their relationship was going to last.

"What was your name again, my daughter?" she asked.

"Mary," she answered.

"And where are you from, Mary?"

"Magdala," she replied.

REFLECTIONS

Matthew 5

Seeing the crowds, he went up on the mountain, and when he sat down his disciples came to him. And he opened his mouth and taught them, saying:

"Blessed are the poor in spirit, for theirs is the kingdom of heaven.

"Blessed are those who mourn, for they shall be comforted.

"Blessed are the meek, for they shall inherit the earth.

"Blessed are those who hunger and thirst for righteousness, for they shall be satisfied.

"Blessed are the merciful, for they shall obtain mercy.

"Blessed are the pure in heart, for they shall see God.

"Blessed are the peacemakers, for they shall be called sons of God.

"Blessed are those who are persecuted for righteousness' sake, for theirs is the kingdom of heaven.

"Blessed are you when men revile you and persecute you and utter all kinds of evil against you falsely on my account. Rejoice and be glad, for your reward is great in heaven, for so men persecuted the prophets who were before you.

(Mt 5:1–12)

There is so much that can be said and read about chapter 5 of Matthew's Gospel. It is the new covenant of the Bible that supersedes the old covenant on Sinai. It is the preamble of a new constitution for the new people of God. It is the blueprint for the kingdom of heaven Jesus came to establish on earth. It is how all God's people are meant to live. No treatise on the New Testament or Jesus can fail to take this keystone of his ministry into account. It explains who he is and what he was about.

The beatitudes and the teaching by way of "You have heard it said...but what I say to you is..." are grist for every expositor's mill. The passage is also fertile ground for mythmakers who prefer to leave identification, codification, itemization, and rationalization to the specialists while they teach by telling stories.

Jesus was creating a new outlook on life. The old perspective had taken the people as far as it could, and it was time to forge ahead. Jesus begins with the familiar. A leap into the new kingdom is what Jesus is calling for — a leap of faith.

Was the old wrong? Not at all. Jesus himself said that he had not come to do away with it but to fulfill it (Mt 5:17). They had let their outlook on it go awry.

When I was asked to lead a penance celebration at a local Catholic boys' high school, I struggled and prayed for a way to illustrate this important point to them. It occurred to me that I might be able to do it with water. I held two glasses of water before them, one clean and the other dirty. The clean one I told them contained ordinary tap water. There was nothing special or exotic about it except that if they were thirsty it would slake their thirst. The dirty water on the other hand, while it contained all kinds of filthy things from cigarette ashes to moldy food, also contained several shots of very potent liquors. I told them that it was guaranteed to give them a zing. Before I offered them the choice of which one they wanted to drink from, I said that I thought it only fair to inform them that if they drank the dirty water, they would most surely die because of it.

"The choice is yours," I said, holding the glasses aloft one at a time. They booed the dirty water. I told them that unfortunately that is not the choice most of us make in life. When Adam and Eve were given the choice and told that they could eat from all the clean trees in the garden and were warned that if they ate from the bad one "they would most surely die," they chose the dirty one. Since that time, we all have done the same and when we get sick from it, when we begin to die because of it, we blame God for our plight. We say, "How can God be a God of Love if this happens to us?" Jesus came to teach us that the Father would not have been a God of Love if He had seen the danger and not warned us, not told us to stay away from it. It is precisely because He cautioned us against drinking the dirty water that He shows Himself to be a God of Love. The don'ts of the old law were the warnings against drinking dirty water and signs of God's love for His people.

The people had not only lost that perspective in Jesus' time but had reverted to their old ways. They had forgotten the vows God and Moses had exchanged on Mount Sinai. What Jesus was calling for on the Mount of Beatitudes was more than a renewal of vows; it was a new contract based no longer on laws but love. Love is not measured on the scales of justice like fish. It is given freely and without cost the way the Father gives it.

One Sunday morning, to illustrate the reasoning behind Matthew 5, I held up balance scales for the congregation to see. I stood two people, one on either side of them. I gave them each a set of envelopes with the same labels on them. SWEAR, LIE, CHEAT, CURSE, HIT, KILL, and so on. But the envelopes were not weighted the same. I told Ann that Frank had done something to upset her and that she might get even with him by throwing one of the envelopes on his side of the scale. She chose SWEAR and the scales were balanced against Frank. I told Frank that since the scales were now balanced in favor of Ann, he might want to get even with her by throwing an envelope on her side of the scale. He chose CURSE. Only it didn't weigh enough to put the scales in balance. I told him that his curse wasn't near as powerful or weighty as Ann's swearing. So he took HIT and threw it on her side of the scale. The balance was now against her. She countered with LIE and CHEAT and the scales flip flopped again. This continued until they had no more envelopes and the scales were still not even.

"Were you able to get even?" I asked. They both said, "No."

That's what Jesus was trying to show the people when he told them that they had been taught "an eye for an eye and a tooth for a tooth," but it didn't work. How much longer would they continue to apply it? How can one weigh a lie against a curse? How can one measure the force of one blow against that of another? There are always degrees and interpretations. To get beyond that dead end would take a leap of love.

I held up the scales again and demonstrated the Jesus method of getting even. I asked Ann to begin the process again. She threw the SWEAR envelope on Frank's side of the scale. I asked Frank if he wanted to get even. He said, "Yes." I told him not to look in his arsenal because that didn't work, and we didn't want to get on that merry-go-round again. I told him that Jesus said that he should take her envelope and throw it away. He looked puzzled at first and then did it. The scales balanced out. Ann then continued to throw her envelopes one at a time at him. He kept throwing them away, and the scales continued balancing out.

"That's the only way we can be sure of getting even," Jesus said.

God had brought the Hebrew people out of the slavery of Egypt to a new country, a Promised Land where they were supposed to leave old ways behind, learn new ways, and become a mighty nation. Jesus was calling them to do the same. It is not always easy to leave "the old country."

In 1910, when my father was still a teenager, he left his small hometown in Sicily and worked his way across the ocean to America. He settled in New York City, where he worked as a laborer. At the outbreak of the First World War he served in the American armed forces. After completing his tour of duty, he was discharged and given a certificate that made him a United States citizen. Shortly thereafter he returned to his hometown, where he met and married my mother. He brought her back to New York City with him. He then began an odyssey that was to continue for most of his adult life. He could never really decide in his heart where he wanted to live — America or Sicily. So time and again he traveled back and forth across the Atlantic, sometimes with the family, many times alone.

In 1947, after the Second World War, he decided that the family would settle in "the old country" for good. We packed up our bags and mattresses and moved to Sicily. There we were meant to remain for the rest of our days.

For a nine-year-old boy this was an exciting adventure. But after a few months the lark began to wear thin, and my brothers and I were getting homesick. After all, in the Sicily of 1947 there were no hot dogs and milk shakes. Pleading with my father got us nowhere. My mother in her wisdom simply said, "Wait."

Of course, she knew Papa even better than he knew himself. He was a man without a country. He was forever torn between being a card-carrying American and a native Sicilian. When he was in the United States, he was homesick for Italy. When he was in Italy, he was restless for the United States. My relatives said he had a glass behind and if he sat too long in one place, it would shatter.

But something happened to Papa that year of 1947. Mama saw it, and upon mature reflection later in my life I began to realize it. That was a year of decision for him. He had to make up his mind once and for all. He thought it was to be the old country, but America had become too much a part of him. It was present in the way he thought and talked. It was there in his attitude and in the way he did things. Papa was an American from his soles to his soul. It was inevitable that we would return, and Mama knew that.

That was the year Papa really became an American citizen. It wasn't simply a piece of paper that declared it. It was a conviction and a commitment he made after years of wandering between two countries. Later, when we got turned back at the Canadian border because he forgot his passport, he said to us children, "It's okay. We don't need to go there. We belong to the best country in the world."

What I saw as Papa's plight when I was a boy, I later discovered was everyone's problem. We are born into this world and this world is our country. Then we were brought by our parents to a new place, God's country, and we were baptized. Our certificate of baptism made us citizens of God's kingdom. Then our odyssey began. We could never really settle down in one place, so we travelled back and forth between the two. On Sundays, Holy Days, and catechism days we sojourned for a while in God's country. Then we went back to "the Old Country." We lived this dual life into adolescence, when we wanted to decide for ourselves where we wanted to belong. Unfortunately, adolescence is not the best time for decision making. We saw citizenship in God's country as inhibiting, restricting, and demanding. It was a place of don'ts. There seemed to be a don't for everything we wanted to do. The choice was easily made. Perhaps far too easily. We opted for the old country where we thought we could do anything we wanted. We soon discovered that while the prospect was inviting, it wasn't possible or even feasible. Life calls us to maturity. Eventually we have to settle down.

That puts us at the point of decision making. How are we to decide? The lure of the world is still strong. Citizenship in the kingdom is enticing. What will turn the tide for us, one way or another?

Time and again Jesus said, "To what can I compare the children of this generation?" Following his lead we might ask today, "What can we say of the citizens of the world?"

They are like the man who rises in the morning and gets ready to go out and face the day. Before he leaves he picks up his bag, the one that he will carry with him throughout the day. It has his initials on it: ME. When he gets to work, he encounters his boss. Before he responds, he opens up his bag to see how he should act. There is a little bag inside his bag that says, BOSS. He reaches inside to see what it tells him to do. It says, SMILE. He smiles. He reaches in again. It says, GREET. He says, "Good morning." A third time he reaches in. It says, GO DIRECTLY TO YOUR DESK. Of course, the situation could be different. He could reach in and get instructions telling him that he is labor and the boss is management and he that should frown and pass him by.

On his way to his desk, he stops at the coffee urn and encounters a pretty woman. Immediately, he reaches into his bag and pulls out another little bag that says, PRETTY WOMAN. He pulls out a slip that says, SMILE. He smiles and reaches in for another slip of advice. It says, FLIRT. This he does and gets put down hard and fast. He did not realize that she was married. Had he known he would have reached in for the little bag that says, PRETTY WOMAN BUT MARRIED. Of course, that too might not have been enough, because there are other PRETTY WOMAN bags inside that make further stipulations like PRETTY WOMAN — MARRIED BUT FLIRT or ON THE ROCKS or VIRTUOUS. There are an awful lot of little bags inside his bag, so one could easily get confused and make mistakes. Soon, he discovers that there are any number of little bags inside his bag with all sorts of responses for all kinds of situations with all manner of different people. There are different bags for fellow employees and family or relatives. Different instructions for business and pleasure. Endless little bags with a host of varying advice. At the end of the day, he needs time to sort all this out, as do his wife and children who have also spent their day opening their little bags. Sometimes, it's no wonder that they all have to go to counseling to help them sort out their lives. They can get pretty complicated and confusing.

There is an option. It is one taken on occasion by the citizens of God's kingdom. It starts out differently. When this citizen is ready to go out and face his day, he too, reaches for his bag. Only the initials on it are different. They read, GOD. Bear in mind that this man is a simple citizen like our other man and not a religious fanatic as he is often characterized. He does not wear his religion on his sleeve or go around talking incessantly about God, quoting scripture, or saving souls. It's just that his bag is different.

When he gets to work and encounters his boss, he too reaches inside for advice about what to do. However, the inside of his bag is not cluttered with a host of other little bags. It has only one. It says, LOVE ONE ANOTHER. That's all! No countless little bags that make distinctions between labor and management, family and friends, married, divorced, or single. No searching frantically for just the right response for differing situations. Just LOVE ONE ANOTHER, honestly, purely, everywhere, for everyone, all the time. It's amazingly simple. Nothing to sort out. And the bag is light and wonderfully portable. That's all it means to be a citizen of God's kingdom.

If you're tired of being a traveling man or woman, then it's time to decide. It's time to make up your mind. "The time is at hand," Jesus tells the crowd.

There is another consideration to bear in mind. We don't have to leave "the old country" to accept citizenship in the country we were baptized into. We just bring a different bag into it. That's what is at the heart of Matthew Five.

There is something else I learned in those halcyon days in Sicily. When we arrived I could not speak the language. That is catastrophic for a young boy with endless vacation in sight and no one to communicate with except brothers. Learning the language was a necessity for survival. First came the simple but essential things like food, play, and toilet. These were followed by enough phrases to get by — "pigeon" language. Unfortunately, that was not enough to deal with the broader base of the society we were living in. Conversations were required with non-children. My knowledge of Sicilian grew as did my facility with it. After several months I discovered that I had begun to think in that language. You have really arrived when you begin thinking in a foreign language. By the end of the year, I was actually dreaming in Sicilian. I suppose at that point I was what you would call a real Sicilian. I had even begun to forget English.

Now it strikes me that God Himself is a different language. This language is certainly different from that of the "old country." Kingdom language is a new language. We began learning it as children with simple phrases like "sharing," "helping," and "loving." But as time passed we needed to know more of the language to deal with the society we were living in. Many of us are still at the threshold of the next step, learning to think in God's language. But we have to know enough of the language to be able to think in it. Matthew 5 is the primer for that language. Even as we learn it, there is a constant tendency to fall back to the old language.

One winter's eve I went Christmas shopping at a local department store. As I pulled my car into the large parking lot, I was lucky enough to pull into a place where someone else was pulling out. What I didn't see was that there was a car waiting on the other side and I had taken the spot the driver had been waiting for. Before I could make a move I saw through the steamed windshield the driver of that car mouth an obscenity at me. My first reaction was an "old country" reaction. Since I was not dressed clerically, I could have given curse for curse without detriment to my calling. After all, I reasoned, I did not see her waiting there. I did not cut in front of her. I innocently pulled into a vacating spot. She was about to pull away angrily when I told myself to think in God's language. I honked my horn and motioned that I was pulling out. I parked further down in another spot and hurried back to apologize to her. When I finished I could see remorse for what she said written all over her face.

"Did you see what I said?" she asked.

"Yes," I answered.

"I feel bad now," she confessed.

"Good," I laughed.

Later we bumped into each other while shopping and exchanged greetings and smiles. Imagine if I had given an eye for an eye what our Christmas shopping would have been like? I was convinced that I had to continue trying harder to think in God's language. I want to learn to automatically give back a blessing for a curse, praise for criticism, love for hate. I want to think instinctively about turning the other cheek, walking the additional mile, and giving the extra measure. I want to do this because if thinking in God's language can be so rewarding, I can't imagine how wonderful it will be to begin dreaming in it.

The Problem with Miracles

What is a miracle? There are as many answers to that as there are authorities on scripture and angels dancing on the heads of pins. While everyone has a "feel" for what it is, it defies definition for that very reason. Consensus is impossible. I have sat in the midst of endless debates from parish halls to the hallowed halls of theology and have concluded that miracles like beauty are in the eye of the beholder. The most one can hope to do is explain one's own viewpoint and leave acceptance, rejection, or modification to the beholder.

I define a miracle as a wondrous event in which God plays a part. I find that this definition is no better or worse than the countless others that have been offered through the centuries. It has the advantage of simplicity and what I would consider the three key ingredients: God, a happening, and a certain uniqueness.

A miracle of necessity must include God. Atheists, agnostics, and other nonbelievers will have to come up with their own word to describe such special occurrences. The miracle must also be a historical fact, as differentiated from an imagined or fabled happening. Its uniqueness need not be unexplainable without divine intervention. The boundaries of the unexplainable are in a constant state of flux and we must not relegate God only to areas of human ignorance. On the other hand because something can be explained naturally, it does not automatically exclude God's intervention. Finally, I say wondrous and not wonderful because while many things in life are wonderful they are not all miracles in the more refined sense. There should be a certain uniqueness to them that raises them above the ordinary and expected.

Illustrations, of course, abound and are admittedly debatable. I have yet to discover any that aren't. I offer them simply to exemplify my point.

We had spent almost a year of careful planning with numerous civil and government groups for the first ever grandiose outdoor carnival for the retarded people of our state institution. Just before the carnival date arrived a devastating hurricane hit the area. It made its way slowly toward the institution and struck the night before the carnival. At exactly noon a big parade was scheduled to open the festivities. Thousands of people were involved in the success of the venture and a cancellation would have scuttled it, as there were no possible alternative dates. Heaven was as inundated with prayers as the grounds were with flooding. In spite of a morning downpour, the booths were set up and the marching units assembled. At exactly noon (no exaggeration, as thousands will testify) when the mayor cut the ribbon to begin the parade, the cloud cover broke and sunlight came flooding through. The entire event took place in scorching sunlight, and most of the participants went home with sunburns, while not a mile away all around us the city and county were still being deluged.

Miracle? Or was it simply the eye of the hurricane? Unquestionably the latter, many would say. But does that remove it from the rank of miracle? The fact that the eye, if indeed it was that, arrived at precisely the right moment in exactly the right place does give it a certain uniqueness. But there was also something else. The event was scheduled to end at 4:00 p.m. and everything was to be disassembled by 5:00 p.m. Because of the extraordinary volume of people that attended, food and prizes ran out an hour early. As the very last booth was torn down and put on a truck to be taken back, there was an ear-splitting thunderclap followed immediately by a torrential downpour. Miracle or coincidence? It was certainly wondrous.

The gulls that appeared in the desert after the prayers of the Mormon community of Utah can be explained by an occasional, erratic movement of the jet stream that trapped them. This does not take away from the fact that this event happened at exactly the right time, in precisely the right place, making it a truly wondrous event. Even if a totally unexpected and unaccounted for cure is later reasoned away by some scientific explanation, this does not exclude God's having had a hand in it at the time. Once again, miracles, like faith, are in the eye of the beholder. How can any miraculous event ever be attributed to God unquestionably when God Himself is a matter of question and of faith?

With that in mind we should consider the miracles of Jesus. It is most debatable which of his miracles is the greatest, apart from the resurrection that is. While I have chosen the miracle at Bethsaida for illustration, it is not what I would consider the best example. However, since it deals with healing it is one that is the most timely.

Five porches filled with sick people. Still Jesus treads his way past all of them — over this one, around that one, past another and another until he gets to the one he wants. Even with all that, he was a poor choice, a man whose condition was due to his own sinfulness, according to the Gospel. Then to top it off, he reports Jesus to the Jews.

What about all the rest of those sick and suffering people Jesus left behind? There are a number of possible explanations for this that I consider in detail in *Mosquitoes in Paradise*. Suffice it to say here that John's Gospel, as well as the others, gives details of only certain cures that had relevance for teaching or evangelizing. After all, when you do so many, a cure is a cure is a cure. In such cases the Evangelists merely lump them all together and state that "he cured all who came to him."

What was there in this healing that was noteworthy? The man had been sick a long time, thirty-eight years. Consider the hopelessness of his situation. Like the bleeding woman who had been sick for a long time (twelve years), had squandered her money in futile cures (Mt 9:20), and who finally touched Jesus' cloak on the road, Jesus was his only hope. Like the paralytic whose friends lowered him through the roof (Mk 2:4), it was his own sins that had caused his affliction. In this case there was even the added note of ingratitude and betrayal after Jesus had cured him. "The man went away and reported to the Jews that it was Jesus who had healed him" (Jn 5:15).

It is important to remember that in the Old Testament God always dealt with the people as a corporate entity, a group. The theology of the Old Testament was "all for one and one for all." What Yahweh did for and with individuals was always done for the sake of Israel. Individuals were important only insofar as they were a part of the whole. As the king went, so went the nation. In the New Testament we are once again a corporate reality, the body of Christ. If one member is exalted, the whole body is exalted. If one member suffers, all the members suffer with it (1 Cor 13:26). It is difficult for our twentieth-century individualism to appreciate this concept. Rugged individualism is the priority of the day. What's good for me is good for the community and not vice versa. The idea is not new. It has been around since Adam and Eve. It is also at the heart of our sin.

Of all the miracles I could have chosen to represent Jesus' healing ministry, I chose this one, as John the Evangelist did, for its teaching value. A peculiar phenomenon of current Western Christianity is an overpreoccupation with Jesus as healer. So much of our present sickness is what modern prophets call "systemic." On the larger scale, our mega-systems pollute the environment, squander resources, and oppress the poor. On the smaller scale, individuals within these megasystems fall prey and acquiesce to the corruption. We blind ourselves to that sin that makes us all sick.

We also have become a people obsessed with personal healing. Much of this is due to fundamentalism and televangelism, which tout miracle after miracle for those who are born again and profess their faith in Jesus. Our prayers are increasingly directed toward our own health or the recovery of sick members of our families and friends. We have made of Jesus not a rabbi (a teacher, with more enduring value), which he himself claims to be, but a doctor, some sort of divine physician who goes around curing illnesses. While a doctor can be good, it is not what Jesus claimed to be. It is also much too individualistic a role for a religion whose purpose is to build up the body of Christ. While my good health is beneficial to me, it must also be seen as good for the whole.

There is also a danger in all this healing. The body and this life alone are not all we are about. If they were, then Jesus should have healed everyone under the five porches and everybody else he came into contact with. Our preoccupation with our bodies could very well be a masked form of idolatry, making everything of this life and doing anything we can to hold on to it. What does that say about our trust in God and our faith in the resurrection? We might do well to remember that everyone Jesus healed got sick again. The cures were at best temporary, just as they are today. We are healed of one thing and another sickness comes along. If healer is the role we have cast Jesus in, and all too many of us have, then he would be relegated to a mission of futility. Sickness, like the poor, we will always have with us (Mt 26:11).

The miracle of healing at the pool of Bethsaida, like all the healing miracles, is important for the lessons it teaches the community. Of all the wondrous deeds heralded by the Gospels, however, the multiplication of the loaves and fish receives the most attention and is the richest in symbolism and significance. To the Jews the wilderness was as much symbol as inescapable reality. It was the domain of Satan as Tester. Desert existence was survival living. The ultimate desert decision, as Moses told them, was either for life or death, and they were continually exhorted to choose life (Dt 30:19). Life in the wilderness depended on two things — food and the Law. One could not count on the vicissitudes of nature or human fickleness for them. One had to depend on God. God provided both and Moses was God's instrument. The quail, the water from the rock, and the manna were signs that God was with them. So too was the Law given on Mount Sinai. In the desert as well as in life, people must have food for the body and food for the soul.

That the multiplication of the loaves and fish took place in the desert was no mere coincidence. Jesus led the crowd there just as Moses did the Israelites. They would be tested just as their ancestors had been. What was expected was the same as generations before — food for the body and the soul and a decision about life and death. God would provide and they must respond.

They had been out there for three days. Numbers were also rich in symbolic significance. The scriptures seldom used them without some symbolic meaning. Only statisticians were concerned with literal figures, and even these were often exaggerated. Storytellers see how much more figures can mean. If there were five baskets of food left over, why not make them twelve and by doing so imply that there was enough left over from this wondrous event to feed all twelve tribes of Israel? We're speaking of a reality different from one that would concern a tax collector. There were five loaves and two fish. Remember who feeds the people in the desert. God does. Seven is the perfect number, implying that there was enough to satisfy all of them. It also hearkens back to the seven days of creation. God formed a creation out of primeval chaos and a new creation in the wilderness with Moses; the parallel with Jesus' action becomes increasingly apparent in the unfolding of the account.

Even the fact that a child leads them into the miracle is reminiscent of Isaiah. There are also overtones of the messianic banquet that will happen in the end times that Jesus had come to inaugurate. Nor can we fail to see the unmistakable allusion to the Eucharist, of which this event serves as a prelude and foretaste.

Obviously, then, this is more than merely a miracle account. It is also a pedagogical event, one of immense significance.

I remember once in my younger days when I was a fledgling in scripture studies I was confronted by a rationalist who dismissed this miracle with the most offhand and simplest explanation. He said that people in those days carried food along with them; otherwise, where would the boy have gotten it? When he offered his food, he simply shamed the others into offering theirs. "Nothing miraculous about that," he said. I remember coming back at him with something profoundly clever like "What is gratuitously asserted is gratuitously denied," which I had learned in philosophy or debate, and walked away with a niggling little doubt. Today that explanation serves me better than all the explanations I have since read or heard about and all the dramatizations in all the movies I have ever seen. What I say now is that if it didn't happen that way, it should have.

Taken in context a miracle was never the sole focus of an event, although there has always been a tendency to make it so. It was a vehicle used in teaching, either to illustrate or to vindicate it. After all, a miracle of and by itself only serves those who are the recipients of it. When Jesus healed the paralytic or the leper or the man with the withered hand, it benefited only them. The rest would have to stand in line and await their turn. This, however, flies in the face of almost everything that was taught in the Old Testament. A miracle had to have a group significance, or else who would care? Jesus, who was so eminently conscious of their Old Testament roots, would hardly deviate from that tradition. If each time an Apostle broke off a piece of bread or fish it were to grow back in his hand, that would have no impact beyond what it did for those who ate there. Another hungry group would have to wait their turn. Such miracles lead only to an endless proliferation of miracles in order to supply a never diminishing demand. God would be trapped into personal servitude to every individual for all days or forever be accused of blatant favoritism. This is the trap modern "healers" fall into.

The miracles of Jesus were wondrous events Jesus used for the sake of the community. For a boy to be so touched by the preaching of Jesus that he led the way to an outpouring of generosity from this group of "followers" is to me far more significant than for that same group of people, as they hide their bread, to be awestruck by fish and loaves doubling themselves so that they could have more. I suppose it could have happened the way we visualized it from our youth, but that would say nothing more to a group of Christians today than this: "Even though you probably have some goodies stashed away you don't have to help those who are hungry around you because God will come and give to everybody, including you." For the crowd to be touched by the sacrifice of that boy into sharing what they had was what the teaching of God and Jesus was all about. That to me is a miracle and not a rationalization. But of course, the miracle is in the eye of the beholder.

Poverty: Bitter/Sweet

Truth is universal. The word "universal" means one, everywhere. When something is true, it is true everywhere and for all times. The ultimate truth is that everything is one. This should be read slowly and perhaps again before proceeding on.

It is not true because I said it or think it. It is the consensus of all humankind since human beings began to express their thoughts. In the beginning everything was one. In the end everything will all be one. Everything is all one now except for our perception of things. We see things separately. This redwood, that maple, these evergreens, those boxwood — but they are all trees. Saint Paul expresses this in his letter to the Corinthians when he says there is one body but it has many parts (1 Cor 13). The analogy of the body is easier to comprehend because all the parts are attached. The analogy of the trees expresses the same reality in a wider sense. Definitions are made up of what are called genus (main category) and species (subdivisions, or what makes them specifically different). Dog is the genus; beagle and bloodhound are species of dog.

If everything is One then all things we know are species of the great One. Even though we perceive things as separate and distinct, they are all somehow part of and manifestations of God. Theologically, this is expressed by saying that everything comes from God, is sustained in being by God, and returns to God. Even this doesn't adequately express the reality since we have never "left" God and therefore have no need to "return" to God. Saint Augustine merely states that in the end there will be one God loving Himself.

The reason for all this philosophical banter is not to wax eloquent but to lay the groundwork for understanding life and especially the death and resurrection of Jesus. If everything is one and that One is God, then the more we diminish our multiplicity the closer we get to the ultimate reality. All the great spiritual masters of all faiths and traditions have deduced that one gets to God not by addition but by subtraction. If we start to eliminate from a million and get to a thousand and then to a hundred and then to ten, we draw closer and closer to one. When we get down to two we are as close as we can be. We are at the beginning. "In the beginning God created the heavens and the earth" (Gn 1:1). For us that's where it started. God and creation. Duality is the last threshold we must cross to get to God. But it is the most difficult one. However, the crossing can be made. It has been made. Jesus made the crossing in his death/resurrection.

Duality is where we are physically, historically, philosophically. God and creation. Spirit and matter. Created and uncreated. Light and darkness. Yin and yang. There is a fundamental truth here that should be reflected upon. It might well be illustrated by a glass half full of water. It is half full and at the same time half empty. While the optimist is said to see it half full and the pessimist half empty, there is another deeper significance that is being overlooked. It is *one* glass. If we pour some of the water out, it is *at the same time* being filled with emptiness. If we add water, it is losing its emptiness. The one is always balancing the other. Let us change the example to matter and spirit, the duality of nature. If we add to the matter, we empty out the spirit. If we add spirit, we empty out the matter. Herein lies the wisdom of the mystics. By subtracting the accretions of the world, we are at the same time filling in with the spirit.

We seem to sense this in our own common way when we say that things have been going too well for us. We expect life to balance out with some sort of tragedy. When we've had too much sweet, we anticipate the bitter. By the same token then, when we've been experiencing the bitter, we should be confident that there is also sweet. But where is the sweet? When we have been pouring out pain and suffering, should not sweetness be pouring in? Sweetness is the spirit that flows in behind our sacrifices.

This is the immeasurable significance of Jesus in the history of human struggle — that emptying ourselves for him is at the same time filling us with him. A cup of water given in his name, clothing the naked, feeding the hungry, comforting the sick are tantamount to doing these things to him. No other philosophy or theology has ever bridged that gap. The more we strip ourselves for him the more we fill ourselves with him. No one who gives up father, mother, brother, or sister for his sake fails to receive a hundred times more fathers, mothers, brothers, and sisters (Mk 10:29). We can become all that he is. The resurrection makes it possible and at the same time makes it so.

Adam came into this world naked and because of sin began adding layer upon layer to himself. More and more of the world continues to fill our cup. The more we add on, the further removed we get from the One. We move from double to triple to quadruple. We multiply until the multiplicity becomes overwhelming. Everything we add only separates us further from one another. It makes for more layers between us. My wealth separates me from the poor, my health from the sick, my intelligence from the simple, my color, my creed, my nationality. Even my name is an encumbrance upon me. The more I strip away the closer I get to oneness.

It is only fitting that on the cross Jesus is stripped of everything. Everything has been poured out. Humankind is once again naked and innocent. There is nothing of this world left. On the cross there is just Jesus.

Parables on Poverty

PINPRICKS

Once upon a time in the jungle there lived a naked man. He didn't know he was naked, for as far as he knew he was the only man in the jungle so he had no way of telling. Life was pleasant enough for him, wandering about eating during the day and resting comfortably at night.

One dawn while he was eating from an apple tree he saw a beautiful, bright red leaf in the midst of a tree full of ordinary green leaves. Perhaps it was the way it caught the early light of the sun, or perhaps it was just because he was tired of seeing only green leaves that at that moment this particular leaf captured his attention. Well, for whatever reason, he eventually climbed the tree and took the leaf. Thus came his very first dilemma. How was he to carry this first possession with him? After all, naked men have no pockets to put things in. In the end he had no alternative but to hold it in his hand and carry it with him wherever he went.

It was quite by chance that he later discovered another way of carrying the leaf about. It happened that while he was picking some wild berries a thorn pricked his finger. It wasn't much of a wound, just a pinprick, and it only hurt for a brief moment. But it brought a little blood to the surface of his skin. The man discovered quite by accident that his blood made the leaf stick to his finger. It was really a remarkable discovery, for now he could carry his leaf around with him without having to put it down and pick it up every time he reached for something. But it was not convenient to carry the leaf on his finger, so he made a small pinprick on his belly just below his navel and stuck the leaf there.

The man had found a unique way of always carrying his captivating red leaf with him everywhere. He also discovered that there was room on his body for other acquisitions. Next came a pretty flower. Then an attractive butterfly. Just little pinpricks and he could get attached to all sorts of things. And he did. Soon his body was covered with pretty things.

Eventually, however, he ran out of available space.

This was when he discovered another remarkable bit of knowledge. When he decided to remove the bright red leaf because he had long since grown tired of looking at it and he wanted to make room for something new, he found that it was extremely painful to remove it. Pulling it off caused him severe bleeding, so he immediately put it back on. But that was when he made the incredible discovery that the leaf had been nurturing itself on his blood. It had been living off him. When he checked the other accumulations he had put on his body, he found that it was the same with all of them too. They had all somehow leeched onto him. His life's blood was sustaining everything he had attached himself to.

One would think that this would have been sufficient reason for the man to stop accumulating new treasures, but for some foolish reason known only to him, it didn't. Because removing what he had already become attached to was much too painful, he simply continued to add on to what was there. More pinpricks for more acquisitions. Layer upon layer of them.

Only the more he accumulated, the heavier all these things were to bear. And the more of his life's blood was being drained from him. The more he added, the weaker he became. Even this didn't stop him. He continued to prick himself and add to all that he already had until he was completely spent and drained. Finally, he fell in a heap on the jungle floor.

Then one day a naked man walking through the jungle stumbled upon him. It was a remarkable discovery for him to find all these wonderful treasures just lying there in a heap. He would have liked to take them all with him, but since naked men have no pockets to put things in, he had to rummage about for just one thing to take with him. At the bottom of the heap, there was a beautiful red leaf. He decided on that. But before he left this treasure trove he wanted to make sure there was nothing else beneath the leaf. There was nothing beneath it. Absolutely nothing.

So the naked man walked off into the jungle carrying a bright red leaf in the palm of his hand.

I DISCOVERED A WONDERFUL PIE

I discovered a wonderful pie. I must admit that at first it didn't appear at all appealing. It wasn't covered with a mouth-watering mountain of delicious whipped cream or an eye-appealing brown peaked meringue. It didn't even have a tantalizing golden baked crust. In fact, there was nothing attractive about it whatsoever. It was just a simple, unadorned pie. But someone urged me to try it and I did.

It had a strange taste. One might even say it was distasteful. It had none of the accustomed sweetness of pies. If anything, it was bitter. Bittersweet. But there was a strange, unexplainable pleasing quality to it. Something that made you want to try a little more.

Upon reflection I can say that after eating that first piece of pie, I could take it or leave it. I had eaten countless pies in my day, any one of which tasted immeasurably better than this one did at first bite. Maybe that was what led me to have another piece. Other pies either left me with a much too sweet aftertaste or uncomfortably bloated because I could never seem to eat enough of them. This pie, while not sweet or alluring, seemed strangely satisfying. There was no compulsion to eat more and finish the whole pie in one sitting. There was no unbearable craving for the next piece. The odd thing about this wonderful pie was that it didn't seem to please the body as much as it did the soul.

I was to discover later that one piece at a sitting was more than enough. When I tried two or more pieces I felt decidedly uncomfortable.

The strangest thing of all was that eventually the less I ate, the more satisfied I became. In my heart I knew that what I wanted was to consume the entire pie. Only now it would take longer. There was no rushing it, however, because I had come to the point where only a nibble would satisfy me for an incredibly long period. Longer by far than the two full pieces I ate when I first tried that remarkable pie.

I know that in the end I will finish the pie. I also realize that when it is done there will be no more. Still, I can't wait for the day when I will have consumed the last tiniest morsel. For now I know at last that when it is all gone and there is nothing left, I will have it all. I will never be hungry again.

Moral: The name of the pie is Poverty.

Death is the ultimate unburdening, the final stripping away. When you have nothing left, like Jesus on the cross, you have gained everything.

Celibacy and Virginity

A few years ago a young woman told me that she refused to believe that Mary was a virgin. I told her that there was no way I could prove two thousand years later that she was. All I could say was that those who were closest to the situation held that she was and the tradition went unchallenged for a millennium and a half.

There are numerous biblical reasons to ascribe to the virginity of Mary. For one, God had consistently used the impossibility of odds to prove His actions divine. Time and again, God chose barren and sterile women to be the mother of special people. I have illustrated this amply in foregoing texts.* As easily as one can say, "Why a virgin for the mother of His son?" I can say, "Why not?" In fact, there is greater biblical reason to assert the virginity of Mary than her fecundity or sterility. The greater the end, the greater the means.

There is no question that the scriptures speak of the brothers and sisters of Jesus. Were they speaking literally by blood or figuratively? If we say that they were blood brothers and sisters, we could still assert that the birth of Jesus was divine and that of the others was human and physical. This still does not diminish the priority of Mary in the divine plan of salvation. If a groom (or bride) chooses a mate carefully, would not God, who had the prerogative of choosing the future mother of His Son, do so with even more care? There is no question that Mary was selected from eternity and has a position of priority. If my mother is so important to me, is not the mother of Jesus important as well?

Those closest to the time of Jesus maintained the perpetual virginity of Mary. Many reasons may account for this. One, that it was true. This is what had been handed down. Two, sex had always seemed to be cast in a negative light, and the mother of the Son of God could never be tainted. This is pure and patent nonsense. Mary could have had other children naturally, without negative or sinful connotation. Her virginity alone is not what makes her special, any more than it makes a celibate priest, nun, or anyone else special. Virginity for the kingdom is another matter. Virginity and God have been linked, not just in Christianity but in almost all other religions.

We know that there was a time-honored custom that spoke of relatives as brothers and sisters. It is a practice still in use today. Jesus himself said that those who do the will of the Father are his brothers and sisters.

But there is still another possibility: that Mary married a widower and his children were raised as her own. If Judaic law required that a childless widow marry her husband's brother and the child be considered that of the deceased, do we even begin to understand the Semitic mentality toward relationships?

What about the celibacy of Jesus? There are some who would want to infer from this that he was a homosexual. I have even read modern psychoanalytic assessments of his personality that deduce such a conclusion. Certainly, celibacy in the time of Jesus was not the preferred

---

*See also John R. Aurelio, "Gideon — Give Me a Sign," in *Skipping Stones* (New York: Crossroad, 1990), pp. 102–4.

option, especially given the Mosaic tradition that "it is not good for man to be alone" (Gn 2:18), coupled with the divine mandate to "increase and multiply" (Gn 1:28).

Still there is the apparent evidence of other prophets (Jeremiah, Elijah) for whom the prophetic call precluded marriage. Jesus was a prophet who had given up everything for the sake of the kingdom. Poverty and the kingdom of God were inseparable in the teaching of Jesus.

> And he lifted up his eyes on his disciples, and said: "Blessed are you poor, for yours is the kingdom of God."
>
> (Lk 6:20)

> And he said to them, "Take nothing for your journey, no staff, nor bag, nor bread, nor money; and do not have two tunics."
>
> (Lk 9:3)

Would not total commitment to poverty extend even to the denial of a spouse, who in Judaic law was considered a man's possession?

Then there is the tradition of those who give themselves totally to God. This has been a tradition in both pagan and Judeo/Christian cultures.

> For there are eunuchs who have been so from birth, and there are eunuchs who have been made eunuchs by men, *and there are eunuchs who have made themselves eunuchs for the sake of the kingdom of heaven.* He who is able to receive this, let him receive it.
>
> (Mt 19:12; emphasis added)

God would then make the recompense.

> Jesus said, "Truly, I say to you, there is no one who has left house or brothers or sisters or mother or father or children or lands, for my sake and for the Gospel, who will not receive a hundredfold now in this time, houses and brothers and sisters and mothers and children and lands, with persecutions, and in the age to come eternal life.
>
> (Mk 10:29–30)

Jesus was also an eschatologist, which gave his message urgency and immediacy. The recurrent theme of Jesus' preaching was that the kingdom of God was at hand. Would not the scenario as I presented it be a real possibility, namely, that the final battle was about to be joined and soldiers going into battle were to refrain from sexual activity?

And the priest answered David, "I have no common bread at hand, but there is holy bread; if only the young men have kept themselves from women." And David answered the priest, "Of a truth women have been kept from us as always when I go on an expedition; the vessels of the young men are holy, even when it is a common journey; how much more today will their vessels be holy?"

(1 Sm 21:4–5)

Finally, one may justifiably assert that Jesus was an all-or-nothing person. His poverty was total:

Jesus said to him, "Foxes have holes, and birds of the air have nests; but the Son of man has nowhere to lay his head."

(Mt 8:20)

And his commitment was total:

You, therefore, must be perfect, as your heavenly Father is perfect.

(Mt 5:48)

There is nothing in life more beautiful and powerful than virgin love. It is a sparkling crystal, a flawless diamond that rivals the very moon and stars for pure and pristine beauty. The fire of its ardor makes a mockery of the sun's inestimable heat. There is no power on earth that can compare to it. There is nothing in the universe that can withstand it. It is the Holy Grail.

Words falter in attempting to convey virgin love's ineffable beauty, its indescribable power, its peerless magnificence, so one is forced to resort to poetry. Yet no strophe can capture it any more than it can snare the power of God that radiates through it. Other than the gift of life itself, nothing is its equal and nothing can compare to it. Strength is in awe of it. Wisdom is mute before it. Angels bow down to it. Virgin love stands radiant before the very face of God. Virgin love is the face of God.

But this is no mere poetic myth. It is an inescapable fact of life. When young people enter puberty they are near the peak of their potential in the natural order. Their physical strength will never be greater, their emotions more intense, their dedication more total. There is no more all-consuming passion than that of an adolescent. And nothing encompasses this passion more or captures the heart of it better than pure, unblemished, virgin love.

Every generation of humankind since earliest recorded civilization has held the pure virgin in singular and highest esteem. There must be a reason. It can't be put aside as insignificant when virginity has been considered the prize of every race, culture, and tradition from time immemorial. Virgins were considered the choice of the gods. They have been held in esteem by every people. They have been the priests and priestesses of choice from pagan temples to Christian cathedrals. Even in the realm of magic there are none considered more powerful. And in the eyes of the Devil there are none more hated.

The world hates the light and struggles mightily to quench its flame. And nothing shines brighter than a virgin. To understand this simply in sexual (reproductive) terms is to minimize its total breadth and power. Virgin love is pure power, unselfish and untainted. It is consuming love selflessly given. It is freely given seeking no recompense, but lives and delights in the giving. It is the immaculate mirror of trinitarian love.

When it is captured in the adolescent state it is at its youngest, most innocent, and most powerful. If the darkness hates the light as scripture tells us, then nowhere does it hate it more than in innocent youth. It will do everything in its power to seduce and contaminate the young. It will use every means at its disposal to despoil them. But such virginity is not lost by rape or coercion. Such virginity goes beyond the simply sexual, which is why giving birth did not change Mary's status as virgin any more than being raped changed Maria Goretti's title as Virgin and Martyr. Nor does such fiery virginity diminish after adolescence any more than did the ardor of Teresa of Avila's in her mature years.

Pure virgin love is lost in marriage. But that does not make marriage sinful or selfish and its power need not be diminished. Pure conjugal love is itself a masterpiece of human and divine achievement. If it is any less than virgin love it is because the mutual commitment of marriage may make the total dedication of one's love of God slightly more difficult. This is no doubt why Saint Paul preferred virginity to marriage and celibacy after one of the partners dies. Still married conjugal love is a power for evil to contend with.

When virgin love remains unselfish, uncontaminated, uncynical, and directed, no power on earth can stop it. Its power carries it beyond death. This is why Jesus had to be a virgin.

4

TRANSFIGURATION

TABOR

He was running, actually running up the Mount. Peter and John were trying to keep up with him, but he had far outdistanced them. Even the young John could not keep up with him when his spirit soared. He was going to run to the top of the hill and beyond. Nothing could hold him down. He was going to fly up to heaven without waiting for a fiery chariot. When he got to the summit, he would simply extend his arms and the wind would carry him aloft like an eagle.

The miracle of the loaves and the fish had done this to him. The crowd had done this to him. The Father had done this to him. The excitement and joy were overwhelming. His cup was full measure and more. Much more.

"Moses!" he shouted as he scrambled over some rocks pressing forward and ever upward. "It is the wilderness like before. We have covenanted again and have been fed. Blessed be the name of the Lord!"

Peter, James, and John were panting heavily trying to keep up with him. They had never seen Jesus this excited. Had he gone mad, as his relatives once feared? They heard him call for Moses. Perhaps he was mad. If he was, then they wanted to be mad too. The wilderness miracle had done to them what it did to Jesus. Everything Jesus did in Galilee seemed to be leading to this point. The remarkable teachings. The wondrous miracles. And the love. Especially the love. Who would have dreamed that so many people could be so deeply emotional toward one another, that they themselves could reach out and embrace Gentiles as well as Jews, John thought. He had followed Jesus to fight the heathens to the death. Now all he wanted to do was love them to death.

Peter was falling behind. He was remembering Cana. How different this was from then.

"They have no wine."

The bridal couple was poor, the food was sparse, and the wine was cheap. Still, this is what the children of Israel had come to expect in these trying times. Jesus was no more than a dreamer as far as he was concerned, but he needed to dream a little every now and then just as they all did. There had been so much talk of the Day of the Lord and the destruction that would accompany it that it was novel to hear someone talk about the hopeful part of it once in a while. The banquet part. Food and drink shared in fellowship. Israel feasting on the mountaintop while the world looked on. He had painted that picture again and again in the synagogues of Galilee. "Feast on love," he would say. "Let God take care of justice."

He called it the great nuptial feast. Well, this nuptial had run out of feast. There was no more wine. Would his messianic banquet fall short like this one did?

"Why do you come to me? Have I not told you what to do?" he said to the guests who had begun whispering among themselves. "Will you let the nuptial banquet of Israel be like this, without wine?"

"So be it," he said, his voice laden with disappointment. "Then let her drink water."

Peter had never seen anything like it. This was no ordinary man. This one was Elijah, who kept the oil flowing. Had Elijah now taken possession of him and he was about to ascend to heaven once more?

When they reached the mountaintop, Jesus with his arms extended was dancing and laughing and calling out to Elijah to carry him home. The wind was blowing and the dust he kicked up swirled around him like a great cloud. The sun blazed behind him so that they had to squint to see him.

"I have never seen him like this," Peter said to John.

"Nor I. Isn't it wonderful?" John and James took Jesus by the hand and they circled and danced together.

"Master," Peter called to Jesus. "Let us never leave this place. Let's stay here forever. Let us set up our tents ... in Galilee."

They sat down to rest. The effort had exhausted all of them. They were still breathing heavily yet still relishing this magnificent moment.

"Master," Peter said again. "Why not stay here?" He tried not to look in the direction Jesus had set his gaze, south toward Jerusalem.

The sun was setting. It had been an extraordinary and eventful day. They were tired and happy. Jesus stared toward Jerusalem.

"There is one more mountain to climb," he said. "In Jerusalem."

REFLECTIONS

Transfiguration

After six days Jesus took with him Peter and James and John his brother, and led them up a high mountain apart. And he was transfigured before them, and his face shone like the sun, and his garments became white as light.

(Mt 17:1–2)

Loneliness. Estrangement. Solitude. Alienation. Once God decided to create the great universe, there were no alternatives. There could be no other possibilities.

Unity. Infinity. Fullness. It cannot be cut up and parceled out in pieces, each one total and complete. Throw a ring into the ocean. It is there. It is not the ocean. The ocean stops where the ring begins. Even though the water fills the ring, it is not the ocean. It is disparate. Cut off. Draw a square on an infinitely large sheet of paper. The box stops the endless flow of iridescent white. Even though the square is written on the paper, even though it has its being because of the paper, even though it embodies the paper, the flow ceases at the lines. The square can never be erased. The mark will always be there. Like a chip off a block of granite glued back on. The scar remains.

So it would be once creation began. It was inevitable. Unavoidable. When the first star was born, if indeed a star was the firstborn of creation, the line was drawn. Even had it been simply cosmic gas, the separation began. And with it the unquenchable desire to return. To become one again unblemished within the infinite. Yet once created being exists, that can never be. But neither can the desire to return be erased. Nothing in creation can ever pass without leaving its mark. Nothing from a galaxy to a blade of grass is ever lost. Once it has made its impression, it is there eternally. That too is inevitable.

Therein lies the plight and the hope of all creation.

The primal instinct to return to the womb is not the reason behind humankind's creating God, as certain psychological theorists maintain, since the instinct pre-exists humankind and even the earth. To say that God is nothing more than a human projection into the sky of what is simply a human phenomenon is to close one's eyes to a truth that is abundantly apparent throughout the universe. Theories of natural selection, which purportedly account for the miracle that is humankind, take no account of the driving force behind that selection, nor the attraction of all chemical compounds or all celestial bodies. The separation from the infinite brought about the finite. The disparateness from the perfect occasioned the hunger within the imperfect. There is no denying the turmoil. But there is also no denying the attraction to perfection. Where does it come from if not God? This is not just metaphysical, philosophical truth. One need only observe the universe from the atom to the galaxies. Nothing is wasted. Nothing is lost.

The fact that humanity acts out the drive physically, psychologically, and emotionally is not the reason for the creation of the spiritual. It is precisely the opposite. The spiritual reality gives rise to the other hungers. Any attempt to reverse the order, to explain us and creation apart from God, is doomed to ultimate frustration. It is not just the first commandment of biblical revelation. It is the first commandment of the universe.

Humankind hungers for God and God is love and love is infinite. My skin marks the line between me and the infinite, the imperfect and perfection. It is there irrevocably and unavoidably. The obsession is to get through the line, even if it must be there. A man has the craving. A woman has the craving. They bring it together. Still the lines remain between them. Their bodies can penetrate only so far. There is always the separation. Always the loneliness. Even the fusion of their hearts and minds and wills can only go so far. His every thought is not hers. Her every desire is not his. The alienation returns and with it the frustration. Even the child, which represents a moment's fusion of their beings, draws lines of its own. And the quest continues.

Is there no hope? Can this eternal need to get through the line ever be satisfied? Through the line — not some sort of out-of-the-body experience past it, for to get past it would be to leave yourself behind.

It can be done. It was done. Such was the transfiguration of Jesus Christ. What else could the transfiguration mean? What other significance can so singular an event in scripture have? Light passed through him, yet there he remained. He became like glass, and the light of the Infinite penetrated, permeated, and radiated through him. He became translucent and, here is the point, *so can we*, for he was truly one of us. What happened to Jesus is the promise extended to any and all of us. Therein lies our hope. The end of our separation, our alienation, our loneliness.

Jesus describes the great abyss in the story of the dead Lazarus:

> And that is not all. Between you and us there is fixed a great abyss, so that who might wish to come from here to you cannot do so, nor can anyone cross from your side to us.
>
> (Lk 16:26)

And the epistle to the Hebrews refers to it as a veil:

> Like a sure and firm anchor that hope extends beyond the veil *through* which Jesus, our forerunner, has entered on our behalf. . . .
>
> (Heb 6:19; emphasis added)

> Brothers, since the blood of Jesus assures our entrance into the sanctuary by the new and living path he has opened for us *through* the veil (the "veil" meaning his flesh) . . .
>
> (Heb 10:20; parentheses in original)

This separation is like a wall between us and God and the wall is like glass. Our original innocence was lost and the glass became clouded. Whenever we affirm our separateness, whenever we sin, we add layer upon layer of opaqueness to the glass wall. The process of cleansing and purifying is a lengthy one. It begins when we express true, selfless love for one another and for all creation. Such love can eventually polish the glass to transparency. We become radiant, transfigured.

When the desert father Abba Joseph encountered his own rich young man who told him that he had kept the commandments and given up everything to follow Jesus, it is reported that he held up his hands toward heaven and his fingers, thin and transparent after years of sacrifice and fasting, became like ten lighted candles. He told the boy, "If you want, you can become a living flame."

Even if that transfiguration were to last just a moment, it would be an infinite moment. That transfiguration will carry us ultimately to the resurrection, where nothing is wasted and nothing is lost. We will be who we are, who we have become, gloriously and forever.

Helen and the Special People

I have always felt that there was a deeper meaning to the transfiguration of Jesus on Mount Tabor than most people and I had given to it. After all, I realized that all the Gospel events had greater significance than for just those of Jesus' time or for just Jesus himself. God deals with His people as a unity, a body, so that everything Jesus did or everything that happened to him went beyond him. To interpret this singular event as for the edification of the Apostles or even of Jesus himself, as a way of bolstering his courage before his impending suffering and death, seemed far too personal and limited. Miracles, I reasoned, weren't just for the benefit of those who were there, or why should anyone else ever care? The same must hold true for the transfiguration. It was too one-sided. It was too Jesus-sided. It took time and patience to discover a deeper meaning.

The first week I was assigned as Catholic chaplain to a large state institution for mentally retarded people outside Buffalo, New York, I was taken on a personal tour of the extensive buildings and grounds. Eventually, we got to the "back wards," where visitors seldom went and I was overwhelmed by what I saw. Here were the severely disabled, the terribly disfigured, the appalling sights that the pubic is sheltered from. In Building Eleven, Ward Two, we came upon a pitiful sight, an elderly woman lying on a mattress on the day room floor. Her arms and legs were permanently fused in a fetal position. She wore a faded gray institutional gown that matched her fading gray hair. Even now, twenty years later, I can still sense the overwhelming grayness of that encounter. The walls were gray, the floors were gray, the bare mattress she lay on was gray, and my mood was gray. We approached her from the side so that she was unable to see us or even turn around if she wanted to. I was consumed with sadness.

"How old is she?" I asked the ward charge.

"Fifty-five," she answered.

"How long has she been that way?" I asked rather naively.

The charge looked at me quizzically and said, "She was born that way."

"Poor thing," I blurted out unable to hide my feelings.

"Not Helen," she immediately corrected me. "She's everybody's favorite on this ward. Come around and meet her."

I admit I hesitated to regain my composure. The nurse walked ahead of me into Helen's line of vision. At that moment she called her name.

"Helen!"

Helen's whole body jerked into action as we might if we had suddenly been startled. But it wasn't unexpectedness that caused her reaction. It was love. There was a look of affection between the two of them that was overpowering. You could see it on both of their faces. Helen responded by breaking into a mammoth, toothless grin that spread across her entire face. Only she wasn't toothless. She had one big tooth left in the middle of her mouth that sparkled whiter than any bleacher could make it. Her entire body shook with excitement. Her hands fused at right angles with her wrists shook. Her arms fused at right angles shook. Her legs forever fused in a sitting position shook. She was no longer, "Poor Helen." She was radiant. Love had transformed her in a way few of us "normal" people allow it to do in us. She was transfigured, and for a moment I got a peek into Mount Tabor and what love can do.

But the fullness of the revelation wasn't to come to me until much later in 1981. It was the International Year of the Disabled and a group of us decided to celebrate the event by escorting some handicapped people to Rome for a holiday. One cannot do something quietly in the handicapped community. Word spread rapidly until there were over a hundred applicants knocking at our door. Against all advice and odds we decided to charter a jet and go. It is no exaggeration to say that the obstacles were Herculean. We had to call for volunteers who would be willing to pay their own way — and work! They had to push wheelchairs (forty of them), bathe, dress, feed, carry, load and unload buses, bind up wounds, lend ears to bend, and shoulders to cry on. People responded. A hundred twenty of them so that we went one on one. Boarding the plane took over two and a half hours.

Rome itself proved to be an inaccessible nightmare. Narrow streets and doors. Out of the way lavatories when there were any. And steps. Everywhere an endless succession of steps ... that only went up.

Still we made our way everywhere and saw everything that all tourists get to see. Until it came to the Fountain of Trevi. While there was a way our buses could get near, the site itself it was restricted to pedestrian traffic. The police made exceptions but only for VIPs. We were refused permission and told that there was a public parking area a few blocks down the road. Pushing wheelchairs that long a distance would have been an extraordinary hardship, especially since that would have been our last stop of the day.

As every tourist to Rome knows, the trip is not complete without tossing a coin into this famous fountain. We too wanted to share the tradition, but I knew that we would be taxing our wheelchair pushers beyond the limit, even though they insisted on going. There was only one other possibility. There was a street that passed very close to the fountain, but it was an extremely busy thoroughfare with only two lanes, one in each direction, and absolutely no standing permitted. Besides, we would be arriving at the height of the afternoon rush.

At the very last moment we made the decision to stop and unload the wheelchairs right onto the street. We reasoned that if VIPs who could walk didn't, then those who couldn't walk shouldn't, or something like that. Over the vociferous protests of our drivers who feared getting summonses, we set out for destiny.

The congestion we caused that afternoon was monumental. Our six buses stopped in mid-block and we began immediate unloading. Roman drivers are not renowned for their patience, and we weren't stopped fifteen seconds into it when horns started blaring, curses began flying, and uniformed *carabinieri* came running. It was like a scene from a comic opera. When the drivers directed the police to me, I gave the only irrefutable tourist reply I could think of, "No capisce!" By the time they found someone who could speak English, we had finished unloading the wheelchairs and I thanked them for their patience. The buses beat a hasty retreat and I made my way to the fountain.

What I saw when I arrived I will carry with me into eternity. The entire Fountain of Trevi was ringed with wheelchairs. It was a sight Rome had never seen before and only God knows if it will ever again. Everyone was radiant! We were *all* transfigured. The tears I cried were tears of joy when I tossed the coin into the fountain on behalf of all those present.

That evening as we relived that special moment in our hotel room I understood the significance of Mount Tabor. When God's people work together for good, we all become transfigured. That's what the transfiguration of Jesus meant. If it can happen to him, it can happen to us.

Like the Apostles, if we could have, we would have stayed at Trevi forever. Before we called it a night, a delegation came to see me.

"We want to go to Jerusalem next," they said.

So did Jesus.

5

THE DEATH OF JESUS

SIGN OF CONTRADICTION

Born of love,
  Yet death played a hand;
Sent from birth,
  To a contradictory land.

Dust from the earth,
  Bound to the ground;
Breathed to life,
  By heaven's hound.

Spirit trapped in consuming flesh,
  Joy and pain in one enmeshed.
Sea of ecstasy, land of gloom.
  Wedded in a human tomb.

Divine in man,
  In man divine;
Devil too,
  In him combine.

Lofty thoughts and airy deeds,
  Solipsism to satisfy needs.
Heaven bound with earthly scent,

Kingdoms built, then torn and rent.
Pray to God, if God there be,
   Is it willed or mere destiny?

Is it gain or is it loss?
The answer lies upon a cross.

Refulgent light in mirrored radiance,
   Transfigured beauty, nobly visaged.
Virtue, honor, courage, valor,
   Love combined and deity imaged.

Deepest darkness in opaqued decadence,
   Inverted comeliness grossly messaged.
Vice, cowardice, treachery, deceit,
   Lust embraced by Writ presaged.

What is man that you are mindful?
   Less than angels yet so sinful.
Earthly bound but heaven meant,
   Irresistible to love's own bent.
Hate breeds e'er within the well,
   Hound of ground with scent for hell.

Is it gain or is it loss?
Death hangs upon a cross.

Noble deeds by love embraced,
   Gallantry, daring, and beau geste.
White-plumed courage, yet self-effaced,
   Sacrifice that's passed the test.

Idle words in darkness spoken,
   Tombs left open in their wake.
Vainglory remnant token,
   Death taken for death's own sake.

Is it loss or is it gain?
The answer's hid on cross of pain.

Virtue is by vice defined,
   Fools declare heaven's mind.
Celibates teach connubial bliss,
   While they themselves the mark have missed.

Capons gorge on widow's milk,
   Sow's ears purses made of silk.

Men declare by God what's holy,
   Mitered prelates or "anointed" solely.
Infallible man for God unerring,
   Earthly shoes divines are wearing.
Wars declared by fools like these,
   While God's own sons are nailed to trees.

Beauty and comeliness are ope' to all,
   Given or taken after the Fall.
What man rejects the self declares,
   Inner eye that puts on airs.
No rule nor law doth man restrain,
   But only God can see his pain.

Is it loss or is it gain?
On a gibbet lies our shame.

What kings by right divine declare,
   Noble men are for reasons knighted.
Lowest poor can also share,
   No one ever needs be slighted.
For those who toast exalted fate,
   With libations most potable,
Fare no better than the unfortunate,
   Whose joys God has made portable.

Caparisoned peacocks with heads held high,
   Prancing through this vale of sighs.
Lowly knighted before heaven's gate,
   Kingly blighted by fickle fate.
Virtue, vice, truth, and lies,
   Gall made sweet in compromise.

Lofty heights and mountain peaks,
   Regal popes and Arab sheiks,
Hidden valleys and darkened caves,
   Paupers, beggars, and blighted knaves,
Child of earth yet glory given,
   Touched with grace and now forgiven,

Many scattered in God made one,
   On the cross a contradiction.

There it is for all to see,
   God made man in agony.
Life fastened to a tree,
   Alas set free in ecstasy.
In death lies hope if hope there be,
   Adam pierced immortally.

Is it gain or is it loss?
The answer lies upon a cross.

Flesh through God by word made holy,
   Men by deeds do make unclean.
Spirit One more truly wholly,
   Restored by love in breath unseen.

Died by hate,
   Yet life played a hand.
Sent from death,
   to the promised land.

Breath from heaven sent earthbound,
   Returned thereto by heaven's hound.
Christ in Adam, cross and tree,
   Man and God eternally.

Is it gain or is it loss?
God reborn upon a cross.

FROM BETHANY TO CALVARY

Peter: Raising of Lazarus

"Why not now?" Peter thought. The work had been going remarkably
well. Jesus had become more popular than John ever was. He drew larger

crowds. And the miracles! The miracles would keep them coming. Their numbers would grow into an army.

But Judea was questionable. The Judeans did not like Galileans. Galileans were considered hardly more than Samaritans in that stiff-necked country. He had never liked the Judeans. They acted like peacocks before others while they licked the Romans feet. There was no love lost between the Galileans and Judeans. Not that there was ever any to begin with. To add to it, Jesus was a Nazarean. His enemies had made sport of that fact often enough. Why not stay in Galilee where he was considered a Messiah? What did they need to go to Judea for? The Herodians were very strong there.

When the news reached them that Lazarus was sick unto death, Jesus had shocked them by deliberately delaying. Was he having second thoughts? Was he afraid that his power would fail him? Peter would just as gladly have turned back for Capernaum until Jesus informed them that this sickness would not end in death. So they stayed there and rested while Jesus prayed. When the news came that Lazarus had died, they were all stunned. All except Jesus. Once again, he chided them for their lack of faith. Death had hovered over them from the moment they entered Judea and now it beckoned them. Jesus would not be deterred. Thomas told them that they were going to their own deaths.

Martha came to meet them. Distress and frustration were written on her face. Mary didn't even bother to come, so great was her anger over Jesus' failure to heed their plea.

Martha's words cut into them all.

"If you had been here, he wouldn't have died."

How typically Judean! When the chips are down they show their true colors. He would have told her that they wouldn't come back here again until pigs could fly.

But not Jesus. He cried. Cried! Martha softened. She left them to get Mary. Mary came and wept at Jesus' feet. She too knew that Jesus could have done something. Should have done something. Her words were the same as Martha's. They had discussed this with one another. Now it was too late. But they still loved him.

When they went to the tomb, like the others Peter thought that they were going there to mourn. He did not expect to be told to roll back the stone. "There will be a stink." "It's been three days."

"Did I not tell you to have faith!"

What happened next was like a dream. "Lazarus! Come out!" He said it as if Lazarus hadn't been there rotting for days. He ordered him out as if he was ordering a child to run an errand. Or a demon to leave a possessed man. Would wonders never cease with this man?

Lazarus staggered out. The crowd scattered like frightened sheep. The disciples themselves almost ran off.

"Untie him and set him free."

It was then that Peter understood. They had all worried about going to Jerusalem to die. Jesus was showing them that he had power even over death. There was nothing to fear. Nothing could stop them now. Jerusalem and all Judea would fall before them as had Galilee. The news of this miracle was sure to precede them to Jerusalem. They would be waiting for him with open arms. Jesus would go there with open arms. The new kingdom was about to commence. All his hesitations and doubts were suddenly gone.

Why not go up to Jerusalem?

Why not now?

Jesus: Bethany

He quietly slipped out of the house and made his way to the summit of the hill to the place where all Jerusalem lay spread out before him. It was his favorite place and had been since he was a child when they used to come to Jerusalem for the festivals. They would always lodge with their cousins in Bethany on the Mount of Olives. The first time he came to this spot and saw the city stretched out like a jewel before him, he stood there immobilized staring open-mouthed. His cousins had made absolutely nothing of such a magnificent view of the city. They just laughed at him standing there gawking. He wasn't sure if it was simply because they were so used to seeing the city this way, or because they were showing off, putting on that sophistication Judeans reserved for outsiders, especially Galileans. Besides, Nazareans were considered nothing more than country bumpkins. But this remarkable view had made a permanent impression on him and he carried it with him wherever he went.

Dawn was breaking and the morning sun hurried its way up the horizon, changing the silver glow of the city to gold. It had a way of rising and setting much too quickly in Judea, especially here at the edge of the wilderness. Perhaps it was portentous of how everything happened in this troubled city. He had awakened from a fitful sleep and slipped away quietly so as not to rouse any of the others. He needed to be alone. As much as he loved his disciples and the crowds milling about him, he also craved solitude and time for silent reflection. It was his time for nourishment, to drink from the well of the Father so that he would have living water to give to those who came thirsting.

This morning, however, his spirit was not pensive but morose. He had an overwhelming sense of foreboding. The fear that surged violently within him was so strong he could taste it. He sat on his customary stone, only when he looked at the city this time it brought up such a dread that he had to turn away. Suddenly, it gave him the feeling you get when you see food that once made you violently sick.

Of course he was afraid. He had reason to be. Deep inside he knew what was going to happen. Somehow he had always known. But it had always been a remote possibility. Nothing for immediate concern. It's easy to be brave and indifferent when you're sure nothing can hurt you for the moment. This morning that certitude was gone and he trembled. What he needed was prayer. He fell to his knees and touched his forehead to the ground.

"Hear, Oh, Israel, the Lord is God and Him alone!"

He said it again. And then again and again. It had always been the touchstone for a flood of seemingly endless inspirations. But nothing was happening. No thoughts. No consoling aphorisms, repartees, witticisms. Instead, dread was taking hold of him. He opened his eyes and looked about frantically. Perhaps something would strike him, a bird or a flower, and usher in a whole host of lessons he could teach his disciples. He saw nothing about which he hadn't already spoken endlessly. In defeat he cast his eyes to the ground.

A tiny ant was struggling along carrying an oversized load. Some- times he carried it before him and at other times he dragged it along walking backward. Just ahead was a large ant, at least double its size. Jesus saw that there was trouble ahead for the tiny creature but the little ant walking backward was unaware of it. He was on a collision course with catastrophe....

≈

He had left Jerusalem for Jericho. He was returning to Nazareth by way of the trans-Jordan so as not to be defiled by crossing through Samaria.

But he had lingered too long in the Temple precincts, listening and discussing with some of the great teachers who like himself had come to Jerusalem for the Passover. The caravan he was to travel with was now well ahead of him and he would have to hurry if he wanted to catch up with it. He was deep in thought as he hastened down the road arguing mentally about some of the things that had been discussed. The sun was setting and still the caravan was nowhere in sight. He thought of a clever argument he could use against something a Scribe had said and laughed remembering how he had delighted the priests in doing just such a thing on the day of his bar mitzvah. That had probably sealed his fate, as he lingered there relishing the attention he was getting from the elders, to the dismay of his parents who came looking for him.

He was too pleased with himself just now even to consider the possibility of there being any danger ahead. It was there waiting for him. The road curved past a stand of high rocks. He had just come around them scanning the horizon in the fading sunlight for some sight of the caravan. He was startled by a burly looking man who jumped out in front of him. Still, Jesus had no idea that the man might be a robber and innocently asked him for information about the others.

"Passed and gone," he smiled, showing rotted teeth.

"Has it been long, friend?" he asked.

"Long enough," he replied, sizing up his prey. In his hand he held a stick commonly used as a walking staff. When he saw that Jesus was not similarly armed, he quickly wielded it like a club. The realization finally dawned on Jesus that the man was a robber and he was about to be assaulted. An overwhelming fear took hold of him. As quick witted as he was, he could think of nothing to say. He was a man of peace. He had abhorred any sight of cruelty or violence, no matter how slight, even from his earliest childhood. He would often run home in tears when his playmates did anything unkind to one another. Now, for the first time, violence was threatening him and he was dumbfounded. He felt the old urge to cry again. Instead, he turned to run. It was to no avail. Two of the ugly man's accomplices had come up behind him. He was trapped and there was nothing he could do. His utter helplessness made his legs tremble. A club came down on the back of his head. He saw a flash of light like lightning in the night sky. This was followed by searing pain unlike anything he had ever experienced. He turned to say something to his attacker and as he did he was struck again and again by the other two. They pounced on him clubbing, punching, and kicking him until he fell in a heap on the road.

When he awoke the sun was already well into morning. His head ached unbearably and he felt numbing pain in his stomach where they had kicked him. He made a futile effort to stand up but quickly crumpled into a ball once again. He would have to wait out the pain for a while.

It wasn't long before a priest came down the road. Jesus felt a rush of relief. Here was someone who would help him. He had begun to utter a prayer of thanksgiving when through half-closed eyes he saw the man cross over to the other side of the road. What was he doing? Couldn't he see that Jesus was in distress? When he made a feeble attempt to call him the priest didn't even turn to look at him. Instead he hurried away all the faster.

Jesus could not believe it. The man had scurried past him as if he were some filthy beggar at the Temple gate. Couldn't he see that he was no beggar, but a traveler in distress? Couldn't he see...Jesus looked at himself. The robbers had taken everything. He lay there in nothing more than his undergarment. In the bright scorching light of midday, he could see the ugly black and blue welts the beating had left all over his body. The morning breeze had covered his body with desert dust so that he was as terrible a sight as any beggar or leper he had ever seen. Still he felt resentment toward the haughty priest, who turned his nose up at him in the hour of his greatest need. Resentment and anger. Should he not have at least made sure of who Jesus was before he passed on? Then Jesus realized that if the priest were on his way to the Temple, an encounter with a leper would have made him unclean. According to the Law he would have to be purified and made clean himself before he could resume his priestly tasks. For the first time in his life Jesus felt resentment toward the Law. He who had loved it and devoured it since his youth now saw it from the other side. The blow was almost as terrible as the ones that had felled him. He was spiritually crushed. The Law had worked against him. How could the Law be wrong?

"No!" he said shaking his head as if that would straighten out this thinking. The Law wasn't wrong. The priest was. But how many others were there like him, innocent and suffering, and the Law was being misinterpreted against them?

He was still struggling through this reasoning, the physical pain no longer a matter at issue, when a Levite repeated exactly what the priest had done. If Jesus was anything, he was an emotional man. His resentment turned to anger. The Law must never be used against people. It was meant to serve the people. How could it have come to this? In all his zealous study of the Law it had never occurred to him that such a thing could happen. It was the naiveté of youthful innocence. Jesus was consoled that this awful incident had served to make him grow up. Maturity had come at a painful price, but it was worth it. He was feeling better already.

Now that he had learned all there was to learn from this incident, he decided to move on. He struggled to his feet. The pain came back with a vengeance. He had put it out of his mind while he was lost in thought, but it was waiting there for him when he decided to come back to reality. He wasn't going anywhere. At least not yet. But if he didn't get out of this scorching sun, and soon, he was going to be in further trouble. He prayed.

Soon another traveler came along, and from the looks of him Jesus knew that he was the answer to his prayer. He was a bulwark of a man, big and strong enough to ward off an army of bandits. When he saw Jesus lying there, he got off his donkey and hurried over to him. The back of his head had stopped bleeding and the wounds on his arms where he tried to ward off the blows were caked with blood. The stranger gave him some wine to drink although Jesus would have preferred water and tried to tell him so.

"The wine will dull the pain better than water will," he said. When he poured wine over his wounds Jesus passed out.

He awoke slumped over the donkey in the courtyard of an inn. The stranger eased him off the beast and carried him to the common room. Once Jesus was resting comfortably, he poured soothing olive oil on his wounds. Then he gave him some food to eat. While they ate Jesus told him the story about what had happened to him. For a moment he relived the fear of the encounter, but that quickly changed to anger. He berated himself for being so foolish and naive. He should have been traveling with the others and not by himself, only nothing like this had ever happened to him before so he never considered the danger. Danger was something children heard about in stories but never happened to you personally. Now he knew differently.

"What exactly have you learned?" the stranger asked.

Jesus loved to be questioned so that he could show how intelligent he really was. "I'll never travel alone again," he said hastily and then added, "but if I have to you can bet that I will be prepared. I will carry a big stick so that any bandit will think twice before he approaches me."

"What if there's more than one again?"

"Don't worry. I'll make myself strong like you. I'll be able to defend myself the next time." Jesus was surprised at the depth of his anger. He could see himself encountering that ugly, rotten-mouthed thief again and beating him in retribution. It was only just. After all, as you measure, so will it be measured back to you. Jesus was more than ready and willing to measure it back, measure for measure, stripe for stripe, pressed down and even overflowing.

"You are barely more than a boy," the stranger said, "and you still have much to learn." Jesus' face flushed with embarrassment. He was accustomed to being praised for his quick and incisive answers. He was the pride of the rabbi and the learned people of Nazareth. Who did this stranger think he was calling him a boy? Only gratitude for what the man had done kept him from lashing out against him.

"During the course of my travels," the man said, "I once saw a curious thing. A small animal was set upon by one at least three times its size. The end was certain, I thought, when the smaller animal suddenly turned to face its pursuer. Then quite unexpectedly it attacked. The bigger animal was taken by surprise and maneuvered to avoid being bit. It backed up just enough to fall down a ravine. By the time it scrambled back up, the little animal was gone."

"What are you saying?" Jesus asked.

"A man does not run away from his pursuers. A wise man faces them head on even though they are more powerful than himself. But he makes sure that when he attacks there is a pit for them to fall into."

Jesus pondered his words all night long. By morning he considered himself indeed fortunate for learning all that he had from his unfortunate incident. He poured forth a torrent of words and lessons on his attentive benefactor, both his reflections on the Law and what he had learned from the stranger. This was his forte and he was proud to be able to show off what we was best able to do.

"I am glad that you have learned all that there was to learn from your misfortune," the man said. "Tell me, Yeshua. Where were you going when you were set upon by the robbers?"

"To Jericho and thence to Nazareth," he answered.

"Why such a roundabout route? Would it not have been quicker to go straight from Jerusalem to Nazareth?"

"That would take me through Samaria," Jesus answered all too quickly. "And that would have made me unclean."

His benefactor walked toward his waiting donkey, when suddenly he stopped and turned toward Jesus. He looked him straight in the eye and said, "You have not yet learned everything, Yeshua. You see, I am a Samaritan."

Jesus was taken aback. He had not expected this. The Samaritan had backed him into a pit. He had done precisely what he had spoken to Jesus about. Jesus knew that he would never forget that Samaritan. He also resolved never to walk around Samaria again.

He remembered the incident this morning as if it had happened yesterday. He looked down at the ants that had triggered the memory. The little ant lay there dead. Jesus looked at the city of Jerusalem and wept.

Peter: Hosanna!

"He's sullen, again," Peter thought. Sullen and moody. Just when they had all gotten fired up over the raising of Lazarus. What was on his mind?

It was impossible for Peter to try to second-guess Jesus. He could never fully figure out what he was up to. James and John had gone off to make arrangements for the Passover supper, and he brooded while they all waited. Suddenly Jesus had become secretive. Almost cryptic, the way he gave them instructions about where they were to go and what they were to do. Judas had gone off too, probably to buy provisions for the feast. The others were anxious to get started. They were still on fire with the Lazarus miracle. None of them could wait until they got into the city to show off.

Just wait until they hear about Lazarus. What a spectacular way to enter the city! He was sure that the word was already spreading like wildfire. Now the Judeans will know what good can come from Nazareth. Now those haughty bastards will grovel before them.

This was the moment he had been waiting for, praying for, since he had figured out what their mission was really all about. He was eager to get started. What was Jesus waiting for? And why was he brooding when victory seemed so close at hand.

Finally they returned. All this time just to wait for an ass. But Matthew set him straight. "Behold Jerusalem! Your savior comes to you astride an ass, a beast of burden." He wasn't sure of the scripture, but he knew what it meant. Jesus was always one step ahead of him.

As they neared the city, the shouts began. They recognized him. At first, it was just Galileans. He recognized some of them. But as they proceeded, others joined their ranks until the road ahead was swollen with a tremendous crowd. They could barely pass for the shoving and the shouting and the palms.

"My God!" Peter thought. This is it. He had thought it was premature, but, as usual, Jesus knew better. The kingdom is at hand! Hadn't he repeated it time and again. It was beginning and he was riding the crest of the wave. All Jerusalem lay before them. They were entering it on palm branches, the greeting reserved for a conquering hero. A pagan custom, but put to good use.

They entered the gates to the hosannas of all Jerusalem. The shouts followed them right into the Temple. But Peter wasn't expecting what happened next. No one was. Jesus made a whip and flailed away at the money changers, kicking over their tables. He was challenging them right off. The action was so startling that the hosannas stopped abruptly. What was he doing? Why was he doing this? He was acting too precipitously. The insurrection can't start now. They're not prepared for it.

Peter stood there aghast. He couldn't move. Everything had gone from joy to confusion. Coins were clattering over the cobblestones to the curses of the vendors. Pigeon cages were overturned and frantic doves were making good their escape. People were shouting, "Who is that man?" "What does he think he's doing?"

By the time the Temple guards got there Jesus was gone. He had entered and left like a bolt of lightning, leaving destruction behind him. Peter snaked his way slowly through the milling crowd looking and listening to their charges. None of them could identify Jesus. There were no Galileans among them. The guards hurried off to make their report.

Peter made his way out of the Temple, a dazed man. Jesus had done it to him again. He wanted to scream out in anger and frustration. What a hell of a way to begin a kingdom!

Judas

"The trouble with you, Judas, is that you think too much."

"The trouble with you, Simon, is that you don't think."

Simon clenched his fist and scowled at him. He was going to take a swipe at Judas but that would have only affirmed what he had said. Actually, he didn't care. He was a man of emotion and not of intellect, and it was of no consequence to him who knew it. Once he was convinced of something, Simon was unshakeable. He was a doggedly loyal friend and a rapacious foe. At times, Judas was justifiably afraid of him. Judas would never have baited or intimidated him if it weren't for Jesus. Jesus had somehow soothed the beast that raged in Simon the Zealot.

Judas couldn't help it if he was a plotter. That's the way his mind worked. He was gifted with brains, not brawn. Let the Samsons conquer. It was the Judases who were the power behind the throne. Trying to talk to Zealots was like trying to reason with mules. What did Simon care about Jesus' motives for entering Jerusalem in triumph. Like the others he had wallowed in the glory of it. They all had. Without giving a second thought to *how* he had done it. "If the master wants to ride an ass into Jerusalem, then we get him an ass to ride on." That's all there was to it for him. He might just as well have ridden you, Judas thought. There was more to it than that, my friend, only you're too dense and hot-headed to know it.

Jesus didn't always confide in Judas. But he was that way with the others too. Sometimes he shared intimacies with John. Sometimes with Peter or Andrew. Judas knew that Jesus' moves were always calculated, always deliberate. It was a strategy that kept the Apostles off balance and in competition with one another. Of course, the others didn't realize this. Only he was perceptive enough to assess the situation. And perhaps Thomas. But Thomas was difficult to talk to. Judas had tried to enlighten him.

"Moses was a true genius," Judas began in a way that would ingratiate himself to the skeptic. "Not simply because he was a law-giver. There were many before and many after him who did likewise but never achieved the status he did.

"It was because God chose him," Thomas answered. Succinct and to the point. It was so like him.

"I dare say that God has chosen others, too. Others who never attained his stature."

"What are you getting at, Judas?"

Judas continued not so much seeking affirmation for his theory as to impress Thomas with it. "Kingdoms rise and fall, dynasties ebb and flow with the tide. Great ones come and go and there is barely a remembrance of them."

"Get on with it, Qoheleth."

A truly worthy debater, Judas thought. If only Thomas could delve more deeply, beyond the superficial, he would be a truly worthwhile associate. Therein lay his fatal flaw. Did he really think that he was merely going to wax eloquent about a time for this and a time for that? They had trained Thomas well. He could react but not grasp, think but not reason.

"What has made Moses enduring is that he did not grasp for power. He never made himself king, although he easily could have. He set up no dynasty in his own blood. Instead, he chose Joshua to succeed him. He conquered no land he could call his own. Nor did he even enter the promised land."

"That was because of his sin!"

"Yes, Thomas, yes." Judas sighed impatiently. He was dealing with a boy who had learned his catechism. But only that. "The point is that he did what others who were stronger and greater than he never did."

"And what was that?" Thomas asked, impatient with Judas's dawdling.

"He endured. He will continue to endure long after we and our time are no more than a fading memory. And why?"

"Because of God," Thomas interjected before Judas could continue. The question was simply rhetorical and Thomas knew it, but he could not abide Judas's lecturing.

"Because he went for the bigger prize — human hearts. The genius of Moses was that he didn't waste his time conquering lands and setting up buildings or monuments. These come and go, and Moses knew that before Qoheleth. His genius was that he made his people not merely a nation but a religion. Religion binds people beyond period and place. Even beyond time. That is why Moses has endured while the pharaohs are mummified in their tombs and Alexander rots in the earth."

"So what does that have to do with us?"

"Nothing. Never mind." It was like casting pearls to swine. It has everything to do with us if you could see beyond your nose. Couldn't any of them see what was happening? Judas felt on the verge of a great discovery, but he couldn't quite nail it down. Talking to someone usually helped. More often than not he went to Jesus, because the others were not as keen or perceptive as he was. This time he couldn't go to Jesus, because he was trying to figure out what Jesus was up to. If Jesus had wanted them to know, he would have told them. There was a kind of frenzy all about them but Judas seemed to be the only one aware of it. Things were definitely coming to a head. But where? How? Take the spectacular raising of Lazarus before entering Jerusalem. There was a reason for doing it then. Otherwise why did Jesus wait? The others made nothing of Jesus' delay after he had been informed of his cousin's fatal condition. Jesus never acted without reason. When were they going to learn that? Then there was all that cryptic talk about getting the donkey and securing the room for them to celebrate the Passover meal. There was definitely something to all that, but Jesus shared it only with a few of the Apostles. Again, was it simply to keep them off balance or was it to make sure that with only partial knowledge none of them would be able to put it all together and figure out what he was up to?

He was so close he could taste it. He tried talking to James and John who were "in" on the upper room but they were as tight as clams. He had to go on his own instincts.

The entry into Jerusalem bothered him. It was so out of character for Jesus. It was the triumphal entry of a conquering king, but Jesus had consistently and adamantly eschewed any such honors. Why then did he go through with such a charade?

That's it! Judas thought. That's exactly it. It was all a charade. It had to be. Nothing else made sense. A charade. But why? Why would he deliberately antagonize the Scribes and the Pharisees, excite the Zealots, and give the Romans pause to wonder who this man was with such a vociferous following? No half-thinking Jew could miss the obvious allusion to David and messiahship. And if there was ever a time the Romans were nervous about uprisings, it was at Passover, when the city teemed with extra Jews. Jesus had to be deliberately baiting all of them. He kept asking himself over and over again why would he act that way.

There was only one possible answer. There could be no other answer and Judas knew it. Jesus *wanted* to start trouble! He wanted to be arrested. He wanted to be put to death.

The realization left Judas trembling. All Jesus' veiled allusions about death now began to make sense. This was all part of his plan. What plan? What was the plan? He felt certain that he was on the verge of discovering it, but there was still a piece missing. It was the essential piece. The piece that would unlock the entire puzzle. Judas wanted to scream, he felt he was so close to it. He paced back and forth talking to himself. The others would be waiting for him, wondering what happened to him. Let them wait. In a moment he would uncover the truth. He just knew it.

Why would Jesus deliberately set in motion the events that could very likely lead to his death? All his work would have been in vain. All his teaching would be forgotten. It would all be for nothing just as Qoheleth said. Unless...Unless...

My God! It couldn't be! It couldn't possibly be! Jesus won't be forgotten. Not any more than Moses. He doesn't want to set up a kingdom. Jesus is after the hearts and minds of people. Did he not say so himself? *He wants to set up a religion!* It was the only possible answer. It was the only one that made sense.

The discovery astounded him. His mind raced furiously considering the possibility. The possibilities. It was absolutely unbelievable. A new religion with Jesus as the new Moses. He saw it all now, as clear as day. This was the missing piece that solved the riddle and completed the puzzle. Everything was falling into place. Of course, Jesus as the new Moses. The plagues were nothing more than the signs and wonders that preceded the exodus of the Israelites from Egypt. Those had been the prelude for the beginning of Judaism. Were the miracles of Jesus meant to be the start of something similar? That would mean then that the teachings of Jesus were supposed to be reflective of the teachings of Sinai. They were to be the new rules of faith. Why even the twelve Apostles were meant to hearken back to the establishment of the twelve tribes once they crossed the Jordan and took possession of the Promised Land.

Everything pointed to it — a new religion. Why did it weigh so heavily on his heart? Was it because Judas had seen so many religions come and go? The idea of another religion was certainly not new. Every conqueror brought a new religion with him. But being false, they were all doomed to oblivion. Judaism had outlasted them all.

Thus far. Those were all attacks from without. They had only served to make the faith of the Jews stronger. This, however, would be coming from within. This was not simply a reform movement. Jesus was more than just a reformer like the countless others who had gone before him. No one had ever done what he has done. This would be a whole new beginning of another religion. He had no doubt about it. The old one would have to die for the new one to be born from it. It would be a case of the mother dying in childbirth.

Dying. That's why Jesus could not be dissuaded from going to Jerusalem in spite of all their protestations. *He has to die — like Moses — for the new birth to begin.* The timing was perfect. Passover! The symbolism would be unmistakable. This Jesus was either the greatest prophet that ever lived — or the worst devil!

Then his mind became clouded. What about Moses? Did Jesus mean to usurp Moses? That would be too much even for Judas to bear, let alone the people. Jesus didn't want to overthrow Rome. He meant to overthrow Moses! My God, how could that be? This was too much, even for Jesus. Judas was willing to give up father, mother, brother, and sister to follow him. But Moses? Never! That would mean the end of them all. The end of everything Jewish. The remembrance of them would be wiped off the face of the earth. This could not be the will of God. God had made a covenant with them and God will not break it.

Judas trembled uncontrollably now, but it was more than the cool night breeze that made him wring his hands. He had uncovered Jesus' secret plan, and he knew that he must do something about it. Did he have any choice? Was there any other avenue open to him? If there were he would try it, for he truly loved Jesus. His disciple-ship had always been sincere. If he thought there was any possibility of dissuading Jesus, he would try. But he knew what Jesus was like once he made up his mind. "If you take the plow in hand, don't look back."

Now his dilemma was complete. He couldn't go to Jesus with his discovery, because that would tip his hand and Jesus would stop him. He couldn't go to the Apostles because they either wouldn't believe him or they might inform Jesus. Why did the burden have to fall on his shoulders? It was too much to bear. The choice was his to make — Jesus or Judaism?

Jesus or Judaism? God was on the side of the Jews. There was no question of it in his mind. Was God on the side of Jesus? How could God be if it meant the destruction of everything that God had done for a thousand years? If it meant the end of everything Judas held precious and dear. Jesus had said it to them time and again. You must give up everything to follow him. For the first time Judas had to confront what that really meant.

And he couldn't do it.

The future of Judaism was in his hands. He knew what he had to do. The others were calling him. He had to make an appearance or they might get suspicious. He walked slowly up the stairs, dreading having to look at them. Dreading having to see Jesus. As he entered the room his heart beat wildly. Suddenly, he felt like a spy in the enemy camp. If he didn't leave quickly he was afraid that cowardice would overtake him. Strange. That was the one thing Jesus despised.

Jesus looked him in the eye. Judas knew that he knew.

"What you have to do, do quickly," Jesus said.

Judas left. As he hurried down the stairs he wondered for a brief moment if there was something in that look of Jesus' that said this too was part of the plan.

John: The Last Supper

"This night is certainly different from every other night," John thought.

There was something about it he couldn't quite put his finger on. It was there from the moment they entered the room — an air of excitement, of expectancy, but he couldn't tell if it was for good or ill.

Jesus once told them about how excited the people must have been listening to Amos prophesy about what would happen to the bad people on the Day of the Lord, only to discover that he was talking about them. Whenever Jesus talked about the Day of the Lord, John would get a strange feeling like he wanted it to happen but at the same time he was afraid of what would happen to him. He had that same feeling tonight.

He also felt drained from all the excitement. Their entry into Jerusalem had been spectacular. When Simon the Zealot brought the mule to Jesus, he wondered what that was all about. Jesus always walked wherever they went. But no sooner had they begun the ascent from Kidron Valley than he understood. There was just no way Jesus could have walked through that crowd. They came running at him from everywhere, hemming him in, blocking their passage, shouting excitedly. The Apostles tried to keep the crowd back but it was futile. They had to inch their way along.

Someone then shouted, "Hosanna to the son of David!" John reacted instinctively. It was as if a fist had suddenly grabbed his stomach inside him. It was the first time that day "the prophet feeling" had come over him. There was no mistaking what the shout meant. Trouble. Although he couldn't swear to it, it seemed to have come from Simon. He wanted to stop him, but it was like a signal that triggered an immediate reaction in the crowd that began the chorus: "Hosanna to the son of David!" It got louder and louder as they approached the city gate. Here was a mob openly flaunting their defiance at the soldiers and the guard.

A centurion and some soldiers were standing nearby intently watching the scene. John knew what they would be thinking. He had to do something to put some balance into this, to get it into perspective. He shouted at the top of his lungs to make sure that they heard it, "Blessed is he who comes in the name of the Lord!" Some others picked up the chant along with him, but Simon and his crowd drowned them out as they passed the group. When John looked back he saw them hurry off toward the Antonianum.

When he looked ahead he saw the Day of the Lord. On several occasions in his young life he had seen military parades staged by the Romans. But there were never any cheers, any joyous shouts other than from a few of their own or their flunkies. The crowds that lined the streets, when they were forced to, watched in sullen silence. But here was a victory march the likes of which he had only imagined. People were shouting jubilantly and strewing palm branches before them. It was what it must have been like when David entered the city in triumph. If this was the Day of the Lord, then his question was answered and his fears put to rest. He was on the right side.

"Hosanna to the son of David!"

The scene in the Temple was quite another matter. John had never seen Jesus that violent. It was as if he got caught up in the wave of his own making. He couldn't believe his eyes when Jesus began overturning the sellers' tables. This wasn't merely stirring up trouble, as he had done so often in the past. This was starting a war. The Apostles and some others began to follow suit. He felt as if he was in the midst of a violent storm on the Sea of Galilee. Jesus had calmed the storm for them then, and John knew what he had to do now. He forced his way through the shouting mob and took hold of Jesus. They stood there for the briefest moment, their eyes locked together. Jesus' eyes softened. The storm was over. As he led Jesus away, he noticed the eyes of Simon the Zealot. The storm still raged in them.

Jesus was pensive when they entered the upper room. As they sat waiting a bit impatiently for the women to serve them, Jesus did a strange thing. He put on a servant's smock and washed the feet of each of them — over Peter's protest. There were times when John was so attuned to Jesus that he could have said or done what Jesus did. This was one of those times. The Apostles were treating the women as servants and not with dignity the way Jesus taught them. All that had happened was making them a bit heady, so they needed to be reminded and humbled again. It was so typical of Jesus that John could have laughed. It was also so typical of Peter that he did laugh.

There was a pleasant air of celebration about the gathering. Beyond a doubt this was Jesus' favorite holiday — and theirs. He had made it especially so for them because of his intimate knowledge of the scriptures and his vivid accounts of their people's history. When he spoke about Moses and the desert community, it was as if he was there. No one can relate an event the way an eyewitness can and somehow Jesus seemed to have been an eyewitness to history. He made it come alive for them. It came as no surprise when he told them of how much he desired to eat this meal with them. They looked forward to it just as much.

But there was something else afoot. John sensed it perhaps more than the others. Jesus spoke at great length about the importance of remembering, which was what Passover was all about. He tried to remind them of all the special things he had taught them, the lessons he had carefully explained to them. Some of the others were getting just a little weary with the discourse. There wasn't the usual banter among them. This was more serious than usual.

It was when they got to the lamb that John knew something was up. He got that "prophet feeling" again. While Jesus seemed to be mentioning it in passing, John was positive he was telling them something in that parabolic way he had.

Jesus was reminding them of the importance of repentance when he digressed on the Day of Atonement. It was only a momentary thing about the scapegoat but that was when the gut wrench struck him. John looked questioningly at Jesus, who seemed to sense his anguish. Jesus leaned over and embraced him so that he rested against Jesus' chest. There was something very paternal about the way he did it that made John feel like the boy he really still was. At any rate, it was enough to distract him from trying to remember something, a memory that the scapegoat and something Jesus said had triggered.

They took a little break to stretch their legs. Judas went off to get something that someone must have forgotten. They would wait for him before going on with the meal. The Apostles broke off into little groups while he went to the women to ask if they needed any help.

Jesus didn't move from his place at the head of the table. He was lost in a world of his own thoughts, something they were all very used to. John took the amphora of wine and filled the cups. When he got to Jesus' he smiled at him.

"Remember Cana?" he said.

Jesus looked up at him. Tears began to fill his eyes. He thought remembering Cana would make Jesus happy. Ordinarily, it would have. But tonight it made him cry. How was he to know? Before he could say anything else, Jesus called them back to the table.

John didn't return to his place right away, he felt so bad. He stood in the back of the room trying to sort out his feelings. His anxiety was overpowering.

Jesus ate some of the lamb along with the others. The "prophet feeling" in John was overwhelming. There was something he was trying to remember, just on the edge of his consciousness, something having to do with the lamb and the goat that was erupting to the surface.

Jesus held up the bread.

"Take and eat," he said. "This is my body."

"That's it!" John almost screamed out loud. Suddenly it all made sense. The strangeness of Jesus, the unusual discourse, that undeniable "prophet feeling" tearing at his innards begging to know if this would be for good or ill.

What he was trying to remember boiled to the surface. It was a fable he had heard a long time ago. It was about a lamb that was invited to a banquet only to discover that he was the meal.

Jesus: Gethsemane

"Why is this happening to me? Oh, God! Why is this happening?"

He was kneeling on the rough earth, his body bent over, his head almost touching the ground. He rocked back and forth, moaning. He cried out again, out loud.

"Why?"

The others didn't hear him. He had moved off away from them so that he could be alone. He didn't want them to hear him. It made no difference. They were sleeping.

It was coming to an end and he knew it. He had always known it. It hung over him like an ominous cloud even in his moments of greatest triumph. It cast a shadow over everything he did. Death. It was always there, always waiting for him. It made him brood at times. The others made excuses, saying that he was just being pensive. They didn't know. How could they?

Did they ever understand? Did he himself understand? How could he expect them to when he wasn't sure himself. They were expecting more. Was he just leading them on? He tried to tell them. Over and over he tried, but they didn't see. Wouldn't see. The miracles blinded them. The excitement was too much for them.

"These were all You gave me!" he shouted.

In the near distance, the Apostles stirred, but fell fast asleep again.

What did God expect from him? What could he expect from fishermen, shepherds, and tax collectors? And these were the best among them. In spite of all his teaching, they still fought among themselves. They still harbored childhood dreams of glory.

But so did he. He dreamt of glory that day on the plain with the loaves and the fish. The crowd had listened. They were one with him. And the boy had led them. With just a few loaves and some fish. They were eating and sharing together as one. One family. One nation. God's people as they should be. With him at their head. Like Moses in the desert. It was the best of his miracles. He had reveled in it for a long time. Yet deep down he knew this was not to be. The temptation was so great he had to flee and remonstrate with himself because of it. It would have been so easy to succumb.

The kingdom is not there. Not that way, he reminded himself as he lay hunched over on the ground. It is not an earthly kingdom. Not with all its allurements. Not with all its glory. He understood that in the desert, but it didn't make the honey any less sweet.

The end was near and he began to tremble. He needed support. As feeble as it might be, he needed it. Needed them in his dark hour. He rose haltingly and went over to where they slept.

"Why are you sleeping? Stay up with me."

John asked if he wanted them to join him in his prayer. Peter grumbled. Yes, he wanted them. He desperately wanted them close to him. He wanted to grab hold of them tightly. He wanted them to embrace him and never let him go. But he didn't want them to know it. Their faith was not strong enough. It might undo everything he had worked for.

"Just stay awake and pray," he said and stumbled back into the grove.

The Passover supper would be their last meal together. He had prepared carefully for it. He knew the scriptures. He knew the mind of the Father in revelation inside out. Like Ezekiel he had eaten it.

The memories came now in a torrent flooding over him. His life was passing before him. Before Abraham was I am. He saw Ezekiel eating the parchment. He saw his people eating the manna in the desert. He saw the Passover lamb being slain, its blood spewing forth covering the earth. He writhed as he saw the knife dig in deep. He heard the pitiful cry of the innocent lamb. He saw the people eating the lamb. Raw. It's blood on their faces dripping down on their tunics. There was blood everywhere. Blood on the doorposts. Blood dripping from the fruit that Adam and Eve ate.

Then he saw the crowds coming toward him. Broken bodies, twisted limbs, grotesque faces eaten up with leprosy. They came reaching out to him. Pawing at him. He tried to break away. There were too many of them. They kept coming. Heal me. Touch me. Their pleas became demands. They shouted at him. They screamed like hungry birds of prey.

He was now a lamb bleating frantically, trying to flee through an impenetrable forest of legs. They grabbed hold of him. The lamb became a goat. They held him aloft for everyone to see. Then he screamed as blood spurted out of him, covering their heads and faces and clothes.

He bent over and vomited.

"Let me be the last one, Father. No more after me."

They were still sleeping. A gentle breeze rustled the olive leaves above him. He felt a quiet calm come over him. There would be no more sacrifices. No more blood. His would be the last. He had seen to it at the supper. He had changed the flesh to bread. He had changed the blood to wine. His flesh. His blood. His last sign to them. Or was it?

The soldiers were coming. It was easy to hear them in the quiet night. Death approached. The final battle was about to be joined.

THE LAST WORDS OF CHRIST:
A DRAMATIC READING

CAST:

Christ	*Woman 2*
Commentator 1	*Man 1*
Commentator 2	*Man 2*
Chorus of Six	*Man 3*
Woman 1	*Boy*

I

COMMENTATOR 1:

The next day the crowds who had come up for the festival heard that Jesus was on his way to Jerusalem. They took branches of palms and went out to meet him shouting, "Hosanna! Blessings on the king of Israel who comes in the name of the Lord."

Then the Pharisees said to one another, "You see, there is nothing you can do. The whole world is running after him."

Pause

CHORUS: Hosanna! All hail, the King of the Jews!

CHRIST: (*Pensive*) The crowds are cheering me. How good I feel. How wonderful this is.

I do well with crowds. I seem to work best with them. There are always crowds around me. They want to see signs so I show them signs. They bring me their sick. I heal them and they go away happy.

I remember once they followed me for three days and had no more food. They brought a boy to me who had just a few loaves and some fish. I showed them what it meant to be generous. I fed five thousand. Oh, how they marveled! They buzzed and buzzed like happy bees in a field of flowers.

When I spoke to them on the hillside, they called me a new Moses. So I gave them new commandments. Blessed are the poor. Blessed are the peacemakers. Turn the other cheek. Love one another. Yes. They listened and they marveled. Oh, God, how I love the crowds!

Loudly, commandingly

I tell you that if they were to stop cheering, the very stones would shout hosanna!

Pensive

Listen to them, Father. I have done Your will and they are shouting with joy. I could live with this excitement forever. Is there anything else You want me to do?

CHORUS: *All six chorus members cry out:*

All hail, King of the Jews!

In unison five chorus members shout it, while one cries:

Crucify him!

Then four shout, "All hail..." and two cry, "Crucify him." Then three and three, until at the end all six shout out, "Crucify him!"

Pause

COMMENTATOR 2:

It is finished.

II

COMMENTATOR 1:

The chief priests and the elders, however, had persuaded the crowd to demand the release of Barabbas and the execution of Jesus. So Pilate had Jesus taken away and scourged. After this, the soldiers twisted some thorns into a crown and put it on his head and dressed him in a purple robe. Again Pilate asked them, "Which of the two do you want me to release for you?" They said, "Barabbas." But in that case, Pilate said to them, "What am I to do with Jesus?" They all said, "Crucify him!" "Why?" he asked. "What harm has he done?" But they shouted out all the louder, "Crucify him!"

Then Pilate saw that he was making no impression on them, that, in fact, a riot was imminent. So he took some water, washed his hands in front of the crowd, and said, "I am innocent of this man's blood." And the people shouted back, "His blood be on us and on our children."

Pause

CHRIST: He is washing his hands of me. How strange! I am in such pain from the flogging, and yet I seem oddly detached from everything. It is as if I were watching things happen to someone else.

How refreshing that water looks.

Pause

WOMAN 1: They have no more wine.

CHRIST: Bring me the water jars.

Pause

How clear and cool the water looks. Father, the time is now. It must begin.

Draw some water and take it to the chief steward. "The best wine," he said. "The very best wine and it was saved until last." How they drank and celebrated. I was drunk with the miracle.

Pause

Woman, give me a drink.

She doesn't understand. This water will refresh but for a short time and you will be thirsty again. I have a deeper thirst.

WOMAN 2: Sir, give me of that water.

CHRIST: Unless you drink my blood, you shall not have life in you.

Will you walk away, too? I am so thirsty.

Pause

COMMENTATOR 2:
I thirst.

III

COMMENTATOR 1:
When they reached the place called the Skull, Golgotha, they crucified him there.

Pause

CHRIST: Ah, the pain! My hand. Ooohhh! My hands. How they hurt! Try not to think about it. Think of something pleasant. Quick! It will ease the pain.

Here comes a man with a withered hand. Ah, yes, I remember the man with the withered hand. He looked so frightened. What did he think I would do?

Stretch out your hand.

See the amazement in his eyes as his fingers stretched out whole and good. He wiggled them like a baby who just discovered that he has fingers.

Is it lawful to heal on the Sabbath or not? The Pharisees are mad at me but what can they do? His hand is healed... (*He screams*) Ah! Ahh. Aaahhh, my feet. God, how that hurts. Think. Think. Think. It will take away the pain. Think of the crippled ones who came to me. How many they were.

Pick up your pallet and walk!

Walk? Why they jumped and danced for joy.

Go and sin no more lest something worse befall you.

He shouts:

For which cripple are you nailing my feet to this cross!

Pause

The thorn is just above my eye. I can barely open it, it hurts so much.

Pause

MAN 1:   Sir, that I may see.

CHRIST: Go wash in the pool.

MAN 1:   I see people like tall trees.

              I can see! I can see!

CHRIST: God, my whole body is wracked with pain.

              (*Angry*) For which of my miracles have I been put on this cross?

              (*Pleading*) I healed your hands. I restored your limbs. I gave you sight. Is it because I missed some of you? Then bring them here. Quick, before it's too late.

Pause

COMMENTATOR 2:
              Father, forgive them. They do not know what they are doing.

IV

COMMENTATOR 1:

As they were leading him away they seized a man, Simon from Cyrene, who was coming in from the country, and made him shoulder the cross and carry it behind Jesus. Large numbers of people followed him, and women too, who mourned and lamented for him. But Jesus turned to them and said, "Daughters of Jerusalem, do not weep for me. Weep rather, for yourselves and for your children."

Pause

CHRIST:

Ah, poor woman. Poor, poor woman. See how she weeps. Her son is dead. Her only son; and she a widow. In all of Nain is there any sorrow like hers? My heart is moved with pity for her. Who can bear to see those tears? Don't cry.

Stop the procession.

Young man, listen to me. Get up!

Mother, here is your son.

Pause

COMMENTATOR 2:

Woman, behold your son.

V

COMMENTATOR 1:

Near the cross of Jesus stood his mother and his mother's sister, Mary the wife of Clopas, and Mary Magdalene.

Pause

MAN 2:

Lord! She follows after us like a dog. Send her away.

CHRIST: Will they never learn? Will not even my own ever learn?
            There is more faith in this foreigner than in all of Israel.
            I must show them. They must learn before it's too late.

            Woman! What is it you want of me?

WOMAN 1:   My daughter, sir. She is afflicted. Please come and heal
            her.

CHRIST: The food I have is for my family, not for dogs.

WOMAN 1:   Sir, then will you give this dog a crumb?

CHRIST: Is there any love like a mother's love? My people —
            love like that and all will be well. Love just like that.

            Woman, go home. Your child is healed.

            Pause

COMMENTATOR 2:
            Behold your mother.

VI

COMMENTATOR 1:
            It was now about the sixth hour and, with the sun
            eclipsed, a darkness came over the whole land until the
            ninth hour.

            Pause

CHRIST: Listen to the thunder. The sky is so dark. There will be
            a storm — a terrible storm. Like that night on the lake.
            The wind howled and the waves broke over the boat.
            They were frightened like children.

MAN 3:   Lord, will you sleep? We are going down.

CHRIST: Why are you afraid? I am with you.

            Wind — be quiet!

            Waters — be calm!

Why are you afraid?

Pause

Father! Father, I'm afraid. I have this overwhelming sense of foreboding. Blood! Blood. Even my sweat runs red. My hands are trembling. I can't stop them. Something terrible is going to happen to me. I'm afraid. If only I knew what it was. If only I knew.

Father. If it's possible, let this cup pass from me.

What is it? Why am I so frightened?

MAN 1, 2, 3: Crucify him! Crucify him!

Pause

COMMENTATOR 2:

My God! My God! Why have you forsaken me?

VII

COMMENTATOR 1:

The people remained there watching him. As for the leaders, they jeered him. "He saved others," they said, "Let him save himself if he is the Christ of God, the chosen one." The soldiers mocked him too. One of the criminals hanging there said, "Jesus, remember me, when you come into your kingdom."

Pause

MAN 1: Lord, heal me.

WOMAN 1: Lord, cure me.

MAN 2: Crucify him.

WOMAN 2: My daughter is sick.

MAN 3: Jesus, touch me.

BOY: My mother is dying.

WOMAN 1:	Crucify him.
MAN 1:	Lord, forgive me.
WOMAN 2:	Jesus, help me.
BOY:	Crucify him.
MAN 1:	Teach me.
WOMAN 1:	Heal me.
MAN 2:	Hear me.
WOMAN 2:	Pity me.
BOY:	Love me.
MAN 3:	Lord, remember me when you enter your kingdom.

Pause

COMMENTATOR 2:

Today, you will be with me in paradise.

VIII

CHRIST: Father. The pain is almost gone now. There's nothing left to hurt. I'm just numb. It feels good to be numb. Thank you. (*Heavy breathing*)

Father, how they marveled! I was just a boy and they could not believe my wisdom.

MAN 1: Who instructed this boy?

MAN 2: How is it he knows so much?

CHRIST: It was wonderful to be in the midst of so many learned rabbis and to answer all their questions. How I enjoyed their astonishment. I could have stayed there forever. Was it three full days? It seemed like only three minutes.

WOMAN 1: Son, where have you been? Your father and I have searched for you in great sorrow.

BOY: How is it you looked for me? Did you not know that I must be about my Father's business?

                Long pause

MAN 3:   Lord, it is not I who should baptize you. It is you who should baptize me.

CHRIST: Let it be so for the time being. I will do what is fitting and right.

MAN 1:   This is my beloved son, with whom I am well pleased.

                Long pause

CHRIST: Father, How good it is to be with you. How I love you. How I want to please you. Have I pleased you? Have I made you happy?

                (*Slowly*) I am tired now. I am so tired. My body is numb. I no longer feel any pain. The burden is gone from me. I feel almost as if I were floating.

                Pause

MAN 2:   Lord, let us build three tents here. One for you. One for Moses. One for the thief.

                Short pause

CHRIST: Yes, I'm floating. The earth can hold me no longer. I must rise.

                There is light everywhere. It passes through me like air.

                Moses is here. And Elijah. Here too is David and Father Abraham.

                There is no more pain. Just light. All is light. Endless, brilliant light.

                Pause

COMMENTATOR 2:
                Father, into your hands I commend my spirit.

It Is Finished

"Oh, my God, Mamma! He's dead."

She leaned over the bed stretching to get as close as she could, looking into his peaceful, portly face. There was no breathing, no movement. His head lay sunken deep in the pillow. The pain was gone. The labored breathing had stopped. Even the crows' feet around his eyes seemed to relax and fill in now that the struggle was over. It was the kind of peace you would want for him, if only it didn't mean death.

Tears streamed from her swollen eyes and anointed his holy body. He was gone. Such a wonderful man. Wonderful, happy, loving man who filled your life with memories the way his body was filled from the joy of living. When people kidded him about his weight he would say to them, "Every pound was a pleasant experience." And everyone would laugh because it was so true. He was a pleasant experience. He gave meaning to the word "life." If you felt down or depressed about the way life was treating you, just being around him brought you back to life again. He didn't have to say a word, not that he ever shied away from talking. Talking was like eating for him. They were both filling. They were both enjoyable and life-giving. There was never such a man before, and there would probably never be quite another. Now he was gone. The life he gave so freely and generously to others went away. Quietly. Reverently. Respectfully. Just the shell remained. The big, precious relic who even in death left enough to go around. How could it have been otherwise?

"Precious in the eyes of the Lord is the death of His holy ones."

≈

"Skipper!" he screamed.

He was playing in front of the house and the ball his playmate threw flew past him into the street. The big collie rushed by him to retrieve it. He called but Skipper knew his job and was doing it. There would be hugs and kisses and licks when he got back. Joey would scratch him behind the ears with both hands while Skipper licked his face in gratitude. Then they would romp and play together some more.

There was no beep to warn the animal. It happened too fast for that. There was just the terrible, harsh screech of a car grinding to a quick halt. And the awful, sickening thump. Skipper let out an agonizing yelp as the front wheel rolled over his body.

Joey ran out into the middle of the street screaming his name over and over again.

"Skipper!" "Skipper!" "Skipper!"

Skipper tried to get up and go to him. He struggled hard as if he couldn't understand what was holding him down. There was no blood. There didn't even seem to be any more pain after the initial hit. But his eyes told the story. There was a frightened, panicky look in them.

He was Joey's dog and always did what the boy wanted. From the time he was a puppy brought home for Christmas and he licked Joey's face and got kissed in return, there was a bond between them that only dog lovers can understand. They were inseparable, even though Skipper took up most of the bed. When the boy was in school, Skipper waited patiently for him to come home. Summer or winter. If Joey got grounded and confined to his room, Skipper spent the time with him. If the dog got sick, Joey moped around. They were simply made for each other.

Joey was on his knees in the middle of the street holding Skipper's head in his lap.

"Oh, God, please no. Please don't let him die," he cried. Tears came in a steady stream. They were unstoppable.

The others stood around him watching. His mother, his friend, the driver of the car. There was nothing they could do. Joey looked at them pleadingly and back at Skipper again. His breathing was labored. His eyes were getting glazed. He was slipping into shock.

"Please, God, please, please."

Skipper looked up at Joey. He looked hurt and confused. He looked into Joey's eyes as if pleading with him to make it all go away.

"No, Skipper, no. Please don't die. Please don't die."

His breathing got very shallow. His eyes lost their focus and seemed to be staring blankly. His head rolled back as if the effort of holding it up was too much. He stopped breathing. His eyes didn't close. It was his way of showing that he didn't want to take his eyes off this boy he loved so much. His tongue slipped out as if he wanted to give him one last happy, playful lick.

It was over.

"Skipper!" Joey cried one last time. Then he picked up his beloved Collie, carried him into the house, and laid him on his bed.

≈

"I don't think I'm afraid to die any more," she said to the nun who sat at her bedside.

Sister Judith didn't know exactly what to say at the unexpected comment so she said nothing. Laurie was a spritely sixteen-year-old dying of leukemia. They had bonded from the moment she was admitted to the hospice, even though she told herself time and again not to get emotionally involved any more. The fact that Laurie wasn't Catholic made no difference, but it might have made it easier. "Damn the Protestants," she once said in frustration over the death of another precious girl like Laurie. "They took away relics, crucifixes, rosaries, and just about everything else a dying person can hold on to." So instead she let the kids hold on to her. But that was emotionally draining.

Laurie came from a typical upper-middle-income suburban family. The All-American family you might say. Her father was a successful businessman. Her mother sold real estate. She had a younger brother, and naturally he was freckle-faced. A big English sheepdog rounded out the picture. That's exactly what it was. They could have posed for an ad for McDonald's or K-Mart or your local department store. They looked picture perfect.

But the picture wasn't perfect. Laurie had leukemia. It had gone into recession twice. Three times and you're out. By this time, they all knew it. But the All-American family didn't know how to take it. Her father couldn't talk about it at all, except to ask if there was anything he could get her. He stumbled around conversations every time they were together, making them both all the more conscious of her terminal condition. She almost would have preferred he didn't come. Not that she didn't love him. It was just that he made them both so uncomfortable. Her mother cried a lot or was forever talking about new medical advances in cancer research. "They're only an hour away," she said quoting the commercial. "Or is it a minute? Whatever. They're just that close." Her All-American brother was typically too wrapped up in himself to show any real concern for her.

Sister Judith was the only one she could talk to. They had talked a lot over the last few weeks. Laurie was an intelligent girl and had read the books, so she knew she was entering the resignation phase. That was the last stage. At first she had reasoned that if she remained in any of the other stages, she could hold off death. Only death was relentless, and so was the process. She eventually gave in.

"Is there really a life after death, Sister Judith?"

"I think so."

The answer surprised her. She had meant the question to be more rhetorical than anything else.

"You mean to tell me that you only think so when you've given your whole life to being a nun?"

Sister Judith looked at Laurie and smiled. How typical of an adolescent to see life as all or nothing. She had seen a lot of gray in her fifty-five years. In her life and others'. If life had taught her anything it was that nothing was certain. That's what faith was all about. Being able to live and manage in the face of uncertainty.

"You mean you don't believe in God?"

"Yes, I believe in God," she said. "But that doesn't answer all the questions, does it?"

Laurie thought pensively for a moment. "I guess it doesn't."

There was a prolonged silence as each let the weight of what had been said sink in. But adolescents can never bear the quiet for very long.

"What do you think, Sister? Is there life after death?"

"There was a boy here several years ago who was genuinely the most wonderful kid you could ever hope to meet," she said. "He was funny...mischievous...entertaining...and lovable. That was quite a big order for a ten-year-old boy. Just having him around made this place a combination of zoo and circus. Believe me when I tell you that everybody loved Johnny.

"The day he died, his mother wept at his bed for hours. When the undertakers came, she wouldn't let them into the room. They asked me to go in and talk to her. She told me something that I will never forget. She said, 'I know he's dead and I'll never hear his wonderful laugh again or watch him play. I have to accept that and I will. But please, just let me hold on to him. I'll take him even without life. Please, don't let them take him away from me.'

"I think for the first time in my life I understood what love was really about. The one you love has become so much a part of you that you become inseparable. You can no more take losing them then losing your heart or your head. We want to hold on to the ones we love, so much so that every bit of them is precious even if life is gone from them. To his mother Johnny's body was a sacred relic that she wanted to keep and love to her dying day.

"I believe that kind of love overcomes death. Laurie, I believe that's the kind of love Jesus had for people. It made him resurrect and it will make us resurrect."

Laurie had tears in her eyes. "I don't think anybody loves me that way. I know my family loves me. But not that way."

"I know this is going to sound like the party line," Sister Judith answered, "but I'm going to say it anyway, because I believe it. Jesus loved you to death."

Laurie looked at her weighing her words. "Do you think he'd want to hold on to *me* and never let *me* go?"

"I do."

"How do you know?"

"Because I'm here."

Laurie smiled. "Will you hold my hand when the time comes?"

"I will. For him. And for me."

When the time did come Laurie held on to Sister Judith's hand for dear life. Sister Judith held on to Laurie's hand for dear death.

≈

"Damn!"

"Damn, damn, damn this war! Damn every God damn war!"

What were they doing here? What the hell was it all about? What did they know? They were just kids. That's all you are when you're nineteen years old. You're full of life and you're hell bent for leather, whatever the hell that meant. They laughed about it at the induction center.

One of the officers said it during a lecture, and afterward he asked Scott what it meant.

"How the hell should I know. I'm not an officer."

They laughed and became friends from that day on. Through boot camp and all the rest. It was like a game to them. Dressing up in a uniform. Looking and feeling macho. Making moves on girls. "It's all the way with the fightin' A." It was all like a big game. So long as it didn't get serious.

But it did get serious. Deadly serious.

There were no gin mills with waiting girls here. Fatigues didn't look macho here. There was no singing to cadences here. There were no gung-ho slogans. There was just killing and death. That's what war is all about.

Scott lay next to him. Dead. His khaki shirt was red with blood. His eyes were closed and his mouth was open. All he said was, "Jesus!"

≈

When they took him down from the cross, they laid him in his mother's arms as she wept bitter tears in the pouring rain.

> Oh, all you who pass by the way.
> See.
> Is there any sorrow like unto my sorrow?
> My people!
> What have I done to you?
> In what way have I hurt you?
> Answer me!

≈

Goodbye, Pappa.
Goodbye, Skipper.
Goodbye, Laurie.
Goodbye, Scott.
In every death Jesus dies.

The Candy Man

Once upon a time there was a candy man. He was the most wonderful man the world had ever known. Everywhere he went he brought with him the most marvelous candy anyone had ever seen or tasted. There were deep, dark, and rich chocolate parfaits. There were elegant strawberry, raspberry, and lemon pastilles. He had sponge candy, cotton candy, and licorice strips. He had an endless supply of multicolored jelly beans, a bottomless reservoir of candied syrups, and no end of bubble gum and candy bars. All of these he gave away free wherever he went. All you had to do was ask and it was yours. And if for some reason he didn't have what you wanted, he always provided you with some equally delicious substitute. He was a marvel, a wonder, a joy, a delight.

Boys and girls, men and women, old folks, dark folks, wise people, and fools — everyone, everywhere greeted him with great jubilation. He was hailed in every city, town, and village. He brought untold joy and delight wherever he went. There was never anyone quite like the candy man.

I say "was" because a most unfortunate thing happened to the candy man. As he was making his way from one city to another, he was set upon by persons or circumstances unknown and stripped of all his candy. As usual, however, when the people caught sight of him they rejoiced jubilantly and called out to him.

"I would like some coconut marshmallows."

"I want gum drops and spice drops."

"I want chocolate." "I want peanut brittle." I want this and I want that, the familiar cries rang out, and they were always heard and always satisfied. Except this day. This day the candy man had no candy to give. No candy for anyone.

At first the people were startled. Then they thought it just a ruse to tease them. When at last they realized that there really was no candy to be had, they became disgruntled. The more they talked about it, the deeper became their disappointment. This grew into anger and finally rage. So consuming and overwhelming was their wrath at not getting the candy they wanted that they attacked the candy man. And killed him.

They killed the candy man.

Why?

Why do we always kill the candy man?

STATIONS OF THE CROSS

First Station: Jesus Is Condemned to Death

LEADER: We adore you, Oh, Christ, and we praise you.

PEOPLE: Because by your holy cross you have redeemed the world.

LEADER: For which of my miracles do you condemn me? For

which of my good works do you condemn me? For which of my teachings do you condemn me? Answer me!

PEOPLE: We condemn you for all of them because your miracles, your good works, and your teachings condemn us. If you had not done them, we would be free not to do them. Now we are guilty because of them. Your light makes us look like the night. We condemn all those who make us look bad when they look good.

LEADER: My friends, come into the light with me. It is better to become a light than to stumble in darkness.

Kneel

PRAYER: Lord, as we begin this journey of suffering with you, help us to learn that it is only through suffering that we can achieve glory. Teach us by your suffering not to fight one another but help each other to resurrection. Amen.

Second Station: Jesus Carries His Cross

LEADER: We adore you, Oh, Christ, and we praise you.

PEOPLE: Because by your holy cross you have redeemed the world.

LEADER: Life was meant to be a joy. Every sin since Adam and Eve's has added its own special weight. So many sins. So much weight. Why have you placed this burden on my shoulders?

PEOPLE: Someone must pay the price. Would our evil be evil if you were not so good? It is because you are good that we see our faults and feel their weight. So we unload the burden on all those who make us feel bad. It is the price you pay for being good. Someone must pay the price. Who better than you?

LEADER: My friends, what I do can take away your pain and your shame. But not without you. Embrace the cross with me. Then you too will share the ecstasy.

Kneel

PRAYER: Lord, teach us not to blame our faults on others for in doing so we put them on your shoulders. Amen.

Third Station: Jesus Falls the First Time

LEADER: We adore you, Oh, Christ, and we praise you.

PEOPLE: Because by your holy cross you have redeemed the world.

LEADER: When did I fail you the first time? What was it you asked for and didn't receive? What did you want and not get? Is that when I fell the first time in your eyes?

PEOPLE: We have our expectations. Of you and all those who are supposed to be good. Parents, teachers, friends, and especially religious leaders. Your will should be our will if you want to make us happy. When you fall short, it is not so much you who suffer but us.

LEADER: My friends, when you fell the first time, I cried along with you.

Kneel

PRAYER: Lord, forgive us when we fall short of your expectations just as we forgive those who fall short of ours. Amen.

Fourth Station: Jesus Meets His Mother

LEADER: We adore you, Oh, Christ, and we praise you.

PEOPLE: Because by your holy cross you have redeemed the world.

LEADER: When you throw a stone into a pool of water, the ripples go very far. When you hurt someone, you also hurt those close to that person and others too.

PEOPLE: When you give us what we ask for we will shout, "Blessed are the breasts that nursed you!" When you fail to, when anyone fails us, we stand ready to strike back. Is it our fault that those who love you also stand in the way?

LEADER: Someone, please, take my mother home.

Kneel

PRAYER: Hail Mary, full of grace, the Lord is with thee. Blessed art thou among women and blessed is the fruit of thy womb, Jesus.

Holy Mary, mother of God, pray for us sinners, now and at the hour of our death. Amen.

Fifth Station: Simon Helps Jesus Carry the Cross

LEADER: We adore you, Oh, Christ, and we praise you.

PEOPLE: Because by your holy cross you have redeemed the world.

LEADER: Every cross is heavy to bear. If it weren't, it would not be a cross. Every cross is made lighter when someone helps you carry it.

PEOPLE: Simon helped you carry your cross. It is you who now send him to help others. Why else would my mother have sat up all night with me when I was sick? Why else would my friend have comforted me in my sadness? Why else would I bear patiently with those who annoy me? Help us to learn that when we are Simon to one another you will come to help us carry our crosses.

Kneel

PRAYER: Lord, help us to believe that your yoke is sweet and your burden is light. Amen.

Sixth Station: Veronica Wipes the Face of Jesus

LEADER: We adore you, Oh, Christ, and we praise you.

PEOPLE: Because by your holy cross you have redeemed the world.

LEADER: God looked into a mirror and saw you and me. He was very pleased. Sin has marred my beauty and yours too.

PEOPLE: We long for the innocence of our youth. Innocence is what made us all beautiful. We have been betrayed by the world, the flesh, and the devil. If we wipe your face clean, will ours become beautiful once again?

LEADER: Wipe my face clean and you will see your face mirrored there forever.

Kneel

PRAYER: You have promised us that the day will come when every sin will be blotted out. Hurry that day, Lord. Then when you look at us you will see yourself reflected there. Amen.

Seventh Station: Jesus Falls a Second Time

LEADER: We adore you, Oh, Christ, and we praise you.

PEOPLE: Because by your holy cross you have redeemed the world.

LEADER: How many times have I failed you? Am I not like you? Am I not one of you? When I fall will you pick me up?

PEOPLE: It is difficult for us to see a God in pain. We want a triumphant God. A victorious God. If you stumble and fall can there be any hope for us?

LEADER: How can I be like you if I do not stumble the way you do? How can I be one with you if I never suffer? Can I say I love you without sharing especially this? I am truly human only when I fall. God is victorious and there is hope for you when you lift me up again.

Kneel

PRAYER: Lord, help us to remember that as often as we have done it for the lowest, we have done it to you. Let our constant prayer be: Father, treat me the way I treat others. Amen.

Eighth Station: Jesus Speaks to the Women

LEADER: We adore you, Oh, Christ, and we praise you.

PEOPLE: Because by your holy cross you have redeemed the world.

LEADER: You say that you have sought me but cannot find me. It is because you refuse to look for me where I really am — where you prefer not to find me.

PEOPLE: We have looked for you among men. Why are you among women? We have searched for you among the beautiful. Why do you choose to be ugly? In our ceaseless struggle for wealth, why do you choose to be poor? We have sought you among the healthy, the intelligent, and the privileged but you prefer to be with the sick, the ignorant, and the outcast. Is it any wonder we cannot find you?

LEADER: Ask honestly and you will receive. Seek sincerely and you shall find. Knock faithfully and it will be opened for you.

Kneel

PRAYER: Lord Jesus, how easily we would be drawn to you if you had a beautiful house, a fine car, stylish clothes, an attractive wife, a handsome son, and a pretty daughter. But you ask us to be attracted to the opposite, like a magnet. If we are not, will you repel us? Amen.

Ninth Station: Jesus Falls a Third Time

LEADER: We adore you, Oh, Christ, and we praise you.

PEOPLE: Because by your holy cross you have redeemed the world.

LEADER: I have fallen again.

PEOPLE: The first time we witness someone fall, we hurry to help. The second time, we offer advice. The third time is an annoyance. We have run out of sympathy and patience. How many times can we keep picking you up?

LEADER: As many times as I have picked you up. Seven times seventy times.

Kneel

PRAYER: Father, forgive us our trespasses, as we forgive those who trespass against us. Amen.

Tenth Station: Jesus Is Stripped of His Clothes

LEADER: We adore you, Oh, Christ, and we praise you.

PEOPLE: Because by your holy cross you have redeemed the world.

LEADER: They have stripped me of all my clothes. They have taken away my power. Now they would take away my dignity.

PEOPLE: God makes us feel guilty. If there is no God, there is no guilt. We must depose you so that we can expose ourselves without sin and remorse.

LEADER: There is no sin in me so there is no shame.

PEOPLE: Will anything ever take away ours?

Kneel

PRAYER: Lord, how wonderful is the flesh you have given us. But as good as it is, it is not God. Remind us that when we worship it, it is far more demanding and less forgiving than you have ever been. Amen.

Eleventh Station: Jesus Is Nailed to the Cross

LEADER: We adore you, Oh, Christ, and we praise you.

PEOPLE: Because by your holy cross you have redeemed the world.

LEADER: Lay your charges against me. They are what nail me to this cross.

PEOPLE: You were better than me.
You were smarter than me.
You were promoted instead of me.
You were liked more than me.
You were not the same color as me.
You made more money than me.
You did not act like me.
You were not me.

LEADER: That is the inscription you have nailed over my head along with that of Pilate's.

Kneel

PRAYER: Lord, let us nail over your head, "No one has greater love than to give his life for another." May they also inscribe it on our tombstones. Amen.

Twelfth Station: Jesus Dies

LEADER: We adore you, Oh, Christ, and we praise you.

PEOPLE: Because by your holy cross you have redeemed the world.

LEADER: From atop this cross I see more than you can possibly imagine. I can see from forever to forever and all the lies in between. I can see every good that illuminates the heart of God and every sin that darkens the soul of humanity. History stretches out on both sides of me like a gigantic balance scale with me on the cross at its center. I must set things straight. If it takes my life to do it, then I do it gladly. Father! Into Your hands I commend my spirit.

PRAYER: *Silent prayer*

Thirteenth Station: Jesus Is Taken Down from the Cross

LEADER: We adore you, Oh, Christ, and we praise you.

PEOPLE: Because by your holy cross you have redeemed the world.

PEOPLE: Do we ever really silence those we dislike? Do we ever really kill those we hate? The world looks at you now silent and dead. Are you really silent? Seeing them place you in your mother's arms speaks more loudly than a million words. On the cross we taunted you with our words. "If you are the Son of God, come down from that cross." You have come down. Not in grandeur but in silence. Now even the stones cry out, "Truly, this is the Son of God."

Kneel

PRAYER: Lord, let every mother's tears for a dead child touch me. Let every father's anguish over his loss move me. Let us never allow death to happen needlessly. Amen.

Fourteenth Station: Jesus Is Laid in the Tomb

LEADER: We adore you, Oh, Christ, and we praise you.

PEOPLE: Because by your holy cross you have redeemed the world.

PEOPLE: Are you really dead? You are not dead so long as I am living. If I sent you away in anger, so long as I am living, I can call you back again. If I turned my back on you, so long as I am living, I can turn around again. If I hurt you, so long as I am living, I can apologize. If you hurt me, so long as I am living, I can forgive you. If I do none of these things as long as I am living, you are not dead — I am.

Kneel

PRAYER: Lord, for you no tomb is sealed permanently. For you no door is closed eternally. May the same be said of us. Amen.

Fifteenth Station: The Resurrection

LEADER: We adore you, Oh, Christ, and we praise you.

PEOPLE: Because by your holy cross you have redeemed the world.

LEADER: So long as I am living, I will forgive every sin against me when you ask for pardon. So long as I am living, I will help you carry every cross you must bear, if you help others carry their crosses. So long as I am living I will bring you peace, if you bring peace; joy if you give joy; love if you love me wherever you find me. Then your death will be mine and my resurrection will be yours forever.

Kneel

PRAYER: In Christ we are the resurrection and the life. Even if we die, we shall live. Amen.

REFLECTIONS

God and Time

Theologically speaking, there has been and there will only be one death to sin, and Jesus died it two thousand years ago. Humanly speaking countless generations of people lived before it and after it. How could his death affect any of them?

Theologically speaking there is only one resurrection from sin, and Jesus accomplished it two thousand years ago. Historically speaking countless generations of people came either before it or after it? What has his resurrection to do with all of them when they came either too early or too late?

There is perhaps no more important notion to the understanding of Jesus and his mission than the notion of time. Time affects everything Jesus did and his relationship to us and all of history. Unless we understand time, we cannot appreciate the most singular events in the history of the world — the incarnation, death, and resurrection of Jesus. Saint Paul says that everything depends on faith. I might further add that that very faith is severely impaired, if not fatally flawed, without an understanding of Jesus' relationship to human time and divine time.

Time as we know it, human time, moves from minute to minute to minute. There is a past, a present, and a future. Once something happens it immediately passes into the past. It is gone. Irretrievable! No amount of willing, wishing, or contriving can make the past present. We cannot touch the past. Nor can we alter it, science fiction notwithstanding. Dreaming of it or thinking about it does not make it a present reality. It is *forever* past. This is human time as we know it and live it.

But this is not so for God! God's time is different from human time. God lives in another sphere, another dimension entirely. To God there is no past or future. There is only present. To God everything is now. God is the eternal now. The forever now. From the dawn of creation when time began until its last moment, even if that should encompass a trillion, trillion years and more, God sees the entire span of it in an instant. In a forever instant. To God eternity is not uncountable trillions of years, not an accumulation of time, but a moment. God penetrates a moment and forever is in that moment. Like a microdot that is almost invisible to the naked eye yet contains within it an incredible amount of information, God's micromoment contains all of everything.

This is not science fiction. This is philosophical and theological truth, as well as biblical fact.

For a thousand years in thy sight are but as yesterday when it is past, or as a watch in the night.

(Ps 90:4)

But do not ignore this one fact, beloved, that with the Lord one day
is as a thousand years, and a thousand years as one day.

(2 Pt 3:8)

An understanding of time is essential to the understanding of God.
God sees all the past and all the future and God sees it now. Nothing
is hidden from God. Nothing can be hidden from God. Before anything
happens (human time) God knows the whole of it.

Even before a word is on my tongue, behold,
Oh, Lord, you know the whole of it.

(Ps 139:4)

Knowing everything that will happen, however, is not the same as
willing it. God does not will sin even though God sees it happen. I see
a robbery take place but I do not will it. That God doesn't prevent it is
wrapped up in the mystery of freedom. If God should step in every time
a wrong is to be done, we would be no more than a puppet creation. Our
consolation in the face of evil is that God will not allow it to triumph.
God will set things right *in God's time*. God has the first word and God
will have the last.

This notion of human time and God's time is not merely a curiosity. It
affects everything we believe as Christians. It will become increasingly
obvious as it is applied.

Consider that at this very moment God is creating Adam and Eve.
Not a million years ago or ten million years ago *but at this very moment*.
At this very moment God is breathing His spirit into them and telling
them to take dominion over the earth. What is long past for us is present
to God. God sees us and God sees Adam and Eve at the same time.
What is depicted for us in the movies as a split-image screen, such as a
bustling metropolis on the one side and Indians accepting trinkets for
Manhattan on the other, is an ever-present reality to God. God's vision
is global. It takes in the whole world from top to bottom and all the way
around in an instant sweep. At the same time it sees all of history from
the beginning to the end.

At this very moment, then, God is showing Abraham the stars and
promising him that He will give him descendants more numerous than
these through his barren wife Sarai.

At this very moment, God is leading Moses and the Israelites through the Red Sea with the waters standing like a wall to their right and to their left.

At this very moment, God sees David dancing before the Ark of the Covenant as it is being carried in procession into the city of Jerusalem.

We must bear in mind that this is not the past to God. It is happening before Him right now. God sees us and God sees Adam and Abraham and Moses and David at the same time — us here and them there, but at the same time. Let us continue the progression.

Right now, God is listening to the wisdom of Solomon offering to split a child in two to settle a dispute between two mothers.

Right now, the great prophet Isaiah is pleading with God to send someone else to do God's bidding because he is a man of unclean lips.

Right now, Jeremiah is crying.

Again, we must try to see these things as God does. In human time all these events are long since passed. In God's time they are taking place right now. The importance of this revelation will have its full impact with Jesus. Meanwhile, let us continue the progression.

At this precise moment, Jesus is being born at Bethlehem. Not two thousand years ago, but *right now.* God sees Jesus being born of Mary and us here today and to God both are taking place at the same time. Christmas is forever happening to God.

At this very moment God sees:

> Jesus' baptism by John in the Jordan;
> the miracle of the loaves and the fish;
> the healing of the man born blind;
> the raising of Lazarus;
> the betrayal of Judas;
> Jesus' crucifixion and death.

In the eyes of God, Jesus did not die 2000 years ago, but right now. Jesus is dying on Calvary at this very moment. We here and Jesus there but to God now.

At this very moment God sees: the resurrection of Jesus on Easter morn.

God sees the two events — the death and resurrection of Jesus — as one. They are happening before Him at the same time. *If we could somehow freeze the moment when death changes to resurrection, we would understand what is called the Paschal Mystery from the perspective of God.* This is why they are increasingly written as one — death/resurrection.

I might further add that the ascension of Jesus to the Father is also included in this Passover event — death/resurrection/ascension. From God's perspective they are one event, happening at the same time and happening forever.

There is still more to the progression, for at this very moment:

Paul is beginning his missionary journeys;
the emperor Constantine is converting to Christianity;
Martin Luther is tacking his theses to the cathedral door at Wittenberg;
the atomic bomb is falling on the cities of Hiroshima and Nagasaki;
I am being born from my mother's womb.

So much for the past. Let us move to the other side, the future. What can we say of the future?

At this very moment, God sees:

me on my death bed;
I am already dead and buried;
your children and your children's children to the hundredth generation;
the last man and woman.

God sees all time, the whole of it and every moment of it, and God sees it all right now. Nothing is lost to God. God cannot forget anything that happened since it is happening before Him all the time. Nor can we sneak something past God in the future since it is already happening before Him. In God's time everything is now — forever now!

This notion assumes its full importance for us in Jesus. Jesus is both God and a human being. This means, then, that he has one foot in God's time and one foot in human time. He stands with us in the space/time continuum and apart from us in the divine dimension.

As a human being, he lives life along with us, minute by minute. Thus he could grow in age and wisdom:

Jesus, for his part, progressed steadily in wisdom and age and grace before God and men.

(Lk 2:52)

As God he lives in the forever now.

Before Abraham was, I am.
(Jn 8:58)

As a human being, he was inescapably bound up with us because of his flesh. As God, he is inescapably bound up with everything from the beginning to the end of time.

> In the beginning was the word ... and the word was made flesh.
>
> (Jn 1:1, 14)

Everything depends on the divinity of Jesus. If he were not divine, he would have no more relevance to us than Julius Caesar or Alexander the Great. Historically important but personally insignificant. Even for all his wonderful teachings, we would have to admit that almost everything he taught was said before and his impact on our lives would have no more relevance than what we accept from the teachings of other great masters such as Plato, Aristotle, or Buddha. His miracles, like many others performed before and after him, would affect only those of his time. If not for the divinity of Jesus, he would be just another man.

The divinity of Jesus makes all the difference in the world once we apply it. Consider that because of the divinity of Jesus:

he was present at the beginning of creation;
he was at the Garden of Eden;
he was with the angels who spoke to Abraham;
he traveled with Moses;
he exalted David, counseled Solomon and wept with Jeremiah.

All this he did because he was one with creation in his flesh. All this he also did because he was one with God in the spirit. As God/Man, Jesus' flesh penetrates all flesh and all creation and his spirit permeates creation for all time.

The pinnacle moment for all time and all history is the supreme moment in the life of Christ — the death/resurrection event. It is the high point, the culmination of humankind's relationship to God. This desperately needs to be understood.

As God/Man Jesus was present to every moment of history, to every event in history from the beginning to the end of time. Saint Paul eminently understood this and rhapsodized about it again and again in his letters.

> God has given us the wisdom to understand fully the mystery, the plan he was pleased to decree in Christ, to be carried out in the

fullness of time: namely, to bring all things in the heavens and on the earth into one under Christ's headship.

(Eph 1:9–10)

He is the image of the invisible God, the firstborn of all creation; for in him all things were created, in heaven and on earth, visible and invisible, whether thrones or dominions or principalities or authorities — all things were created through him and for him. He is before all things, and in him all things hold together. He is the head of the body, the church; he is the beginning, the firstborn from the dead, that in everything he might be pre-eminent. For in him all the fulness of God was pleased to dwell.

(Col 1:15–19)

How else could Paul lay claim to being an Apostle since Jesus had already chosen the twelve and was now resurrected and gone?

Paul an Apostle — not from men nor through man, but through Jesus Christ and God the Father. . . .

(Gal 1:1)

When it comes to the salvation of humankind this means that Jesus was present to every sin from the beginning of time to the end of time. He was there. He saw all of them. They affected him because all humanity is present in him. On the cross Jesus had one foot in God's time and one foot in human time.

Understand this in the light of the Jewish custom of Yom Kippur, the Day of Atonement (Lev 23:27ff). From the days of Moses it was decreed that on this day the high priest would stand before the sanctuary of the Lord, and, with arms outstretched to embrace the Israelite nation, he should call out before Yahweh the sins of the people. Standing in front of him was a goat called the Scapegoat. After he named the sin, he would symbolically gather all such offenses and then lower his hands to press them onto the head of the goat. Raising his arms again, he would call out another of the sins of the people and press them onto the head of the goat. Again and again, he called out the whole catalogue of sins and pressed them onto the Scapegoat while the people outside fasted and sacrificed, joining themselves with him by doing penance. No sin could be omitted, no offense forgotten lest it should bring ill fortune to the people during the coming year. From sunup to sundown the ritual continued until it was accomplished. Then the Scapegoat, loaded with the sins of the nation, was led out to the jeers and curses of the people into the desert where it suffered a bloody death.

What they did was symbolic. It expressed their inner need to free themselves of the weight and burden of their sins. There is a desire in all of us to set things right, to be free of our sins, to start over — to be born again. This was symbolically accomplished each year on the Day of Atonement, the most sacred day of the Jewish calendar. But it was only symbolic. It expressed the desire but could not accomplish the reality. The innocent goat could not take on the sins of the people then any more than it could today:

> Since the Law had only a shadow of the good things to come, and no real image of them, it was never able to perfect the worshipers by the same sacrifices offered continually year after year. Were matters otherwise, the priests would have stopped offering them, for the worshipers, once cleansed, would have had no sin on their conscience. But through those sacrifices there came only a yearly recalling of sins, because it is impossible for the blood of bulls and goats to take sins away.
>
> (Heb 10:1-4)

But not so Jesus! He is one with all humanity. On the cross Jesus was the Scapegoat for all humankind. He was present to every sin. He felt the crush of sin's burden in the ignominious scourging at the pillar, the searing torture of a crown of thorns, the oppressive weight of the cross, the agonizing humiliation of the jeering crowds, the fiery pain of the nails embedded in his hands and feet, and the degradation of a naked crucifixion. On the cross Jesus saw every sin. The sin of Adam, the sin of Moses, the sin of David, the sin of Solomon, the sin of Judas, the sin of Paul, your sin and my sin. On the cross he saw the sins of our children and our children's children to the last generation. He saw them all and individually as only God can. He accepted them onto himself as only a human being can. This was the great Day of Atonement for all creation, done once and for all time.

> In his own body he brought your sins to the cross so that all of us, dead to sin, could live in accord with God's will.
>
> (1 Pt 2:24)

There is a great veil between God and creation. The death of Jesus tore a hole in the fabric of time, just as it symbolically ripped the veil of the Temple in two:

Brothers, since the blood of Jesus assures our entrance into the sanctuary by the new and living path he has opened up for us through the veil...

(Heb 10:19)

That hole opens the forever moment between God and humankind. The eternity of God enters human temporality through it:

Who, though he was in the form of God, did not count equality with God a thing to be grasped, but *emptied himself*, taking the form of a servant, being born in the likeness of men.

(Phil 2:6–7)

The pinnacle of creation, although it came in human time at the crucifixion of Jesus, is eternal before God. Through the breach God becomes human. Through it humankind becomes eternal. Jesus is the bridge, the wedge through which the two pass.

For there is one God, and there is one mediator between God and men, the man Christ Jesus...

(1 Ti 2:5)

The death/resurrection of Jesus is like the middle of an hour glass, through which all divine and human activity must pass.

Only a fitting apology can satisfy so great an offense (the offense not of individual sins but all sins taken corporately as a single, cumulative "No!" to the Creator). If an ambassador insults a head of state, the state has been offended. Only the other head of state can make recompense. Every human being is an ambassador of humankind. We have that integrity, that oneness through Adam. Our sins have offended God. In the reality of God's time, since God sees all things at once, all our sins coalesce into one universal sin — the sin of humankind. Only the head of state, only one on a par with God, can offer a fitting apology. Only a God/Man can do it. Only Jesus can.

What was symbolically accomplished in the Old Testament was actually achieved by Jesus. The crucifixion is not symbolic. It is real. Sins are forgiven. Restoration is made.

By his wounds you were healed.

(1 Pt 2:24)

And through him to reconcile to himself all things, whether on earth or in heaven, making peace by the blood of his cross.

(Col 1:20)

On the cross Jesus offers the eternal apology for all humankind.

And Jesus said, "Father, forgive them; for they know not what they do."

(Lk 23:34)

Having done this, Jesus dies. The price has been paid. Every sin for all time has been made up for in the death of Jesus. He has given the full measure.

Greater love has no man than this, that a man lay down his life for his friends.

(Jn 15:13)

Radically, the act of reparation has been made. It is up to each person, however, to consent to the apology. If we remain apart from it, then we have no part in it. If we do not say yes to the death of Jesus, we shall live in our sin forever. There is no other death to sin than his. Someone must pay the price. Someone must balance the scales.

It is said that trappers have a unique way of capturing monkeys. They chain a small-necked jar half-filled with beans to the ground. Next, they scatter beans all around to draw the monkeys to it. When the monkeys come along eating the scattered beans they eventually approach the jar. Inside they discover a whole bonanza of beans. When they reach in to grab a handful, they make a fist. Once they make a fist it is impossible for them to extract their hand. So long as they hold on to the beans, they are stuck. They will scream, jump, kick, rant, and rave, but they will not let go of the beans. The trapper simply comes along and carries them off.

When we hold on to our sins, when we stubbornly refuse to give up our faults for whatever reason, we chain ourselves to them. For all our ranting and raving, we will not find freedom until we give them up. Jesus accepted them and paid the price for them on Calvary. If we keep them, we will have to pay the price for them.

But if we deny him he will deny us.

(2 Tm 2:12)

There is sometimes a reluctance or hesitation to confess on the part of those in the habit of sin. What good is it, they claim, to surrender the sin when for all they know they will probably pick it up again tomorrow?

For all they know, there may not be a tomorrow. Besides, Jesus has already paid the price for tomorrow's sins if and when they come. What is important is now. All God asks of us is our *now*. But in reality God is asking for everything, since now is all we truly possess.

> Enough, then, of worrying about tomorrow. Let tomorrow take care of itself. Today has trouble enough of its own.
>
> (Mt 6:34)

When I learned about Jesus as a boy, I was overwhelmed by the account of his passion and death. I can remember thinking what a terrible thing it was for him to be betrayed by one of his close friends. I could not understand how Peter could deny him and the Apostles run off and abandon him. If I had been there, I would have fought off the soldiers. I would have done anything I could to prevent his tragic suffering and death. If only I had been there.

Today I know that Jesus is dying on Calvary *right now* — not two thousand years ago, not with distance lending enchantment. If I truly want to defend him, to alleviate his suffering, I must stop sinning. My sins are killing him. And they're killing him right now. If I wish him to suffer one less buffet, one less derisive insult, one less stumble, one less hurt, I can do so by committing one less sin. Because Jesus accepts my sins on the cross, he is my personal savior. When I stop sinning, I am his.

> In my own flesh I fill up what is lacking in the sufferings of Christ.
>
> (Col 1:24)

Every suffering takes place at the same time as Jesus'. Every pain now is joined with his pain then. They are one if they are joined to his. Since we all must suffer, for such is the human condition, then we should make our suffering one with his suffering. Then the passion of Jesus becomes our passion. Only then does suffering make sense. Only then does it become salvific.

Was there ever so great and wonderful a mystery!

When we say yes to the death of Jesus, we accept our own death. It is unavoidable. It is the pinnacle of his life and becomes the pinnacle of ours. We become intimately bound up in that forever moment. Those who believe in Jesus, die with Jesus. There is no other way. This is our salvation.

> You can depend on this:

> If we have died with him
> > we shall also live with him;
> If we hold out to the end
> > we shall also reign with him.
> > > (2 Tm 2:11)

When we die ten, twenty, or fifty years from now, whenever it happens, we leave human time and enter God's time. The pinnacle moment is the crucifixion. If I lived believing and struggling to conform my life to his, then my death and Jesus' are to God *at the same time and one and the same.*That is me on the cross on Good Friday! It is you! There is only one death to sin and in Jesus we will have died it.

Jesus' apology on the cross is humankind's. It is yours and mine. When Jesus entered the tomb, we entered with him. All creation awaited God's acceptance of our apology.

The resurrection is God's yes. It is God's way of saying, "It is over. All is forgiven. The scales are balanced." Now those who suffered with Jesus will share the consolation of Jesus.

> As we have shared much in the suffering of Christ, so through
> Christ do we share abundantly in his consolation.
> > (2 Cor 1:5)

Now those who died with Jesus, will rise with Jesus. On Easter Sunday, *it is we who are coming out of the tomb.* It is our resurrection as well as Jesus' that we celebrate. Otherwise, what would be the reason for our jubilation? It is no great feat for God to resurrect. It is for us. There is only one death to sin from the beginning of time until the end, and Jesus died it. There is only one resurrection from the beginning of time until the end and Jesus did it. It is the one unrepeatable event in all history. It is the death/resurrection event, the Paschal mystery. We are either in Jesus and a part of it or we are not. This is the ecstatic joy expressed by Paul and sung by the Christian community.

> Have this mind among yourselves, which is yours in Christ Jesus,
> who, though he was in the form of God, did not count equality with
> God a thing to be grasped, but emptied himself, taking the form of

a servant, being born in the likeness of men. And being found in human form he humbled himself and became obedient unto death, even death on a cross. Therefore God has highly exalted him and bestowed on him the name which is above every name, that at the name of Jesus every knee should bow, in heaven and on earth and under the earth, and every tongue confess that Jesus Christ is Lord, to the glory of God the Father.

(Phil 2:5–11)

Death

For people today it is difficult to conceive of a society that has no real concept of a life after death. We speak of heaven and hell as if everyone for all time knew and accepted them. We forget that they are still articles of faith and not everyone believes.

There were, however, from earliest times indications of human belief in a hereafter. Where did it come from? We must suppose that people saw the grass die, plants and trees die, animals and humans die and begin to wonder if that were simply the end of it. Since they lived close to nature, it is logical to assume that they noticed that a plant lived to give birth to the seed, which produced a new plant, and animals produced young meant to endure beyond their own lifespan. They must have deduced that to endure beyond death, one had to leave progeny. Such is life after death in the natural realm.

They must also have experienced the devastation of plagues and wars where entire families and tribes were wiped out. To pin all their hopes on a dynasty was tenuous at best. Storytellers must also have begun to take on status in the human quest for immortality. Great men doing great deeds would be remembered through the stories passed on from generation to generation. These became added insurance.

This was pretty much the status of Old Testament belief. Good people lived long lives and left many children. You were perpetuated in your children and through the stories they passed on about you for generations. We need only consider how long Abraham and Moses have been remembered in human history to appreciate the power of that belief. Then too we can better understand the plight of women who were barren or men who were sterile. Having substitute children through slaves or other family members was provided for in the Law of Moses, with strong sanctions, to assure these people of a posterity. It is essential to understand that in the Old Testament you endured by being remembered.

On the other hand, not to be remembered was to be annihilated. There was no greater curse than the obliteration of your name and remembrance with your death. It was their equivalent of hell. The theme resonates throughout the scriptures.

And the LORD said to Moses, "Write this as a memorial in a book and recite it in the ears of Joshua, that I will utterly blot out the remembrance of Amalek from under heaven."

(Ex 17:14)

I would have said, "I will scatter them afar, I will make the remembrance of them cease from among men."

(Dt 32:26)

Yea, the light of the wicked is put out, and the flame of his fire does not shine. His memory perishes from the earth, and he has no name in the street.

(Jb 18:5, 17)

For in death there is no remembrance of thee; in Sheol who can give thee praise?

(Ps 6:5)

The enemy have vanished in everlasting ruins; their cities thou hast rooted out; the very memory of them has perished.

(Ps 9:6)

The face of the LORD is against evildoers, to cut off the remembrance of them from the earth.

(Ps 34:16)

They are dead, they will not live; they are shades, they will not arise; to that end thou hast visited them with destruction and wiped out all remembrance of them.

(Is 26:14)

To be held in everlasting remembrance was heaven. To be held in everlasting scorn or to be forgotten was hell. Yet all of this depended on storytellers. Was there hope beyond the mortal and transient? There must have been another strain of hope in immortality present among people, or how else can we account for burials in which artifacts of life and food were included in the interment practices of earlier cultures? Sentimental attachment may provide a possible, but only partial, answer. It does not account for the food. With the advent of writing this belief became apparent in sepulchral inscriptions and legends. There was an innate need in humanity to go beyond death without facing the frustration of the death of the storyteller. This need was too universal to be denied and too inhibiting to the progress of humanity to be without a solution.

The death/resurrection of Jesus was the breakthrough. It answered both a human and a theological need. With the sin of Adam (and Eve and all humanity seen as happening at the same time, for our sin did not predate his in the sight of God), death entered the human world in a single stroke.

Therefore as sin came into the world through one man and death through sin, and so death spread to all men because all men sinned.
(Rom 5:12)

So that evil might not triumph, not even for a moment, God uses the same death stroke to bring about life. It is the same stroke, happening at the same time before God. Jesus' death and resurrection are inseparable theologically. They are two sides of the same coin. It is the eternal paradox — the juxtaposition of opposites in western culture and the yin and yang of oriental culture. The very moment of dawn is the very moment of the end of darkness. In every moment of life there is a dying. The darkness of creation encounters the light of eternity at the middle of the hourglass; they meet at the hole in the fabric of time that the death/ resurrection of Jesus made. Theologically speaking, the death of Jesus took place at the last moment of dusk and the resurrection took place at the first moment of daybreak. In the eyes of God, they happened at the same time. Death is not the end. It can never be.

6

THE RESURRECTION OF JESUS

MARY MAGDALENE: THE TOMB

Men are such cowards.

She had risen even earlier than usual to make preparations to go to the tomb. She got the ointment and some fresh linen strips and was ready to leave when she remembered the stone. Someone would have to roll back the stone for her. So she made her way through the still dark streets to the upper room where the Apostles were staying.

"Are you crazy?" Peter screamed.

"Are you cowards?" She glared at them with fire in her eyes. "Have you no respect for the dead? Would you let him lay in the tomb unwashed and unanointed? What kind of men are you?"

The accusation stung but did not move them. "We wouldn't get within fifty feet of that place without being arrested. Then who would roll back the stone for you? Make sense, woman."

What made sense to her was that these men were cowards. How could Jesus have chosen them? Sure, they were brave enough when he was around, but the moment he was gone they reverted to kind.

All the way to the garden she talked to herself, trying at times to think more positively of the Apostles but more often than not failing. She accused them in her heart of trying to cover up their fear. Not one of them had the inner strength and courage of Jesus. Bravado, yes, but courage, never. Had any of them ever confronted the Scribes or the

Pharisees the way Jesus had? Had any of them ever spoken up to the rulers of the Sanhedrin? Where were they when the members of the synagogue in Nazareth wanted to cast Jesus off the cliff? Where were they when Jesus hung on the cross? Not a one of those so-called men was there at his execution. Only the boy, John, came.

She wept in anger and frustration. Now that Jesus was dead, it was all over. Nothing could hold this dispirited group together in his absence. They would all head back to where they came from and Jesus would become a memory.

She didn't want it to end. She desperately wanted it to go on. Exasperated with them or not, they had become a family, her new family, and she wasn't about to give it all up without a fight. Jesus had given them an experience unparalleled in the history of Israel. He created a family with ties that went beyond blood and even the Law because it took in publicans and sinners. They were the only ones who knew this experience, and if these men scattered now, the world might never come to know it and all that Jesus did would have been done in vain. She could never allow that to happen. She loved Jesus too much to let it happen without a fight. If she had to shame these men into continuing the work he had begun, she wouldn't hesitate to do so.

The sun was just beginning to rise as she approached the garden. She resolved to get the sentries to remove the stone even if she had to pay them. Only none were around when she got there. She was more annoyed than alarmed at their absence, regarding it as typical of the unreliability of men.

She passed beyond the gate hoping to find someone, perhaps a workman, to lend her a hand. The garden was empty and quiet. When she rounded the corner of the hill where the tomb was, she saw that the stone was already rolled back. At first, she didn't know what to think. Had some of the others come with his mother Mary and were already inside anointing his body? No doubt that was it, and the soldiers were probably with them keeping an eye on things. She stooped and went inside.

It was empty. There was no one there. Again, she didn't know what to make of it. The linens they had used to hastily wrap his body before the Sabbath were lying on the ground. It made no sense. Where was the body? An icy hand gripped her stomach. Who would have taken it? The soldiers would never have allowed anyone to remove it. Not without official authorization. Anyway, she realized that it could not have been gotten so quickly. Could someone have bribed the soldiers into letting them steal the body? It was the only other possible explanation. But why would anyone want to take it? It certainly would not have been the Jews who sought his execution. He was condemned by them for blaspheming and breaking the Law. Would they be foolish enough to break the Law by becoming grave robbers and doubly defiling themselves? Hardly. Besides, what would they have to gain by it?

She paced back and forth in the small enclosure trying to reason things out. It was the only way she had of fighting back the panic that was trying to take hold of her. Someone had taken Jesus' body, that was certain. But who? And why? Could it have been the family? Where would they get enough money to bribe the soldiers? It would have to be prodigious amount considering the punishment the soldiers would have to undergo for neglecting their duty. Even if someone had bribed them, there was still another problem — the wrappings lying on the floor. Why would anyone bother to strip the body or change the dressings when it was imperative that they get away as quickly as possible? Whether desecration or reinterment was the goal, it would have made no sense to waste time undoing the linen wrappings.

She argued her way around to exactly where she had started. She sat down on the stone slab where Jesus' body had lain and picked up the cloth they had used to wrap his precious head. Reverently she began rolling it up while still trying to sort through her confusion. She had successfully fought off the awful and overwhelming reality that Jesus was gone. She wanted to run. But where? To whom should she go? The Apostles? If they were afraid to come out to anoint him, they would be doubly afraid to venture forth now in the light of this new danger. Should she go to Mary and the family? What if they had not come for the body (and she seriously doubted that they had). This would only cause the dear woman further grief.

Unable to hold back her frustration and anguish any longer, she finally unleashed the dam that held back her tears. She sobbed uncontrollably for a long time before she heard a rustling noise outside. Was it the guards returning? Was it the other women come to meet her? When she emerged from the dark cave, the brilliant sunlight blinded her. She looked up through tear-filled eyes and saw someone standing there directly in the morning sunrise. She shielded her face from the sun and squinting through her tears she tried to make out who it was, but didn't recognize him. "Why are you weeping, woman?" he asked.

She was desperate. Perhaps this stranger knew something.

"Someone has taken the body of my Lord away and I don't know where. Sir, if you know, please tell me and I will go and take care of it."

"Mary," he said.

That's all he said. That's all he had to say. No one can call you by your name the way someone you know and love can and you not recognize him. Even if she weren't sure of the voice, the rush to heart and the tingle throughout her body made it undeniable. It was Jesus. With the sun still blinding her eyes she strained to see him more closely. Instinctively, she reached out to touch him. Even though she didn't need it, it would be the final assurance that it truly was him. But he wouldn't allow it. It was just as well. She probably would have died of excitement if she had touched him.

"Tell them," he said.

The light he stood in was too much for her eyes to bear so she rubbed them. When she looked again, he was gone. It was like a dream. Only it wasn't a dream and she knew it. He had risen. He had made others rise from the dead and now he had risen himself. Her own body vibrated with new life. She had to go and tell the Apostles the wonderful news.

She ran like lightning through the streets all the while remembering Jesus standing before her in the blazing light, saying to her, "Tell them."

"Yes, Lord," she cried as she ran. "Yes, Master."

She flew up the stairs and pounded on the door. No one answered. Again and again she pounded until finally someone opened it. She burst into the room.

"He is risen!" she announced.

PETER: THE UPPER ROOM

The fear was palpable. No one spoke. Peter sat by himself wrapped in such a deep anguish that it brought up bile that burnt his throat and made his mouth bitter. Was it wise to come back here? Damn that traitor Judas! Damn that thieving son of a whore! Had he betrayed the rest of them too before he took his own miserable life? Would the soldiers or the Temple guard come pounding at the door to arrest them? Was it wise to come back here?

The room had not been tidied since the Passover supper. Signs of that night's revelry were still strewn about. Peter stood with his back to the shuttered window wringing his hands. Was it only a day ago that they all sat here celebrating, enjoying the holiday, reveling in their auspicious entry into the city? The memory flooded back. "Hail, Jesus!"

"Hail, son of David!"

He could still hear their cries ringing in his ears. He covered them as if that could block out the mocking cheers. But the very stones in the walls of the room seemed to echo their cries, just as Jesus said they would.

"God damn Judas!" he shouted.

Some of the others were startled by the outburst. The rest were so of a mind with him that they didn't realize it was Peter and not they who cursed.

Peter threw himself down at the head of the table, the place where Jesus had sat. The king and his royal court, with Peter seated at his right hand. That was the plan Jesus had in mind, wasn't it? It had to be, in spite of Jesus' protestations. Why else the elaborate secret arrangements for this upper room? Why else the donkey? The symbolism of David entering Jerusalem the same way was more than obvious.

But who arranged it? Who had staged that triumphal entry without his knowledge? Was it the work of James and John to please Jesus? Is that why Jesus favored John that night? Of course! No doubt it was all their mother's doing. Meddlesome bitch!

"But I sat at his right hand!" Peter said out loud again, unable to contain his inner turmoil. This time the others paid no attention to him, they were so lost in their own consternation. He looked down at the cup Jesus had used. It was still partially filled with wine. Damn! Damn! It could have been. He took the cup in his hand. It almost could have been if it hadn't been for that dog, Judas. Why did he do it? Was it for money? Didn't that greedy, ignorant jackass know that we would have been wallowing in wealth if he had waited? There would have been plenty of money after the insurrection. Was he too dumb to see that? Or was he too greedy to take the chance? Bastard.

Peter noticed John staring at him. Was it only yesterday he said, "Why is this night different from every other night?"

Peter averted his gaze. Because this night was supposed to be the beginning. The beginning of a new reign in Judea. The kingdom of Jesus, son of Joseph son of David.

Even he didn't quite understand it at first. Judas knew, however, and tried to tell him, but he wouldn't listen because he didn't like or trust Judas. When Judas accused him of being dull-witted, he cuffed him a good one to the head. But the realization did come to him eventually as he saw Jesus grow in popularity and strength. Was it his fault he didn't see it at first?

After all, he was a fisherman — a good one. And a good businessman. He was not into politics and could care less about it. Even when John and James had ranted about Jesus, he thought of him as just another baptizer.

He had gone with them to see the baptist. The man was a prophet, no doubt. He had to admit that the mere sight of him was impressive. But the nonsense he spewed out was of no interest to him. What did he care about who Herod was married to? That pig could have all the whores he wanted as far as he was concerned. So long as they left him alone they could all go to hell. Prophet, indeed. If John were a prophet, he should have known what would happen to him if he kept it up. What was it that traitorous dog Judas said when word reached them of his death. "If John knew how to keep his head, he wouldn't have lost it." Even then he was scheming. But what did he a fisherman care about this John and his message. He had a business to run. Besides, there's no profits in prophets.

He had just taken Jesus to be another one, another hapless baptizer who would soon follow in John's footsteps. Until the miracle. That was different. "Cast your net on the other side!" It had brought him to his knees. "Master, stay away from me for I am a sinner."

Yes, the realization did gradually grow on him. He was beginning to put it together. James and John were Zealots always spoiling for a fight, like generals. But they were young and impetuous. Jesus needed someone more level-headed. Someone who could successfully run a business could successfully run a kingdom. He may not be the brightest, but when he was in control he held the tiller firmly. "You are a rock," Jesus said.

Where was that "rock" in the courtyard when a lowly servant girl confronted him? Tears welled up in his eyes. How was he to know? It had all happened too fast. It takes him time to think things through. He wasn't expecting this. He was just getting used to the idea of what it was all really about when they came and arrested Jesus. It was John the Baptist all over again. Only it wasn't supposed to happen this way with Jesus.

Why didn't they stay in Galilee? Why did they have to go to Jerusalem? It was too soon. Jesus needed more time to build up his power base. He was still virtually unknown in Jerusalem. They needed more time. More time to get things ready. He was convinced that James and John didn't know of Jesus' secret plan. Like all Zealots the fools would have wanted to overthrow the Romans. Impossible! Absurd!

He wasn't sure when it dawned on him, but he was absolutely certain that he was right. To overthrow the Romans was unquestionably impossible. They were too great and too strong. But Herod, Herod and his lowly minions, that was another story. John the baptizer had paved the way for that. His beheading was just the spark that was needed to set off the conflagration that could overthrow *Herod*. The people were ready. They were ready. What did Rome care about who sat on the thrones of Israel? So long as they got their taxes. All they needed was a little more time.

Of course, Jesus had never said this. How could he? Why would he? There were spies everywhere. But he knew. He understood. It was all a matter of timing. Jesus made that clear when Peter shot off his mouth in front of the others and Jesus called him a Satan. That's what Judas was. A Satan. Had Judas figured it out? He was a wily one all along. That's why he went to the Jews and not the Romans with his treachery. The traitor!

Now his blood began to boil as he gripped the cup in his hands with all his might. It all made sense. Once the Jews knew they had the edge. They came against him at night. They prepared witnesses. They rushed matters so that we could not organize ourselves. The devils even figured on Barabbas!

Oh, God! It all happened so fast. Damn it! Why did Jesus rush it? Why was he pushing it? What did he know that I hadn't figured out. We could have had it all. And now we have nothing. Now we hide here like frightened dogs not knowing if they'll be coming after us next — when they'll be coming after us, if that traitorous son of a whore told them where we'd be.

Peter looked at the others all lost in their own misery. He looked at the cup in his hand. "Here's to what could have been," he said to himself, and drank down what was left. It had turned to vinegar.

Suddenly, there was a knock on the door. The others scrambled in fear and confusion.

"Don't open it!"

"The window!" someone shouted. They ran toward the windows, which were their only means of escape.

"Stand your ground!" Peter barked. "Are we to run like cowards once again?"

The pounding at the door became more intense. It sounded like thunder in the silent room. Peter walked to the door. He would stand like a man. He would never again run away. With firm determination he lifted the bar and opened the door.

Mary Magdalene rushed past him.

"He is risen!" she said.

EASTER

"He is risen!"

Peter and John ran all the way to the tomb, hearing those words. The others debated among themselves, claiming that Mary was hysterical. Thomas, the skeptic, was the most outspoken, arguing that Jesus' body was very likely removed and that whoever had done it, Jews or Romans, they would come looking for the Apostles next. Mary's trying to reason with him only made him all the more adamant.

"I'm sure they know by now that we are holed up here. This place is no longer safe. We had best scatter and make any attempts to round us up futile."

At that suggestion Mary reacted like a madwoman, accusing them all of cowardice and disloyalty. She ranted on about how that would be tantamount to abandoning all that Jesus had done and taught them. Thomas could never abide the women following the group and "taking on airs." Were it not that Jesus' mother was among them, however, the innuendos about a traveling harem might have been taken more seriously. Only reluctantly did Thomas concede to Judas that their presence was an asset. Over the years their critics had shown themselves to be clever and resourceful. They either attacked the group's morality or their masculinity. "The women," Judas said, "cover both eventualities without our having to say anything." The Jews would sooner accept fornication than the despised pagan practice of sodomy. Jesus' mother as chaperone allayed all such charges. It was another of Jesus' ingenious maneuvers against his enemies, Judas said.

Thomas eventually stormed out of the room in a rage. John suggested that they all calm down while Peter and he go to the tomb to check things out. The others agreed to remain there, at least until the two of them returned.

Neither of them spoke as they rushed to the tomb. They were each lost in their own crisis of faith. Peter wondered if it could possibly be that Jesus had not died on Golgotha. After all, he was not there and did not see Jesus die or brought to the tomb. In fact, it hadn't occurred to him right off that if John weren't leading the way, he wouldn't even know where to go. All John knew was that he wanted to believe that Jesus was alive again more than he wanted anything else in the world. But if what Mary said was true, then where was he?

The tomb was indeed empty. They saw the wrappings. They asked each other what this could mean. Peter questioned John about whether Jesus had really died. Again and again, John reassured Peter that Jesus had undeniably died on Calvary. There wasn't even a need to break his legs to hasten his death, the guards were so certain. They were not likely to be fooled. Besides, when they asked to take his body down, the centurion speared him in the heart just to make sure. This last desecration had triggered an outburst of wailing and moaning from the women.

"There's no question about it," John reaffirmed. "Jesus was dead."

"Then how do you account for this?" Peter asked, holding up some of the linen.

Mary Magdalene had explained to them why she thought that neither the Jews nor the Romans could have been responsible for taking the body, and her arguments seemed plausible. The only other possibility was that he had indeed resurrected as she claimed. But serious and perplexing questions remained. Now that the two of them were at the tomb, they were unavoidable.

"Remove the stone," Jesus had said to the Apostles when he raised Lazarus from the dead. Who removed the stone for Jesus? It was either moved from outside or inside. Supposing he *had* resurrected from the dead. He would have been trapped inside the tomb. No single person could move that stone from its slotted position in front of the entrance. From within, it would take a Samson or Goliath to push it over. But it wasn't pushed over. Outside it would take more than a Mary Magdalene and some women to roll it back up the incline. Who moved the stone?

Had Jesus called from within and startled the guards into rolling back the stone? Then when they saw him alive, they fled in terror? This would account for the missing sentries. It would also account for the stone. The stone had to have at least two strong men to roll it back up the incline. The guards could have done it, but why would they?

Again why? The Romans could care less about removing his body. The Jews had nothing to gain and everything to lose by doing it. They were back where they started when they argued with Mary. They continued discussing it all the way back to the upper room.

≈

A sudden thunderclap, so strong that it shook the ground, woke the sentries with a start. A spring storm was likely coming. They shook the sleep and lethargy from their bodies as they stood up to see where the storm would be coming from. It was still much too dark to tell. The two of them gathered up their cloaks and turned to the tomb. Just as they did lightning flashed. It was so close that they instinctively shielded their eyes. It must have struck somewhere in the garden, because the ensuing thunderclap shook the ground so violently that they fell down. When they looked up, they saw a white figure standing directly in front of the stone that blocked the entrance to the tomb. It was Jesus. He was partially covered with the shroud he had been buried in. As quickly as the lightning had flashed its brilliance, it was dark once again.

They were startled and frightened by the vision. When the next flash of lightning lit the garden a moment later Jesus was standing directly in front of them, not three feet away. The roar of the thunder made the ground quake again just as their bodies now did. They stumbled to their feet and fled in terror.

Jesus was no longer standing there. Instead, Moses and Elijah were at the entrance of the tomb. As the last of the thunder faded into the distance, they effortlessly rolled the stone back.

A few minutes later, the storm having passed, Mary Magdalene made her way into the garden.

≈

"He's gone," Peter declared. "He's not there, just as Mary said."

"What do you think happened?" James asked.

"We don't know," John said. "We've talked about it all the way back and we can't figure it out."

The argument resumed where it had left off. Peter could only convey John's and his suspicions that it had to have been the guards who rolled back that heavy stone, but they had no idea why. Even without Mary Magdalene and Thomas present this time, the discussion became no less volatile.

In the midst of their shouting, someone said, "Peace." It was spoken calmly, just barely above a whisper, but they all heard it. They looked around to see who said it. A stranger was standing in the doorway.

"How did you get in here?" Peter barked, thinking that someone had foolishly neglected to lock the door.

"Peace," he said again, this time to calm Peter. Was this the man Mary Magdalene had spoken to at the tomb? While he didn't look like Jesus, or even sound like him, there was a certain unmistakableness about this stranger that said within them, "It *is* him!" They looked to one another as if for concurrence. In the next instant when they turned back to question the stranger, he was gone.

They gaped at the door dumbfounded. Suddenly, there was harsh, insistent banging upon it. Peter hastened over to open it. It was still barred. The women hastened into the room.

"It's true what Mary told you," Joanna said. "We've been to the tomb and spoken to angels."

The Apostles no sooner began to add their own strange experience to that of the women's when someone knocked at the door again. Peter was so excited by now that he could barely unlatch it. It was Thomas.

"The Lord has risen, Thomas. We have seen him."

Thomas listened patiently to their tales but remained skeptical. "How do you expect me to believe all this? One sees a gardener. Others see angels. The rest of you see a stranger. Have we not spent months and years with him? Do we not know him as well and as intimately as we know ourselves? How is it, then, that none of you recognized him? I'll tell you what I think. I won't believe any of this drivel until I put my hand into his gaping wounds! That's what I think. And I'll tell you what else I think. I think we're all hysterical with grief. I think that we've been shut up here too long. I think we could all use some sunshine and fresh air. I think we could all use it right now."

He rushed past them, pushing them aside, and attacked the shuttered windows, flinging them open. It was a beautiful, sunny day. A midmorning breeze blew into the room. They stared at Thomas in wide-eyed amazement. It was obvious to all that he had reached his limit.

"Now the door!" he shouted. As they all turned toward the door, they saw Jesus standing there.

"Peace," he said.

Thomas had stopped his rush to the door in mid-stride. Jesus held out his hands. "Come, Thomas. Put your hand into mine." He extended his arms toward him showing the holes in his wrists. Then he pointed to the wound in his heart. "Add yours," he said simply.

Thomas fell to his knees. "Oh, my God!" he cried. "My Lord," he wept.

Jesus read into their hearts, just as he always did. He would forgive Thomas just as they must forgive one another. "If you forgive each other's sins, then they are forgiven. But if you should hold back, will not all your sins be held back?"

A sudden gust of wind blew into the room, causing the shutters to bang loudly. Those nearest the windows rushed over to close them but the moment they went to do so, the wind stopped. With the distraction Jesus had disappeared. Their faces glowed as if on fire.

"What are we waiting for?" Peter shouted. "It's time to tell the world. They're out there waiting for us."

Peter rushed to the door expecting to fling it open. It was still locked. He laughed uproariously and burst out into the streets.

John followed close behind. "What *are* we waiting for?" he repeated as he left the upper room.

"Let us go to die with him," Thomas said, echoing what he had said a lifetime ago.

REFLECTIONS

The Seasons of God

Before the universe began, before history ever started, before the beginning of time, there was God. Just God. Only God. There was nothing else but God.

Before anything ever happened God saw the whole span of every-thing that would come to be or could ever be. God saw the whole panorama of creation history played out from the first bang to the last sputtering ember. God saw it all in an instant. In a micro-instant. The countless billion millennia God saw in less than the blinking of an eye, before it ever even came to be. Nothing was hidden to God before God said yes to creation.

Why did creation take place? Why did it happen? We don't know how it took place, but we do know what caused it all. We do know why.

Causes must be traced back to their beginnings, to the first cause, to give a complete answer. For example, I am here because of my parents. My parents are here because of their parents, and so on, until we get to the first parents. In dealing with human history we follow the same process, from what is here to how did it get here. How did all this, from the stars to us, get here?

Consider if you will that there are only two seasons before God — life and death. What is God and of God is life, and what is not is death. Life and death, light and darkness, being (here) and non-being (here), yes and no are the seasons of God.

To God the most meaningful life began on Christmas and ended on Good Friday. Now let us look for causes. Jesus was born on December 25, *during the night*. It happened during the night both scripturally and traditionally. We must not pass over that fact too quickly because it has great significance.

And in that region there were shepherds out in the field, keeping watch over their flock by night.

(Lk 2:8)

It was dark at mid-afternoon when Jesus died. Now from the sixth hour there was darkness over all the land until the ninth hour.

(Mt 27:45)

And when the sixth hour had come, there was darkness over the whole land until the ninth hour.

(Mk 15:33)

It was now about the sixth hour, and there was darkness over the whole land until the ninth hour.

(Lk 23:44)

The resurrection of Jesus also took place at night:

> Now on the first day of the week Mary Magdalene came to the tomb early, *while it was still dark*, and saw that the stone had been taken away from the tomb.
>
> (Jn 20:1)

Creation itself began in darkness:

> In the beginning God created the heavens and the earth. The earth was without form and void, and darkness was upon the face of the deep.
>
> (Gn 1:1,2)

Why darkness? Because it is God who will change the darkness into light, night into day, death into life. The finger of God is present at that critical point between the two. Suddenly, weeping turns to rejoicing and mourning into gladness. This is what is gloriously proclaimed and sung in the Exultet (Exult!) of the Easter liturgy.

> Oh, night more light than day,
> more bright than the sun,
> Oh, night more white then snow
> more brilliant then many torches,
> Oh, night of more delight than is paradise.

The Gospels of Matthew, Mark, and Luke stress that point in the resurrection of Jesus.

> After the Sabbath, as the first day of the week was dawning...
>
> (Mt 28:1)

> Very early, just after sunrise, on the first day of the week they came to the tomb.
>
> (Mk 16:2)

> But on the first day of the week, at early dawn, they went to the tomb, taking the spices which they had prepared.
>
> (Lk 24:1)

Light will change the night of the birth of Jesus:

> Now when Jesus was born in Bethlehem of Judea in the days of Herod the king, behold, wise men from the East came to Jerusalem,

saying, "Where is he who has been born king of the Jews? For *we have seen his star* in the East, and have come to worship him."

(Mt 2:1, 2)

And in that region there were shepherds out in the field, keeping watch over their flock by night. And an angel of the Lord appeared to them, and *the glory of the Lord shone around them*, and they were filled with fear.

(Lk 2:8, 9)

Accordingly, then, Jesus should return at night. He will usher in the dawn.

In the Semitic way of things, life itself begins at night. Conception always took place at night, for the simple reason that men and women were busy working during the day, from sun up to sun down. Nighttime was rest time. It was sabbatical time. Nighttime was for love.

Again we have the contrast. We spend the daytime, which is symbolic of light and life, dying because of our burdensome work. And it is at night, which is symbolic of darkness and death, that we create new life. The two seasons have the necessity for God at the junction point.

To return to our causes, let us look again at the birth of Jesus on December 25. Although Jesus was born on that day, he was conceived nine months before, on March 25 at the time of the Annunciation. The cause of the birth of Jesus was the conception of Jesus. But before you could have the conception of Jesus, you had to have the birth of the universe. By the same token, before you can have the birth of the universe, you must have the conception of the universe. How then was the universe conceived?

We return to God as God existed before time. In His foreknowledge God saw the birth of Christ. In His mind God began planning what He would give Jesus for Christmas. Just as we would carefully think about an appropriate gift for someone we love before we go out to get it, so too, did the Father plan out the gift He would give His son. This is what Paul refers to in his letter to the Ephesians:

For he has made known to us in all wisdom and insight the mystery of his will, according to his purpose which he set forth in Christ as a *plan* for the fulness of time, to unite all things in him, things in heaven and things on earth.

(Eph 1:9, 10)

To me, though I am the very least of all the saints, this grace was given, to preach to the Gentiles the unsearchable riches of Christ, and to make all men see what is the *plan* of the mystery hidden for ages in God who created all things.

(Eph 3:8, 9)

God begins His Christmas shopping in much the same way as an artist considers what to paint. First, she must find an appropriate canvas. There are so many possibilities — large, small, square, rectangular, round, and so on. For her own reasons an artist chooses one. For God's own reason He does the same. His blank canvas is earth:

In the beginning God created the heavens and the earth. The earth was without form and void. . . .

(Gn 1:1, 2)

This is why the creation account begins with the earth. This is the place where His Son will be born. But this is still an idea in God's mind. It has not come to be yet. Not yet. There must be more first. So God paints in the universe. From the very beginning the contrast is made between light and darkness.

. . . and darkness was upon the face of the deep. . . . And God said, "Let there be light"; and there was light. And God saw that the light was good; and God separated the light from the darkness.

(Gn 1:2–4)

Such a contrast could not be made until after creation when the human mind could conceive it. But God saw it all in His mind before it came to be. Under the guidance of inspiration we would mark it at the very dawn of creation.

God liked what He saw. It was good. So God continued to think about it. He continued to paint in His mind. There was a blue sky and a brown earth and waters covering the deep. And it was all good.

The progression continues. Like a woman who plans to give her husband a handsome jacket for his birthday. Then she decides to get him trousers to go with it. And then a shirt to go with the outfit and a tie to go with the shirt. So too does God get carried away with His own ideas, His own goodness. He adds life to His thoughts. Plant life to cover the earth and animal life nourished by the plants. An abundance of life — in the waters, on the earth, in the sky. It was all so good. And,

206 ≈ THE RESURRECTION OF JESUS

of course, humankind. In God's image. Able to give back what would be given. Able to love.

But God also saw that human beings would be free not to give back, not to love. The idea became clouded. Should God bring life to the critical point of freedom or not? Without freedom all the universe would be nothing more than a puppet creation. Would God's Son grow weary of puppets the way children do? Like in the story of Pinocchio, the idea of humankind cried to be without strings. But can God give Jesus a marred gift?

It is still just an idea in the mind of God. But God is a trinity. What God sees in His mind, the Son also sees. The Son loves the idea . . . and adds to it.

When a man loves a woman, he wishes to express the depth of his love for her by giving her a gift. The gift must embody all that she means to him, so he searches for something special, something truly appropriate. For the sake of example let us say it is a ring. Not just any ring but one that is a valuable heirloom and has more meaning to him than anything else in his life. So he gives his loved one this very special ring. The gift overwhelms her because she realizes all that it means to him. Now she must express her love for him in some equally suitable way. She searches among all her possessions to find just the right gift, something that has more meaning to her than anything else. Only one thing fits that description. The ring. Not only because of its value to him but because of what it means to her. It is the only appropriate gift she can give. So she gives him the ring. The ring has just doubled its value to the man because of her selfless act of love. Now there is even greater reason for him to give it back to her. And she gives it back to him, and so on ad infinitum.

The Son sees the intended "good" gift in the mind of the Father and wishes to accept it. He offers not simply to accept it but to become one with it and give it back to Him. The gift takes on added significance because of this and becomes a "very good" idea. In fact, inescapably good, since God cannot resist His own Son.

The planning is over. All God has to do is say the word. Once He says the word it will all happen. To the Father, the Son is irresistible. For the Son He says the word. YES!

In the beginning was the word . . .

(Jn 1:1)

There is something vitally important about the word YES. Every YES has a million little yeses inside it. There is no such thing as a simple YES. Yes is procreative.

God said YES and there are a million little yeses inside it.

YES — and there are millions of stars in millions of galaxies;
YES — and there are millions of birds and fish and animals;
YES — and there are millions of people.

And there are millions of little yeses in all of them.

Human beings were made in the image of God. So it must be that in every one of our YESes there are millions of other little yeses inside.

A man says YES to a woman, and there are a million other yeses.

YES — I will take you home with me;
YES — I will take care of you and provide for you;
YES — It will be for better or for worse, for richer or for poorer, in sickness and in health;
YES — to the curlers and the diets and the clothes.

A woman says YES to a man, and there are a million little yeses inside it.

YES — I will go home with you;
YES — I will cook and sew and wash for you;
YES — I will do it in good times and in bad, for better or for worse, in sickness and in health;
YES — to the paunch and the baldness and the sports.

YES is generative. A man and a woman say YES to each other and there are a million little yeses inside it. My father and mother said YES to each other and five little yeses came out of it. And each one of those little yeses had a million little yeses inside.

YES — I will feed you and bathe you and change you;
YES — I will help you and teach you and clothe you;
YES — to the braces and the glasses;
YES — to the schools and the skates and the bikes and the fads and the parties and the acne and the worrying.

There is no such thing as a simple YES. Since we are made in the image of God there will always be a million little yeses inside every YES.

But there is nothing inside NO — except death. Everything stops at NO! Nothing goes beyond NO! There is no activity, no life beyond a NO. There is only silence. Only darkness. Only death.

There is no life after NO!

> Therefore, he [Adam] must not be allowed to put out his hand to take fruit from the tree of life...
>
> (Gn 3:22)

> Then the Lord asked Cain, "Where is your brother Abel?" He answered, "I do not know. Am I my brother's keeper?" The Lord then said: "What have you done! Listen: Your brother's blood cries out to me from the soil!... If you till the soil, it shall no longer give you its produce (life).
>
> (Gn 9–11; parenthesis added)

There is only silence after NO! Such is the fate of the wicked.

> They are dead, they will not live; they are shades, they will not arise; to that end You have visited them with destruction and wiped out all remembrance of them.
>
> (Is 26:14)

There is only darkness after NO!

> Yea, the light of the wicked is put out,
> and the flame of his fire does not shine.
> (Job 18:5)

But God cannot abide a NO! Before God darkness must change to light, death into life, NO into YES! God had given His word and it will not come back to Him dead.

> So shall my word be
> that goes forth from my mouth;
> It shall not return to me void,
> but shall do my will,
> achieving the end for which I sent it.
> (Is 59:11)

The gift that the Father willed to give to His Son for Christmas must be returned to Him full of goodness and life. Only God's Son can turn it around. Only a divine Son could do it.

It had to happen at the point where NO appears to conquer. At the pinnacle. At the death of Jesus on Good Friday. On the cross the last breath of Jesus is his final YES! That YES had a million little yeses inside.

> YES — to the sickness and the suffering and the pain;
> YES — to all the agony and the anguish;
> YES — to giving to the last measure.

That YES changed the darkness of Good Friday into the brilliance of Easter Sunday. That YES embraced all creation, all time, and gave it back to the Father like a precious ring given by a lover to his beloved. The YES of Jesus on the cross was irresistible to the Father. It was this that the Father saw before the creation of the universe that caused it all to happen.

> You have indeed protected us, Jesus,
> from endless disaster.
> You spread your hands like a Father
> and fatherlike gave cover with your wings.
> Your blood, a God's blood, you poured over the earth,
> sealing a blood bargain for us because you loved us.
> What anger threatened you turned away from us;
> instead you gave us back God's friendship.
>
> The heavens may have your spirit, paradise your soul,
> but Oh, may the earth have your blood.
>
> This feast of the Spirit
> leads the mystic dance through the year.
> The pasch came from God, came from heaven to earth:
> from earth it has gone back to heaven.
> New is this feast and all-embracing;
> all creation assembles at it.
>
> Joy to all creatures, honor, feasting, delight.
> Dark death is destroyed
> and life is restored everywhere.
> The gates of heaven are opened.
>
> (from the Exultet)

Consider now, if you will, that before you had the birth of Jesus on December 25, you had to have the conception of Jesus on March 25. Before you had the conception of Jesus on March 25, you had to have the birth of the universe in which he was to be born. Before you had the birth of the universe, you had to have the conception of the universe. The conception of the universe was the love-act between God and humankind, which found its climax in the death/resurrection sigh of Jesus on the cross on Good Friday. It was that act that the Father saw as an idea before anything ever happened, before anything ever came to be. It was that act in human time that tore a hole through the veil that separates God from creation. It was through that hole that God came pouring through to begin the universe.

The death sigh of Jesus on the Cross tore its way through the curtain toward the Father. The life sigh of the Father returning His love in full measure tore through the curtain toward the Son. At their juncture death and resurrection become one. Like an hourglass, God empties Himself into creation. The universe is born, which leads to the conception of Jesus on March 25, which leads to the birth of Jesus on December 25, which leads to the love-sigh on the cross on Good Friday — the death-sigh event of creation. Through that hole creation empties itself into the resurrection of Jesus and enters the infinity of God.

That YES of Jesus had a million little yeses inside. And each of us was one of them.

In reality, then, there are not two seasons before God. There is just one. It is life. It is Jesus. It is us.

Who Are You?

In 1989 two scientists, B. Stanley Pons and Martin Fleischmann, claimed to have achieved "cold fusion," that is, nuclear fusion in a jar at room temperature — a discovery almost as remarkable as splitting the atom. The news made the front pages across the country. When given the ingredients, however, other scientists were unable to duplicate the process.

What good is an earthshaking discovery if it can't be duplicated? If we can't observe step by step the remarkable process that is taking place? It would be like realizing the ancient alchemists' dream of finding the formula to change a base metal like lead into gold, but then not being able to observe the wonderful transformation that took place and losing the formula.

It only stands to reason that when something that profound happens we would want to observe carefully what transpired and decide if it's worth repeating.

Jesus was the first and only man to resurrect from the dead. Since this incredible event is more remarkable than anything that has ever happened or ever will in human history, it seems only reasonable that we should study the phenomenon carefully, observe what actually happened, and then consider how to duplicate it for ourselves.

> Then the disciples went back to their homes. But Mary stood weeping outside the tomb, and as she wept she stooped to look into the tomb; and she saw two angels in white, sitting where the body of Jesus had lain, one at the head and one at the feet. They said to her, "Woman, why are you weeping?" She said to them, "Because they have taken away my Lord, and I do not know where they have laid him." Saying this, she turned round and saw Jesus standing, *but she did not know that it was Jesus.* Jesus said to her, "Woman, why are you weeping? Whom do you seek?" Supposing him to be the gardener, she said to him, "Sir, if you have carried him away, tell me where you have laid him, and I will take him away." *Jesus said to her, "Mary."* She turned and said to him in Hebrew, "Rabboni!" (which means Teacher).
>
> (Jn 20:10–16; emphasis added)

How is it that Mary Magdalene, a close follower and friend of Jesus, who knew him probably as well as any of the disciples did, did not recognize him? How could she have mistaken him for a gardener?

> Now the eleven disciples went to Galilee, to the mountain to which Jesus had directed them. And when they saw him they worshiped him; *but some doubted.*
>
> (Mt 28:16–17; emphasis added)

The Apostles saw Jesus and worshipped him, but some doubted. How could they doubt what was right before them? What was wrong about the appearance of Jesus that caused this dissension among them?

> That very day two of them were going to a village named Emmaus, about seven miles from Jerusalem, and talking with each other about all these things that had happened. While they were talking and discussing together, Jesus himself drew near and went with them. *But their eyes were kept from recognizing him.*
>
> (Lk 24:13–16; emphasis added)

Again there arises the disturbing question of recognizing the resurrected Jesus. While these disciples were not among the leaders of the community, they were close enough to them to be sufficiently informed about what had happened that very day. Yet they too did not realize that it was he in their midst. The nuance in this account was that they were *prevented* from recognizing him. What could the reason be?

Even the form of Jesus' appearances was different.

As they [the Apostles] were saying this, Jesus himself stood among them. But they were startled and frightened, and *supposed that they saw a spirit.*

(Lk 24:36–37; emphasis added)

After this he appeared *in another form* to two of them, as they were walking into the country.

(Mk 16:12; emphasis added)

Jesus said to them, "Bring some of the fish that you have just caught." So Simon Peter went aboard and hauled the net ashore, full of large fish, a hundred and fifty-three of them; and although there were so many, the net was not torn. Jesus said to them, "Come and have breakfast." *Now none of the disciples dared ask him, "Who are you?"* They knew it was the Lord.

(Jn 21:10–12; emphasis added)

These disturbing questions about the resurrection appearances of Jesus must be faced as forthrightly today as they were then. Did Jesus really resurrect from the dead? Why didn't his own recognize him? Why did they still doubt even in his presence?

We have examined some of the textual accounts (other references are much the same), and now we must try to understand what they mean.

First, we must understand that the New Testament is a document of faith. This means that what was written was the belief of the people of the time, neither provable nor disprovable in our time. The evidence of scripture is that they definitely believed in the resurrection of Jesus even in the midst of disturbing circumstances. What we must examine are the reasons for the confusion and the doubts.

The resurrection of the dead was a hotly disputed issue at the time of Jesus. Saint Paul was able to throw the entire Sanhedrin into utter chaos by merely alluding to it (Acts 23). We may well imagine that, lacking any hard evidence, those who believed speculated about the form this would take in much the same way as we speculate today about what heaven is like. Unfortunately, by doing so, we create our own prejudices.

One such prejudice is based on the illusion of holding onto this life as we know it. This body will simply arise from the grave (of course, free of corruption) and walk the earth again. Even though the practicality of such a solution defies reason (where would we all fit?), it is still the most sought after and preferred option. Ultimately, it is a veiled desire to hold onto this life and hardly more than a disguised form of idolatry.

Such bodily restoration would be nothing other than a form of re-suscitation. There is more than ample evidence of this happening in the scriptures and no doubt accounts in great part for the hypothesis. Elijah, the prophet, repays a favor to the widow of Zarephath by bringing her dead son back to life (1 Kg 17:17). Elisha, his successor, restores the life of the dead son of the woman of Shunem (2 Kg 4:8ff). Jesus restores life to the daughter of Jairus (Mt 5:22ff), the son of the widow of Nain (Lk 7:11ff), and his friend Lazarus (Jn 11:1ff). Such restoring to bodily life continues in the Acts of the Apostles when Paul restores the young man Eutychus when he dies after a fall from a window (Acts 20:9ff). Again, these are accounts of resuscitation and not resurrection since those revived have all died again. Such stories, however, more than likely account for our preference for this type of resurrection. But they do not measure up to the only real account of resurrection we have in the scriptures. To persist in this expectation would be to disregard the textual evidence.

The scriptures express an unshakeable belief in the resurrection of Jesus. But resurrection was a new phenomenon. What the expectations of the eyewitnesses were and what the reality was appear to be different. He was mistaken for someone else; they were afraid to ask him; they thought he was a ghost. That's precisely the point. They knew it was Jesus but the reality was different. Such is the conclusion we must draw from the only eyewitness accounts of the resurrection of Jesus.

Such a phenomenon is not unique to us. We receive a letter from a friend. The reality of his presence is there but different from his bodily presence. We speak to a loved one on the telephone. She is truly present to us but in a different way. We receive a computer message from someone at another terminal. The examples are too numerous to cite, but they serve to illustrate that there are different yet real ways that we can be present to one another. Resurrection is such a reality. The Apostles and followers of Jesus had to drop their preconceived ideas in order to understand what had taken place. Until they did, was there any alternative but to doubt?

Christians have believed in the presence of the resurrected Christ for two thousand years after the fact. They have not looked for some ethereal manifestation of a spirit form with nail holes in his hands and feet, but have found him in the Eucharist, indeed, all the sacraments, in the reading of the scriptures, and wherever two or three are gathered in his name.

So too must be the resurrection of the dead. Scripture and faith tell us that those who died with Jesus will also rise with Jesus. Should we look for some ghost of a deceased relative as a sign of life after death? Would this not put the lie to the resurrection of Jesus as we know it? If his was the only resurrection and all others share in it through him, how could theirs be different? Are we not in the same position as those first eyewitnesses who doubted — unless we see we do not believe?

A friend told me that she was standing in line at a checkout counter in a supermarket behind an elderly woman who whistled while she waited her turn. Her mother used to whistle all the time. For a moment, she said, she felt the presence of her mother again. While on vacation my friends and I commented on how someone looked amazingly like my brother who had recently died. Just seeing him put me in my brother's presence again. Obviously, it was not my brother, or my friend's mother, but there were realities that go beyond mere imagination. The resurrection of Jesus means that wherever Jesus is, those who have resurrected are with him. If he is present in the Eucharist, so too are they. If he is present among his followers, so too are they. If I set up my own conditions for the manifestations of Jesus or the resurrection of the dead, will I not miss the myriad of ways that God and they can use to be present to me? Only God could have come up with so boundless a manifestation of love; and only human beings could so limit it.

If resurrection were simply centered on this body as it is, would we not be giving too much importance to our bodies? Is there not a deeper meaning to this body than just what we see? After all, have we not all wondered what body will eventually resurrect? Our body at eighteen, or twenty-five, or fifty? Will my eternal body be shriveled and wrinkled if I live to be eighty-nine years old?

There must be a deeper meaning to the body than just this fat and short or tall and thin appearance. The body contains all that I am and all that has affected me and made me what I am and all I am meant to be.

The form is merely accidental and not essential. Jesus identifies himself to the doubting Thomas by telling him to put his finger into the holes in his hands and side. The appearance was not important. His passion and death for us were, and they marked him for eternity. Mary Magdalene knew he wasn't the gardener when he called her by name. That loving call could never be mistaken.

When the woman in the checkout counter turned around, when I saw the face of the man I thought to be my brother, the spell was broken. Bodies have a tendency of getting in the way of religious truths. Spiritual realities have always been hampered by physical limitations. This is not reason for disparaging the body, however, for how else would we come to know?

The disciples on the road to Emmaus did not recognize Jesus until he broke bread with them. If they had recognized him by his appearance, what hope would there ever be of recognizing him in others? There can and should never be an actual portrait of Jesus, the shroud notwithstanding. It would fly in the face of the true meaning of resurrection. If we had a picture of Jesus we would forever be looking at others saying that they don't look anything like him. Once we see others face to face, the spell would be broken. We would never see him in women as well as men, in Gentile as well as Jew, in slave as well as free. We would not be able to see him in the poor and the sick and the outcast. The resurrection of Jesus reminds us that there is more to our bodies than what meets the eye. And there is more to resurrected bodies than we can ever even imagine.

> Eye has not seen, nor ear heard, nor has it entered the heart of man, what God has prepared for those who love him.
>
> (1 Cor 2:9)

I know now that this phenomenon, the central point of Christian belief, must of necessity depend upon faith.

> If Christ has not been raised, then our preaching is in vain and your faith is in vain.
>
> (1 Cor 15:14)

Just as Adam needed faith to rely on the word of God not to eat the forbidden fruit, so must we rely on faith to enter the new creation. There can be no shortcut, no irrefutable evidence except that which relies on things unseen. If we see, there is no longer need of faith.

Because we look not to the things that are seen but to the things that are unseen; for the things that are seen are transient, but the things that are unseen are eternal.

(2 Cor 4:18)

Now faith is the assurance of things hoped for, the conviction of things not seen.

(Heb 11:1)

Jesus said to him, "Have you believed because you have seen me? Blessed are those who have not seen and yet believe."

(Jn 20:29)

Even should Jesus appear to us as he was, we would probably take him for an imposter. If we were to have his portrait, we would most likely say that he was merely a look-alike. If he were to perform the same miracles as he did then, we would simply relegate them to faith healings or trickery. How could it be otherwise? If we cannot prove the existence of God who must be accepted on faith, should the Son of God have greater prerogatives?

What about Heaven?

Who among us has never wondered about what heaven is like? When the first thought was conceived about the possibility of life after death, the second one must have been about what it would be like. We have no first-hand accounts. There are those who have had so-called life after death experiences, but these, like so many other "religious" phenomena, are viewed skeptically and must also be accepted on faith. Therefore, lacking historical and scientific evidence we must rely on speculation over faith evidence.

The evidence from scripture is often confusing and symbolic.

For in the resurrection they neither marry nor are given in marriage, but are like angels in heaven.

(Mt 22:30)

Does this mean that marriage is inconsequential in the hereafter? A newlywed once told me that if she died before her husband, she didn't want him to marry again because she wanted him to be her husband in heaven or she would never be happy. She also said that she could never be happy in heaven if he went to hell.

> If your eye causes you to sin, pluck it out; it is better for you to enter the kingdom of God with one eye than with two eyes to be thrown into hell.
>
> (Mk 9:47)

Does this mean that people can still be without bodily members in heaven? Do we take our blindness, lameness, or other incapacities into heaven with us just as Jesus took his wounds?

In Apocalyptic literature (Ezekiel, Revelation) the heavenly Jerusalem is square, made of precious stones, with water flowing around all four sides of it. Does this description give us any indication of what heaven is going to be like?

First, eternity is not a question of time as we know it. It is not a million or a hundred billion years. It is a moment — a moment that once it is penetrated stretches forever. Most of us have expressed the desire at some time in our lives to capture a precious moment, a wonderful, meaningful moment, and have it last forever. Even our advertisements for photographic equipment tell us that we can "capture the moment." Eternity is the moment. It is entering God's time and seeing all history, from the beginning to the end of created time and more as one through God's eye. The eye of God is the death/resurrection of Jesus Christ. We see as much of God as is possible for us through it, and God sees all of us through it.

Since there is only one death to sin and only one resurrection, we enter into the moment through Jesus. There is no other way. When we die we enter God's time. God's time is one. To God our death and Jesus' are at the same time. If we share his death, we share his resurrection. We overcome death and enter eternity through him and with him and in him.

If I were to take a glass of clear water and add a drop of red dye to it, it would have an effect on the water. If later I were to add a drop of blue, that too would affect it. We enter life like that glass of water. People and events shape our lives, leaving their impressions, changing the color of our lives. They and us make us who we are. A parent, a spouse, a child, a teacher, a friend, a passing stranger, and even a pet can shape who we are. There is a hunger in us from the moment of birth that yearns for God. We carry with us every good that fills the void. Even the bad can have a good effect on us. When I was a child, an adult I upset called me a "homely thing." I didn't know what that meant so I looked it up in the dictionary. I was devastated to discover that it meant ugly. The last thing a twelve-year-old wants is to be considered ugly. For months afterward I prayed to God not to have me be ugly. When I finally grew up and learned that there was nothing I could do about my face to make it beautiful, I decided that if I tried I *could* be a beautiful person. That I could do something about. If in some way I have been able to achieve that during my life, I owe part of it to that woman.

So many things have helped shape the person that I am. They have all served to form the color of my life. Now take the glass of colored water and move it to heaven. We take these influences to heaven *with us*. They are a permanent part of us. We could never leave them behind any more than Jesus could leave behind the wounds in his hands and side. They are what makes him who he is and us who we are. We take them into glory with us.

I used to joke with people telling them that when I got to heaven I would be so dashingly goodlooking that my own mother wouldn't recognize me. She wouldn't and neither would God because it wouldn't be me. Whatever we are we bring to heaven with us — gloriously. If we are short, fat, and bald in life, we will be that in eternal life, only we will be gloriously short, fat, and bald. That's what the resurrection of Jesus alludes to. That's what showing his wounds was all about.

Our lives have made a permanent impression on Jesus, so he takes us to heaven with him. Our resurrection is analogous to his. We take all those who have impressed us into him. That would include the newly-wed's husband, even if he should marry again or even go to hell. That emptiness in our lives that someone special filled with love, we take with us gloriously into heaven just as we take it with us wherever we go on earth. That can and never will be lost. Yes, then even dogs go to heaven. We take them with us. The reality of who and what all these are and what they mean to us will be immanent and real to us there, undiminished and forever. In the working out of the kingdom of God, nothing good (of God) is ever lost. It is what theologians refer to as the economy of salvation. It is also what we need to make heaven complete.

We are the body of Christ. We are what fills up Jesus' cup. He takes us up to heaven with him. We take up to heaven with us all those who filled our cup. Nothing of God is ever lost. Not even a drop (Mk 9:41).

7

APOCALYPSE

A great deal has been said and written about the functioning of the human brain. I have no pretensions about adding to this vast storehouse of knowledge. I merely wish to interpret and apply some of that expertise to this work and to do it in lay terms.

It is common knowledge that the left side of the brain controls the right side of the body and vice versa. How ingenious of God to force balance upon us in this way. Each new discovery of science seems to impel us further into God's wondrous design for us and creation.

Recent experimentation into the functionings of the two hemispheres of the brain has revealed considerably more and interesting complex data. It has been demonstrated that the more so-called intellectual and individualized functions of the brain find their origin in the left hemisphere, while the more common and symbolic functions are rooted in the right hemisphere.

Simply put, this means that thinking, reasoning, interpreting, deciphering, and the like are done by the left brain. This part of the brain is at work when we learn the three "Rs," reading, writing, and arithmetic. Logic, science, and mathematics are functions of the left brain. This is where definitions are formed, distinctions are made, and individuality is accounted for. The left brain sees the apple as different from the pear and you as different from me.

The right brain deals in symbolism and consequently commonness. It may link mother and tree together because of their commonness in giving birth. The more universal aspects of life are located in the right brain. Here are found stories, poetry, art, music, dance, sports, and what are usually termed cultural activities. The right brain joins where the left brain separates.

In learning to walk an infant must coordinate both sides of the brain to get balance. At a deeper level one may define a spiral staircase or use gestures to illustrate it in a form of sign language. Both serve a purpose. When we put them together, both hemispheres of the brain are working together in balance. It is difficult to explain a spiral staircase without the gestures. Try it.

This knowledge is important in our study of the scriptures because much of the Bible is a right-brain book. It deals with stories, parable, myths, song, heroic narrative, liturgy, and poetry. Of course, there are ample examples of left-brain data, such as genealogies, dynasties, historical accounts, laws, and prescriptions. But even here the right brain insinuates itself with symbolic names, numbers, and events.

As more is understood about the workings of the human mind, more of the scriptures are revealed to us. The Bible, then, may be approached on two levels — the apparent and surface level of words and their immediate context and meaning, and a beneath level that nurtures and supports the upper one. (I choose to use "surface" and "beneath" rather than other words that may convey a hierarchy of importance I do not intend.) One may liken the distinction to a flower that gives beauty and perfume (surface level) and the stem, leaves, and roots that support and sustain it (beneath level). Both are needed for balance. Simply to dissect the flower, label it, and leave it (left brain), takes away from its beauty and mystery (right brain). To avoid any intellectualization is to be as the fig tree that bears no fruit (Mt 21:19).

The Apocalypse (which means revelation), or the Book of Revelation, is a classic product of the right brain. It is symbolism *par excellence*. It is rampant with bizarre images, symbolic numbers, and liturgical songs. Because of this, it isn't always clear what the author meant. Meanings that we take for granted in our culture can be quite the opposite in another culture. I learned this while I was a boy visiting Sicily. The American gesture for goodbye, the cupped hand waving up and down, in Sicily meant "come here." The color white used to express joy in the West is used for mourning in the East.

We must also take into account the different times. Words change meanings over the years. So do symbols. If an artist paints a green man or an author writes about one, will they know a thousand years from now that what they meant was someone filled with envy? Nor does everything have to be taken as literal, historical fact. Was there a real boy who cried "wolf"? Was there a real Jonah who got swallowed by a whale? Did creation actually take place in seven days? Or was there a different truth at stake here? Even in historical facts the right brain can see beyond to universal significance. A young American hockey team goes up against a seasoned Russian champion and defeats it in the Olympics and the newspaper headlines read, "David slays Goliath." The Christian conflict with Rome, seen as the universal conflict of good against evil, is what the Apocalypse is all about.

We are dealing with the labyrinth of symbolism that is always new and always challenging. It is never easy to know what should be taken literally and what should not. One Sunday I told a fable as my homily and did not explain it as I usually do. Instead I asked the congregation to discuss what it meant. When interpretations began coming back to me, I was amazed at how many varied interpretations there were. Some were much better than what I had intended.

In the absence of the human author to explain what he intended by all that he wrote in the Apocalypse, we will have to rely on the divine Author to continue to inspire and enlighten us.

APOCALYPSE: A PLAY

The stage is set the same as it was for the Nativity Play, except that there are two easels, one at either end of the stage. The ladder is still in the center of the stage as if forgotten there from the last play.

The scene opens with Moses entering from stage right. Elijah is standing at the picture window looking out.

MOSES: Well?

ELIJAH: (*Staring wistfully out the window*) Well, what? (*He turns to Moses*)

MOSES: It's time.

ELIJAH: Already?

MOSES:	Don't you think it's about time?
ELIJAH:	Isn't that what all this has been about? (*Looking out the window*)
MOSES:	It's been one hell of a time, if you ask me.
ELIJAH:	It's also been a glorious time.
MOSES:	Well, now it's time to call it.
ELIJAH:	When, exactly?
MOSES:	You know better than to ask that. You're just stalling for time.
ELIJAH:	Every little bit helps. (*Looking out the window again*) Are you sure?
MOSES:	Positive.

The office door opens and Gabriel emerges. He speaks in his usual efficient manner.

GABRIEL:	It's time, gentlemen.

Moses looks at Elijah.

ELIJAH:	(*Defiantly*) Time for what?
GABRIEL:	Time for the final curtain, of course.
ELIJAH:	(*Looking at Moses*) Well, it was wonderful while it lasted. What will we do when it's over?
GABRIEL:	There's plenty of time to worry about that later. In the meantime, you'd better set the stage.
MOSES:	Same rules?
GABRIEL:	As always. (*He exits*)

Moses sits on the couch. Elijah looks out the window and then at the ladder. He climbs it and looks out at the sweep of the audience. Moses looks up at him.

MOSES:	What are you doing up there? I swear, you prophets are nothing more than children.
ELIJAH:	That's what heaven is made of.
MOSES:	He was speaking metaphorically.

ELIJAH: (*Looking at the audience*) That coming from a literalist, mind you.

MOSES: Let's not get into that again. We have too much work to do. (*He picks up a tablet from the coffee table*)

ELIJAH: Spare me . . . with the tablet again.

MOSES: You know how I am. I like to wrap things up nice and neat. No loose ends. Now how many would you say are in the final scene?

ELIJAH: Better be careful, Moses. You know how He is about numbers. Remember how He got when David started counting. That was one of the bad times.*

MOSES: That's because people count their accomplishments as if they were responsible for them. We know who is. I just want to get a final tally to complete the ledger. You know. The bottom line. That's all.

ELIJAH: I wouldn't push it if I were you.

MOSES: All right, then. How about 144,000? I've got to have a number.

ELIJAH: Is that all? After all these years? You might as well say we've lost.

MOSES: What kind of a prophet are you, Elijah? Don't you recognize a symbol when you see one? It's a symbolic number.

ELIJAH: That's symbolic? Maybe to an accountant. Moses, you are hopeless. A symbol is a dragon chasing after a woman, a book with seals, different colored horsemen coming from heaven. Those are symbols.

MOSES: Seven seals and four horsemen. You prophets think you are the only ones who are clever. Tell me, when God covenanted with people, how many tribes were there?

ELIJAH: Twelve.

---

*In the First Book of Chronicles (chapter 21), David was punished for taking a census.

MOSES:	Precisely! Twelve coming and twelve going. One hundred and forty-four. Then multiply again by a thousand to round it out. How's that for symbolism?
ELIJAH:	Pathetic.
MOSES:	Really? I thought it rather clever myself. As a matter of fact, I'm thinking of making the heavenly Jerusalem square. A rounded number enclosed in a nice, neat square. A perfect square, mind you.
ELIJAH:	Coming from you Moses, that's no surprise at all.
MOSES:	(*Pensive for a moment. Then looks at Elijah still up the ladder.*) Elijah! What are you doing up there?
ELIJAH:	Getting perspective. I can see it all from up here Moses. From the beginning to the end.

Assistant angel #1 puts a sign with an alpha on the right easel while assistant angel #2 puts an omega on the left easel. Elijah waits until they withdraw.

	What better way to write an Apocalypse?
MOSES:	With your feet planted firmly on the ground. Tradition, you know.
ELIJAH:	You keep your feet on the ground and I'll keep my head in the clouds.
MOSES:	Then we are appropriately situated here.

Elijah looks toward the easel with the alpha on it. Then he looks over at Moses.

ELIJAH:	We'll begin with God.

Assistant angel #1 enters and places a sign reading GOD on that easel. Moses and Elijah look toward the office and wait. Eventually, the door to the office opens and a man begins to come through the door, the same man who played Joseph in the Nativity Play.

MOSES: Wait a minute! (*The man turns around and goes back into the office. The angel is about to take the sign off the easel but Elijah motions for him to wait.**)

           Why a man? Why not a pillar of fire or a column of smoke?

ELIJAH: Symbolism.

MOSES: What do you think those are? Before you go any further you'd better tell me what the symbol is that you're going to use. Using a man is going to cause more trouble than you can imagine.

ELIJAH: Marriage. Does that meet with your approval?

MOSES: Marriage is a good symbol.

ELIJAH: Thank you. Now can we get on with it? As I was saying, we begin with God.

           The angel leaves. There is a pause as they wait for God to enter again. The minute the door opens there is lightning and thunder.

           Really, Moses, you do have a flair for the dramatic. This is not Mount Sinai. As a matter of fact, there isn't even an earth yet.

MOSES: You have your thing, Elijah, and I have mine. Now what?

ELIJAH: He needs a bride.

MOSES: Wait a minute! Wait just a minute. Who's the bride?

ELIJAH: Earth. (*The assistant angel puts EARTH on the left easel*)

MOSES: Can't you be a little more personal?

ELIJAH: Remember, she's a symbol.

MOSES: You can still be a little more personal than that. How about Israel?

ELIJAH: All right then. But virgin Israel. (*He looks at Moses as if expecting a comment*)

---

* Once the GOD sign is placed on the right easel, it is never taken down. All other signs are placed on the left easel.

MOSES: (*Throwing his hands up and nodding*) Agreed.

The assistant angel changes the sign to ISRAEL. *There is a short pause and the woman who played Mary in the Nativity Play emerges from stage right and joins the man at center stage. They hold hands facing each other as at a wedding.*

ELIJAH: (*Looking at Mary*) That's a nice touch, Moses. You are a romantic after all.

MOSES: (*Embarrassed*) Let's get on with it, shall we?

ELIJAH: We start with a wedding. God and his bride.

MOSES: Wait a minute!

ELIJAH: Now what?

MOSES: Something's not right here.

ELIJAH: How could it not be right? We haven't done anything yet.

MOSES: That's just it. We haven't done anything and there's light. In the beginning it was dark. It's got to be dark.

The lights go out. The dialogue continues in utter darkness.

ELIJAH: Why does it have to be dark?

MOSES: Symbolism.

ELIJAH: Really, Moses. What are you trying to say?

MOSES: Light and darkness. The beginning and the end. They've all got to connect. Besides, there's just the minor point that the sun hasn't been created yet.

ELIJAH: Details. You lawyers are sticklers for trivial details. You can't have them getting married in the dark.

MOSES: No sun, no light. That's not a minor detail.

ELIJAH: All right then, I'll start with the creation of the sun.

MOSES: You can't do that.

ELIJAH: Why not?

MOSES:	First things first. The first thing in the heart of a groom is his bride. You can't have the sun coming first. It wouldn't be right.
ELIJAH:	Well, you can't have them exchanging their vows in the dark. That wouldn't be right either.
MOSES:	You've boxed yourself in with your symbol.
ELIJAH:	I like it and I'm not going to change it.

There is a long tense silence. A voice over the loudspeaker says, "Let there be light!" The light goes on. The man and the woman are still posed as before.

Thank God! Now we can see what's going on. (*He looks at Moses who is shaking his head*) Well, what's the matter now?

MOSES:	There's going to be trouble over this. We've got light and no sun.
ELIJAH:	Don't be such a literalist. Besides, remember the rules. We can set the scene but we can't write the dialogue. (*He points at the man playing God*) Especially not His.
MOSES:	Yes, but I'm writing all this down and we've got light and no sun. What am I going to call it?
ELIJAH:	Deus ex machina.
MOSES:	Cute.

He gets up and walks to the base of the ladder. He looks up at Elijah with exasperation.

Are you planning to go through everything, all of history from the beginning to the end, for this Apocalypse? It'll take forever!

ELIJAH:	Won't it? (*Then before Moses can object*) We're not going to go through everything. But as you well know, every beginning has the end within it. And every end, the beginning. The rest is history. So we've got to get *this* right to get the end right.
MOSES:	Will you please come down off that ladder. You're even becoming philosophical now.

ELIJAH:	You should come up here for a while. (*Coming down*) It might change your outlook on things.
MOSES:	If what you say is right, we started out up there and will end up there. Let's get down to the meantime.
ELIJAH:	Moses, you'd exasperate God.
MOSES:	I did. (*Looking at the man and woman still holding hands and facing each other*) Are we finished with this scene now?
ELIJAH:	Not yet. They haven't said, "I do," yet.
MOSES:	(*Stands before the two of them like a priest*) Do you agree to take each other and love each other forever?*

The man and woman say "Yes" together. They kiss. The next moment the woman feels her stomach indicating pregnancy and smiles. She places her husband's hand on her womb and he smiles.

Assistant angels #1 and #2 emerge from the office. #1 climbs the ladder and places a sun, moon, and some stars on sky hooks. #2 brings out a potted tree and some flowers.

Elijah comes and stands with Moses assessing the scene.

ELIJAH:	Now it's done. (*The man and woman walk off into the office holding hands. They watch. He turns to Moses and says:*) Wouldn't it have been wonderful if it could have stayed that way, all peaches and cream?
MOSES:	It's because we can never leave well enough alone. And the expression is milk and honey, not peaches and cream.
ELIJAH:	Oh, what's the use. Let's get on with it. We've seen the best time; I suppose we should contrast it.
MOSES:	That would be the bondage of Israel under the Pharaoh of Egypt.
ELIJAH:	Yes, that was a bad time. But in my opinion there was a worse time. The three and a half years under the Greek

---

*Moses is the mediator of the covenant between God and Israel at Mount Sinai.

Antiochus Epiphanes. His desecration of the Temple was an abomination of desolation. It was the epitome of evil in the peoples' eyes. As if killing was not enough and God knows we've seen enough of that in our history. But desecrating the Temple was like desecrating God. Not even Pharaoh did that to us.

MOSES: Yes. (*Sadly*) That was a terrible time.

The assistant angel puts ANTIOCHUS EPIPHANES sign on left easel. The one who played Herod emerges from stage left. Two servants are with him. They place the couch in the center of the stage and he directs them in adjusting it so that it's placed directly beneath the sun. He sits facing Moses and Elijah standing in front of him.

ELIJAH: He looks like Herod.

MOSES: And the Pharaoh.

ELIJAH: And Nero.

MOSES: His name and face are Legion.*.

The scene is frozen with him sitting and them standing quietly for a long time, or at least until the silence gets awkward.

ELIJAH: (*Turning to Moses*) How long will this go on?

MOSES: 1,260 days or 42 months.

ELIJAH: But who's counting? Moses, that kind of symbolism is too specific to him. It needs to be more universal. Evil happens time and again. You can't just limit it to this one beast.

MOSES: All right then, how would you express it universally?

ELIJAH: (*Thinking*) A time and times and half a time.

MOSES: That can mean just about anything?

ELIJAH: There will be those who will know and understand. Trust me. Give me this one, Moses, and I'll give you one.

---

*Satan is the great and only real enemy of Christ and his people (Rev 13:2, 4)

MOSES: Fine. Then I'll stick with numbers. I'll call the beast 666.

ELIJAH: (*Shaking his head*) Okay, you got me on that one. What does it mean?

MOSES: If three and a half years can come out as "a time and times and half a time," then Nero Caesar can come out as 666. That's the number you get when you add up the letters of his name and title. How's that for symbolism?

ELIJAH: No comment.

The assistant angel places NERO CAESAR *over* ANTIOCHUS EPIPHANES *on the easel. While they are distracted by this, a man appears looking in the picture window.*

MOSES: I'm tired of all this talk. Let's get to some action.

ELIJAH: (*Noticing the intruder*) Before we do that, we seem to have company. (*Moses looks and is puzzled*)

GABRIEL: (*Emerging from the office*) Don't be concerned about him. His name is John and he's got permission. Just continue on as before.

ELIJAH: Well, we can't have him standing out there, can we?

GABRIEL: As you wish. (*He leaves*)

Elijah motions for him to enter. John disappears from behind the window and enters stage left. He stands out of the way near the curtain.

The woman comes out of the office bearing her child. She comes to the center of the stage down from where Nero is seated. She sits on the floor as if nursing her child. The three magi emerge, one dressed in the same garb as in the Nativity. The other is dressed in medieval clothes and the third in modern dress. She holds out the child for them to see. They are about to place their gifts at his feet when Nero screams.

NERO: (*Standing, holding both arms up and shaking his fists*) No! No! I won't have it. I won't have it.

The woman huddles protectively over her child. While Nero rages, Gabriel hurries out of the office to the woman. She hands him the child. He hurries back into the office with the child, leaving the door open. Nero follows in pursuit. Just before he enters the door a big, strong angel blocks his entrance by standing in the doorway with his arms folded.

In the meantime John has joined Moses and Elijah.

JOHN: Who is that?

ELIJAH: Michael, the Archangel.

The assistant angel places MICHAEL *on the easel.*

Nero tries to get around Michael but can't. In a fury he turns and runs to the ladder and climbs it. Screaming he throws down the sun, moon, and stars. The magi take the woman and hurry her off stage left. The assistant angel takes the potted tree into the office, then returns for the plants.

NERO: *(Screaming from atop the ladder)* Where are my minions?

Four caped and hooded figures emerge, three from stage left and one (the White Horseman) from stage right, keeping their backs to the audience. They stand at the base of the ladder looking up to Nero. He commands them.

WAR! *(A hooded figure bows deeply, then turns to face the audience. His face and hands are blood red.)* Wreak your havoc upon the earth. Tear, pillage, plunder, rape. Do what you will but bring me the woman. Through her I shall get the child. Go! *(He points in the direction that the woman and magi fled)*

HUNGER! *(Another hooded figure bows and turns. His face and hands are black.)* Follow close behind. See to it that no one who resists me escapes. Go!

PLAGUE! *(The third figure bows low and faces the audience. His face and hands are pale white.)* Pollute their waters. Contaminate their food. Rise even from their dead bodies. Be their resurrection from the dead. Go!

The fourth figure turns without bowing. His face and hands are bright white.

VICTORY! Sweet victory. Are you mine to command or His? (*No command is given. He walks off regally, not in the same direction as the others but where he came from.*)*

Nero comes down the ladder. He turns to Michael and shakes his fist at him. He exits in the same direction as the three horsemen.

JOHN: Are these the signs of things that can be or will be?

MOSES: Both.

Moses and Elijah confer privately so John goes to the window and looks out. After a short pause he turns to them.

JOHN: What is to happen now?

ELIJAH: Watch and learn. Remember what you see here.

Nero enters with a woman dressed in scarlet. She is carrying an empty cup. They act as if they have been carousing for some time. They are followed by two servants carrying jugs of wine. They sit on the couch while the servants pour. They drink from the same cup.

JOHN: Who is she?

MOSES: Her name is Babylon.

ELIJAH: Her name is Rome.

JOHN: Then she is a great harlot.

The assistant angel puts HARLOT on the easel. Nero claps his hands in summons. From both sides of the stage emerge seven figures who act according to their names when given. As each is identified, the angel puts the name on the easel over the harlot's.

Who are these seven creatures?

ELIJAH: Slaves of the beast and friends of the harlot. The first is PRIDE. Pride goes before the fall.

---

* The Parthians (White Horseman) did not overthrow Rome as was expected by the author of Revelation. VICTORY also does not follow because there is never any victory in war, death, or plague.

As PRIDE *is placed on the easel, he walks haughtily past the others and lies on the floor at the feet of Nero.*

MOSES: Then comes GREED, the corrupter of kingdoms. (*He too lies at the feet of Nero*)

ELIJAH: ANGER to set the people against one another, father against son, sister against brother. (*Lies at the feet of Nero*)

MOSES: LUST is the harlot's mistress, corrupting the young as well as the old. (*Lies at the feet of the harlot*)

ELIJAH: GLUTTONY torments so that one can never have enough. (*Lies at the feet of the harlot*)

MOSES: Then there is JEALOUSY to torture the hearts of those who do not have and never will. (*Lies at the feet of the harlot*)

ELIJAH: And the last and the least is SLOTH, which saps purpose from the living making them the living dead. (*Lies down on the spot, going to neither Nero or the harlot. The two watch and laugh.*)

MOSES: Seven deadly sins.

ELIJAH: Each a hill upon which Harlot Rome sits.

JOHN: How well I know, for I have seen the mark of the beast engraved on those who have abandoned the Lord and sworn an oath of fealty to Caesar as God.*

Nero, the harlot, and the others revel for a while together drinking out of the same cup. Moses, Elijah, and John watch in silence.

How long, Oh Lord? How long?

MOSES: Until Armageddon.

JOHN: When will that be?

ELIJAH: In a time and times and half a time.

JOHN: As in the days of Antiochus Epiphanes.

---

* Those who submitted to Caesar were so tattooed.

There is a thunderclap followed by the sounds of an earthquake. The lights go out. Lightning flashes.

MOSES: It is time. I recognize the signs.

ELIJAH: Darkness and light. The beginning and the end.

As the following scene unfolds the stage lights progress from dim to full power.

The three horsemen return. PLAGUE, HUNGER, and DEATH emerge from stage left, wandering about as if drunk and dazed. The door to the office opens. Michael the Archangel and the fourth horseman, VICTORY, exit. Michael points to the other horsemen and sends VICTORY over to them.

VICTORY grabs PLAGUE by the scruff of the neck and points down to those reclining at the feet of the harlot. PLAGUE pulls up LUST, GLUTTONY, JEALOUSY, and SLOTH and marches them off.

VICTORY sends HUNGER after PRIDE, GREED, and ANGER. HUNGER leads them off.

VICTORY sends WAR to seize the harlot. She struggles as WAR forces her off.

Nero stands in a rage. He shakes his fist at VICTORY and then at Michael and storms off.

VICTORY rejoins Michael the Archangel, and they go back into the office. The door is left open.

Gabriel emerges and goes over to the three of them.

GABRIEL: That's it gentlemen. Wrap it up. (*Goes back into the office leaving the door open*)

ELIJAH: Let's give it a big finale.

MOSES: Why not?

Once again the two stand at the apron of the stage supervising the arrangement of the final scene. John is with them but standing a little off to the side. The two assistant angels confer for a moment with Moses and Elijah and then set about their work.

Assistant angel #1 gathers up the fallen sun, moon, and stars. He climbs the ladder and replaces them on their sky hooks. Assistant angel #2 brings in flowers again.

Soft heavenly music emanates from the office.

ELIJAH: Now for the man and the woman.

The man emerges from the office dressed in formal attire. Michael the Archangel similarly dressed escorts him to center stage where they face the audience waiting.

Organ music plays the wedding march as the woman enters dressed as a bride. She is followed by Elizabeth and Hannah as ladies in waiting holding her train.

The assistant angel places a sign on the God easel, a heart with two entwined rings within it.

MOSES: Wonderful! A wedding. Nice touch, Elijah. A very nice touch.

ELIJAH: And for you Moses, three kings!

The three magi dressed in white enter, bearing packages wrapped in wedding paper.

MOSES: And for you Elijah, shepherds.

Shepherds also dressed in white enter.

During this time the assistant angels have been placing standing candelabra around the stage and lighting them.

ELIJAH: (*Calling out*) Let all the invited guests enter! (*Then looking at Moses laughing*) All 144,000 of them.

MOSES: (*Also laughing*) Will they fit on this stage?

ELIJAH: Symbolically, Moses.

MOSES: Metaphorically, Elijah.

Angels dressed in white carrying smoking censors process out of the office while from both stage left and right others arrive dressed in white.

Everyone poses facing the audience as if for a picture.

ELIJAH: Pretty as a picture, isn't it?

MOSES:	Like Bethlehem, only a little more elaborate.
ELIJAH:	Like creation the way it was meant to be.
MOSES:	Only there's something missing.
ELIJAH:	Only the star attraction.

Gabriel comes out of the office with the star of Bethlehem. He climbs the ladder and puts it in place. The Halleluia chorus from Handel's Messiah begins.

Jesus, dressed in white, emerges from the office. He stands a few paces in front of the bride and groom. Everyone on stage joins in the chorus.

The music softens. A voice over the loudspeaker proclaims, "I am the Alpha and the Omega, the First and the Last, the Beginning and the End. Happy are those who will have washed their robes clean so that they will have the right to feed on the tree of life."*

Assistant angels remove all the signs until they get back down to the Alpha and Omega. The tree is returned to the stage.

Elijah then directs Mary and Jesus to sit on the couch. Moses interrupts Joseph from sitting down with them and directs him behind the couch as he did at the Nativity.

MOSES:	Just like Bethlehem.

Jesus turns and looks at Joseph behind the couch. He reaches up with his hand and directs him around the couch and back. Joseph sits on his other side. The three smile and look at the audience.

ELIJAH:	Just like the Apocalypse.

The music ends. Jesus, Mary, and Joseph rise and walk out into the office. They are followed by their entourage and then the others until only Moses, Elijah, and John are left on the stage.

MOSES:	(*To John*) Remember well what you have seen here.

---

*Rev 22:13, 14.

John nods and departs, stage left. A few seconds later he appears in the window. He waves goodbye and is gone.

MOSES: Well?

ELIJAH: Well, what?

MOSES: It's time.

ELIJAH: Time for what?

MOSES: The Sabbath. And on the seventh day God rested.

Moses and Elijah start walking off toward the office.

Elijah, shouldn't the curtain close now. After all, Gabriel said, "The final curtain."

ELIJAH: Moses, he was speaking metaphorically. Do you lawyers have to be so literal?

MOSES: Do you prophets have to be so ambiguous?

They enter the office and leave the door open behind them. Assistant angel #1 comes out and places a sign on the easel. It reads:

THE END